The World's Perspective

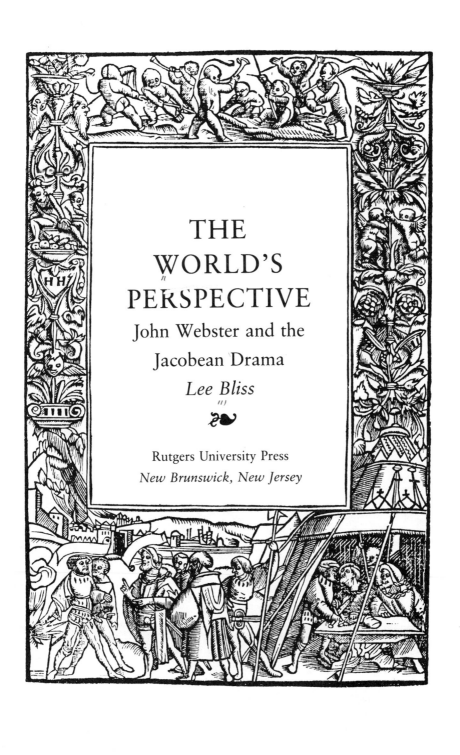

THE
WORLD'S
PERSPECTIVE

John Webster and the
Jacobean Drama

Lee Bliss

Rutgers University Press
New Brunswick, New Jersey

to my parents

Library of Congress Cataloging in Publication Data

Bliss, Lee, 1943–
The world's perspective.

Includes index.
1. Webster, John, 1580?–1625?—Criticism and interpretation.   2. English drama—17th century—History and
criticism.   I. Title.
PR3187.B56 1983   822'.3   82-9119
ISBN 0-8135-0967-X   AACR2

Contents

Notes

Index

Preface

 H I S study grows from my view of John Webster as heir to that brief "tradition" of fertile and explosive experiment which we call Jacobean drama. Although England had spent the late sixteenth century creating its own dramatic tradition out of native and classical forms, later playwrights refused to settle down and tread the paths cleared by Marlowe and Kyd, Greene and Lyly, and then extended by the young Jonson and Shakespeare. In the first decade of the seventeenth century a new and even more hectic theatrical fever raged along the Bankside.

Shakespeare, we all agree, is *the* great experimenter, constantly testing his medium, pushing and pulling at dramatic conventions to discover new possibilities. Looking at Shakespeare's work between *Twelfth Night* and *King Lear*, Philip Edwards finds not steady development but "a single period of intense experimentation" in which "one play contradicts another." In the way new forms are taken up and discarded, the way the author's materials seem repeatedly to resist genre's artistic ordering, Edwards traces Shakespeare's restless pursuit of satisfactory formal expression.[1] We would also agree that in the so-called problem plays particularly, this search becomes acute; there the attempt to enlarge generic boundaries takes "the form of trying to merge comedy and tragedy, or, better, to enclose tragedy within comedy."[2] Yet in our eagerness to celebrate Shakespeare's newness we are often tempted to read contemporary playwrights as mere shapers of those conventions Shakespeare explored: they become the anvils on which we refine our understanding of their master. Such a firm demarcation—Shakespeare in one camp and Jacobean drama in another—has many sources, from personal preference to simple (and simplifying) pedagogical necessity. Whatever its origin, the division itself was not a contemporary one, and it often distorts our perception of each category.

At one extreme stands Shakespeare the lonely genius, confronting his (well-researched) audience and trying to satisfy its expectations without sacrificing his own artistic integrity. Such dragon isolation may require hypothesizing biographical roots for the disturbances so evident in his middle period. We have, after all, adopted the term "problem play" on grounds more relative than the analogy with Ibsen. This ferment need mark no peculiarly bleak stage in Shakespeare's private life; his contemporaries share his artistic restlessness. Yet these men we have, by and large, pushed into a different canon. They stand apart, outcasts from the charmed bardic circle; only in recent years have they enjoyed separate, serious consideration by critical intelligences honed on Shakespeare. The difficulty of encompassing—and impossibility, perhaps, of writing about—the whole dramatic revolution has resulted in a self-fulfilling segregation: when studying a particular play, we are far more likely to look fore and aft within the canon of our chosen dramatist than to glance around at the theatrical landscape to see what might have been in his, and his audience's, recent experience.

Such coarsely woven generalizations fail to net the many fine studies which attempt to bridge this gap. My remarks do point, however, to a critical temptation which haunts us all and continues to tempt by so attractively, tidily, organizing our sprawling materials. Even works that try to study a broad, horizontal slice of the period usually (and understandably) pursue their quarry via chapters on individual authors. Recognizing the difficulties threatening both the scope and coherence of the present undertaking hardly ensures a successful escape; it does suggest specific issues and their likely results. If my primary purpose is to see Webster in his "context," one side effect (or ancillary heresy) will be to relocate Shakespeare in his. For the purposes of this study, at least, Shakespeare's differences—and triumphs—are of degree, not kind.[3] Yet while establishing a new balance between Shakespeare and "the others" only begins to organize the dramatic context, the discussion's scope at the same time imposes its own restrictions; I must forbear exploring significant and shared but nondramatic influences. The next step is to identify in this limited sense Webster's own artistic heritage, that is, those fellow dramatists and competing plays that left their mark on his own work. Pursuing this context, I must inevitably exclude much of great intrinsic interest in the early Jacobean drama. Further, while some connections can be firmly established and documented, others must seem wholly arbitrary—products of my own interpretation or, at worst, caprice. Finally, his contemporaries' innovations must be usefully, illuminatingly balanced against Webster's own work in order to justify such a potentially fragmentary and distracting approach. Since I have myself chosen an individual author as my focus, the difficulty becomes one of persistently seeing his context not as background foil but as an inextricable part of the foreground attraction, which is Webster's dramaturgy.

To see Webster as an exciting and experimental dramatist—one who worked out of and extended the theatrical ferment of his time and not (no matter how long it took him to compose his plays) in studied isolation—has become necessary as well as interesting. If Webster was once hailed and condemned for helping Ford set the decadent seal on Jacobean decline, he is so no longer: the pendulum's swing now labors mightily for rehabilitation. In recent comprehensive studies, Webster's intellectual, moral, and dramatic interests have been pushed back into sixteenth-century didacticism; reinterpreted, he becomes a conservative moralist who portrays the temptations of the World, the Flesh, and the Devil in archaizing, morality-play structures.[4] Even corrective efforts to place Webster in the widest possible context, as part of the European Baroque mainstream, slight his relation to his more immediate contemporaries and their dramatic experiments. He is rescued from decadent sensationalism only to be endowed with an admirable, yet old-fashioned and obsessive commitment to the Law.[5] Ultimately, I too will argue that Webster is more than simply an amoral purveyor of commercial thrills; but it is important to see that Webster's moral stance as well as his experimental dramaturgy grows out of his participation in and response to his contemporaries' political, social, and artistic concerns. In Webster no less than in the best of his contemporaries, form expresses vision; in such a man, at such a time, restless formal experimentation may suggest a search for moral as well as aesthetic solutions. To demonstrate that Webster does not offer simply a morality of aestheticism, either his own or his period's, and that he helps develop an attitude toward the social and political world shared by his peers and revealed in their own evolving artistic careers, is, finally, to place Webster in the broadest and most illuminating context.

Preliminary research for this study, undertaken in England and America, was begun under a summer stipend from the National Endowment for the Humanities; work was completed with generous aid from the Committee on Faculty Development—Affirmative Action of the University of California, Santa Barbara. I would like to express my appreciation to both of these bodies. I am grateful, too, to the staffs of the following libraries for use of the collections in their care: the British Library, Senate House Library (University of London), and the Henry E. Huntington Library, San Marino, California. Parts of Chapter 5 appeared first in *Modern Language Review*, 72 (1977), as "Destructive Will and Social Chaos in *The Devil's Law-Case*," and I thank the editors for permission to quote from this material.

Debts to individuals are both more extensive and less specific or easily articulated. For continued inspiration—as scholars, critics, and models of what the humane study of literature is ultimately about—I want to express a long-standing gratitude to Eugene M. Waith and Norman Rabkin. In more immediate terms, Robert Dent has read parts of this manuscript with his customary diligence, tact, and good sense; he will note the absence of some, at least, of the follies he tried to avert. My research assistant, Jody Millward, spent devoted hours checking, proofing, and in general tidying my loose ends. Finally, for an unforgiving hostility to half-formed ideas or inadequate expression, through inspiration and despair, I thank A. R. Braunmuller.

The Theatrical Setting

 central difficulty in the sixteenth-century reconciliation of classical and Christian ideals is the problem of the will, that aggressive selfishness which casts a dark shadow on Renaissance individualism. This issue becomes particularly acute in the early seventeenth century, as the social and political scope for that will's exercise becomes more apparently circumscribed. In drama, decorum of subject matter and character suggests tragedy as the natural canvas on which to paint the struggle between ego and environment. Certainly the prevalence as well as the nature of tragedy after 1600 reflects this heightened concern, even while the stories being dramatized trace increasingly political and secular preoccupations. The expansive Marlovian vision that pitted and defined man against his cosmos narrows to more difficult and delicate explorations of his social and political relations. Yet this development is not simply linear or direct. In the 1590s the popularity of English chronicle-history plays suggests a transitional, exploratory attitude toward serious political subjects, an attitude presumably encouraged by the dramatists' changing interests as well as by their patriotism. Even more than early tragedy, the chronicle-histories exhibit a growing concern with limitation, with the restrictions placed on individual aspiration by our human environment as well as by our humanity. And an increasingly complex and confining sociopolitical environment also presses more sharply on the individual himself, on those personal limitations which frustrate desired action from within and distort the will that desires. In the seventeenth century, tragedy then turns to probe the power struggles and private temptations of courts more nearly recognizable to its audience, in behavior if not in name. Perhaps as partial legacy of its temporary association with monarchic history, tragedy's interest now lies as much in the irresolvable tensions between the powerful individual and his environment as in the attempts of one to subdue the other.

Perhaps less clearly, comedy comes to share certain subjects with tragedy and creates dramatic worlds increasingly similar to tragedy's. Such convergences finally produce the claustrophobic, antiheroic world of Middleton's late tragedies. Earlier transformations in comedy's form and focus, though less striking than the differences between *Tamburlaine* and *Hamlet*, reveal the pressure of this shift. Indeed, since the major playwrights' comedies either precede or coincide with their tragic writings, we can see how this redefinition and innovation might not only appeal to the audience's changing taste, but at the same time serve individual authors as a transitional form, a testing ground through which they approached new possibilities for tragedy. Serious drama increasingly depicts worlds with clear relevance to the audience's own. Comedy, too, comes to mirror more closely—again, often under aliases—its audience's immediate environment: urban and middle class, competitive both socially and economically.

This is not to suggest that comedy suddenly becomes preeminently "realistic," or that a few place names and con games establish it as social documentary. City comedy is little more realistic in that sense than the verse satire and satirical comedy out of which it partly grew, or than the tragedy with which it shared a stage—even where the tragic subjects are as rigorously contemporary as Chapman's. Except in the most humdrum of domestic dramas or the triumphs of Naturalism, comedy's characters are as distorted and extreme in their own way as tragedy's. Despite some obvious topical references, then, city comedy may not tell us much about Jacobean economic conditions,[1] but its popularity does tell us something about the concerns of its writers and audiences. Its satiric tone and type characters derive from the late 1590s taste for satire, both in and out of drama; it also recycles the intriguing Vice of the old moralities, ever ready to fool Mankind into pursuing the goods of this world. In structure and feeling, however, its conventions reach back into a past that has little to do with Jacobean "realism": Roman New Comedy. Plautus and Terence had long been a part of the Renaissance academic curriculum and later reappeared in Anglicized adaptations and in Christianized prodigal son plays;[2] less directly, perhaps, they influence early Shakespearean comedy, where "the forms of New Comedy . . . reshape medieval romance."[3] But tastes changed, and neither the wanderings of romance nor dramatized verse satire, with its parade of fools and satirical exposer, retained their savor. Playwrights set about refurbishing and updating the form which had expressed their classical masters' more cynical attitude toward amatory and financial intrigue. Thus while realistic settings bear no necessary relationship to realism of plot and character, the dramatists' new subjects and locales made different conventions appropriate; where none satisfied, hybrids were created.

In both pure and mixed forms, generic conventions shape the artistic product. Genres offer ways of interpreting and recording life. In Rosalie Colie's terms, their social force and function are like "abbreviations for a 'set' on the world"; they constitute a variety of "tiny subcultures with their own habits, habitats, and structures of ideas as well as their own forms."[4] Within themselves the main dramatic "kinds" also offered choices, and a shift from one set of conventions to another—from romance comedy to Roman intrigue and farce—may indicate rejection of popular earlier modes as inadequate ("unrealistic" in this sense only) for current needs. Other experiments questioned traditional modes even more radically: if generic conventions governed, generic distinctions met frequent defeat. The increasing overlap of subject in comedy and tragedy—romantic intrigue, adultery, and domestic affairs, even revenge—indicates a certain self-conscious delight in challenging the critics' formalist poetic. Increasingly we feel this confident self-awareness: a sense that the dramatist's perspective on his material, rather than that material itself, determines the play's nature; that his manipulation of conventions throughout, not just in the plot's conclusion, can and will control his audience's response.[5] Among the more educated (or pretentious), this heady sense of having violated canons of acceptability, even probability, provoked a spate of prefatory letters, prologues, and inductions which defended, explained, or apologized for the drama that followed. Even apparently stern conservatives and purists join the progressive vanguard. They fight their theoretical battles largely, in good English fashion, by changing or "reinterpreting" theory to justify the immediate example. England's cheerful disregard of critical theory's prohibitions provided fertile soil for such experimentation. When the final test is the box office, success has a way of erasing careful theoretical distinctions. After all, English drama had always been one of mixed modes—alternating comic and tragic actions, even spilling clowns over into the presence chamber.[6] Sidney had failed to stem the tide of mongrelization, and the gap separating mingled kings and clowns from a Janus-faced action, one which blended their deeds and characteristics, presented a leap of no great difficulty.

Commerical conditions encouraged this rapid proliferation of hybrid forms in other ways. To be sure, such conditions put a premium on novelty itself, as well as inviting the lucrative repetition of previous successes; yet writing plays for an age, not for all time, encourages the best as well as the worst experiments and can push a creative dramatist repeatedly to stretch himself and his medium. Thus newcomers like Marston and Middleton specialize in new *kinds* of plays, but Jonson, Chapman, and Shakespeare, who shared an Elizabethan experience and reputation, prove to be equally experimental.

Two additional features contribute to both the rate and scope of this theatrical flowering. The revival and commercialization of the children's troupes at the turn of the century provided more than merely two extra competing theaters. Differences in the child actors' capabilities, in their audiences' demand for sophisticated and courtly entertainment, in the theatrical setting itself, all fostered innovative play writing as well as adaptations of the older, Lylyesque fare.[7] The little eyases' success in turn encouraged the adult companies to copy, to match, to overgo them in originality and appeal. In discussing this synergistic effect, R. A. Foakes concludes that the reestablished boys' companies "challenged the adult stages strongly enough to force them to take over and use in their own way styles and techniques of drama first exploited in the plays put on by the boys; that in order to maintain their challenge to the older and more solidly established adult theatres, the children and their dramatists were driven, especially at first, to bold experiment; and that, during the decade following their revival, the children's theatres and the dramatists who wrote for them formed a major influence in determining the course English drama was to take."[8] The different theaters partly shared their audience, so commercial self-interest and artistic curiosity would both ensure close attention to rival offerings. The constant "upping the ante" which Foakes describes demanded a rapid rate of cross-fertilization between public and private companies as well as between rival theaters of either persuasion. In the latter category, such a high degree of self-consciousness, on the audience's part as well as the dramatists', produced in-group sequences full of jokes for the cognoscenti, like the so-called War of the Theaters' plays and the even more closely related *Ho* exchange between Paul's and Blackfriars in 1604 and 1605.

Influence might not be a matter of such distant scrutiny and adaptation. The maddeningly free-lance status of most of the period's dramatists frustrates our attempt to pin certain kinds of troupes to certain kinds of repertoires and playwrights, but it surely helps explain the broad currency of many intellectual attitudes as well as dramatic techniques. Shakespeare is unusual in the close financial involvement which tied him to one acting company; criticism's older, categorical separation of public and private traditions obscures the predictable result of peddling one's talents on the open market. The adaptability of playwrights—and plays—suggests a lower threshold of division and a higher degree of interchange and cross-influence than was once assumed. Jonson, Chapman, Beaumont, Fletcher, Middleton,[9] Dekker, and Webster all wrote for both the children's troupes and for adult companies; Jonson and Webster wrote for not one but several adult companies, and Marston migrated from Paul's to Blackfriars. That the King's Men happily raided the private sector for Marston's *Malcontent* (in retaliation for the boys' theft of *The Spanish Tragedy*) and that other plays (e.g., *Satiromastix*) were also performed by different troupes on both public and private stages, suggests an at least partially interchangeable repertoire. Indeed, after 1608 the King's Men often acted the same plays for both the Blackfriars' private and the Globe's public audience—not only Shakespearean romance, but *Philaster* and Webster's own *Duchess of Malfi*.[10]

Doubtless related to such open-market conditions—and to the payment of low wages for a product in which quantity and speedy execution mattered most—are the period's many collaborative dramatic efforts. The ease with which even the most crankily independent dramatists attuned themselves to the exigencies of multiple authorship still taxes our romantic ideas about solitary genius.[11] That Chapman and Jonson (of all people) should be able to sit down with Marston to produce the accomplished *Eastward Ho* borders on the fantastic, yet the very unlikelihood of such a successful artistic interchange suggests its pertinent origin: a challenge, both commercial and artistic, to answer and improve upon the new type of play which Dekker and Webster had just launched with the boys at Paul's.[12] As critics, we readily cite genre's prime importance—in organizing dramatic material, in providing subjects and conventions of proven commercial worth for adaptation or rebuttal; we accept art's debt to art as well as to that more nebulous entity, reality. Successful "kinds" spawn fads—revenge plays, comical satires, and romances, as well as *Ho* plays—and a new triumph might require imitation by a different company. Given the almost indiscriminate nature of collaboration in this period, financial reasons alone would direct a keen interest to style and technique as well as to generic innovation. Yet the impetus to artistic creation, even where it includes theft and imitation, can hardly derive from monetary considerations alone. We cannot escape the sense of excitement generated by such interplay between playwrights and companies; it is reflected in the plays which are our legacy. At least as significant a motive is simply the effect of one man of talent on another. Clifford Leech rightly maintains that the "nature of major dramatic writing in our period is often largely determined by the effect of dramatist on dramatist and by the effect of a man's own sense of his growth."[13]

The *Ho* interchange demonstrates Webster's early theatrical involvement.[14] Even though his own independent work comes later and our records of him are scanty, Webster's art stands firmly rooted in this early period of heady innovation and exchange; indeed, his career exemplifies that world's fluidity and reflects the constant challenges posed by switching between collaborators, genres, acting companies, and their appropriate clientele. His apprenticeship was served in a number of genres and for both public and private theaters. Though the preface to *The White Devil* acknowledges his early partners Dekker and Heywood, Webster seems to have worked with most of the period's middle and lesser lights. Early collaborations were on popular and historical subjects: according to Henslowe, in 1602 Webster worked on *Caesar's Fall* with Middleton, Munday, Drayton, and Dekker; later in that year he joined Dekker, Heywood, Smith, and Chettle both on *Lady Jane* (in altered form probably *Sir Thomas Wyatt*) for the Earl of Worcester's Men and (minus Wentworth Smith) with the same collaborators on *Christmas Comes But Once a Year*.[15] Quite probably he again worked with Heywood on *Appius and Virginia*, though whether early or late remains a mystery,[16] and in the 1620s with Rowley, Ford, Middleton, and perhaps Massinger. The association with the Earl of Worcester's Men was later reestablished, after they had become the Queen's Men; they staged both *The White Devil* and *The Devil's Law-Case*. The *Ho* plays of 1604–1605 offered the challenge of writing city comedy for the

Paul's boys with Dekker, while at the same time Webster contributed a witty, theatrically self-conscious Induction to the Globe's plundered *Malcontent*. The Globe connection, too, was reestablished with *The Duchess of Malfi*, revived at least twice before its 1623 publication; and about 1621, at the Blackfriars, Shakespeare's former company staged a Middleton-Webster city comedy, *Anything for a Quiet Life*. Thus if Webster's unaided plays show an awareness of what his contemporaries had already done, he had himself been involved with, and helped shape, the traditions on which he later drew.

In the early years of James's reign, then, London's theatrical world immersed Webster in an extraordinarily innovative, creative milieu. Foakes helpfully identifies the crucial impact of the children's troupes on the adult companies' offerings, and the plays which seem to me to cast the most light on Webster's dramaturgy are, to a large extent, products of this challenge. Any definite sequence of influence would be difficult to establish, given our uncertain knowledge about dates of first performances and largely hypothesized contacts, however plausible, resulting from proximity and friendship; chronology is also less significant for my purposes than analyzing the new kinds of plays that absorbed the most talented dramatists in those years and the ways in which subjects, attitudes, and character types as well as techniques developed in both public and private playhouses. Thus Marston's *Antonio and Mellida* may derive structural and thematic inspiration from Jonson's comical satires, but we also trace in its second part, *Antonio's Revenge,* similarities with Shakespeare's contemporary work *Hamlet*; although cross-influence here is uncertain, *Hamlet* definitely affected the later *Malcontent*.[17]

If a theatrical revolution seems to get under way at the turn of the century in the works of Shakespeare and Marston and in the widespread experiments with comical satire (which may include *Troilus and Cressida* as well as *Hamlet* and the *Antonio* plays), a period of truly explosive creativity follows in the years 1604–1607. When the theaters reopened after the plague in 1604, they rapidly developed a topical and urban satiric comedy, impelled by the *Ho* authors as well as by Middleton. Yet in both substance and mood, *The Dutch Courtesan* and *The Widow's Tears* seem closer to *Measure for Measure* than to Middleton, though Shakespeare's play may owe something to the popular disguised dukes of Middleton's earlier *Phoenix* as well as Marston's *Malcontent*. City comedy is itself, of course, a notably slippery genre concept, and definitions vary: to some, it means satiric urban comedy of financial and sexual intrigue, perfected by Middleton for the boys' companies but including Jonson's comedies of financial chicanery for the adults; for others the parameters broaden to include another development in the public theaters' heartily optimistic, morally didactic citizen comedies.[18] While *The Dutch Courtesan* probably falls within any definition of the genre, and financial and sexual intrigues reveal connections with Chapman's *Widow's Tears* (despite its uncommercial, Cyprian setting), the probing philosophical substratum in both plays also suggests their affinity with Shakespeare's exploration of the muddled relations among passion, judgment, and social order.

The links among these three plays extend beyond their striking similarity of tone and subject matter and prove more illuminating for Webster than the mere fact of chronological proximity suggests. In the years 1604–1605 he was involved with the King's Men as well as with the boys' companies and likely to be interested in Shakespeare's latest efforts as well as in what Chapman and Marston were doing to stay out of trouble.[19] This, despite the fact that we have long held the latter two dramatists at a critical distance—from each other, from Shakespeare, from us—for reasons in one case of personal antipathy, in both for failure to control or fulfill their obvious talent. That at one moment in such very different careers similar thematic concerns should lead to comparable tragicomic solutions, even specific dramatic devices, fascinates us, all the more in that they are such apparently dissimilar men. And if our traditional classifications and separation—by preferred genre, by theatrical affiliation, by personal temperament—seem here to be unsatisfactory, we must consider why certain dramatists and plays suggest such pertinent connections with each other and with Webster. What carpet includes Webster in its pattern?

Despite undeniable continuity in dramatic forms and playwrights, the first years of the seventeenth century are marked, as I have noted, by some startling theatrical departures, distinctive in tone, iconoclastic and unsettling in form. They vary in popular as well as artistic success and influence: *Hamlet* as well as *Troilus and Cressida*, *The Malcontent* as well as the *Antonio* plays. Yet these plays seem in retrospect to be already quintessentially "Jacobean"; certainly they are harbingers of things to come. A period of intense creativity succeeds, and each of the most innovative dramatists—Jonson, Chapman, Marston, Shakespeare—seems to experience a critical and unsettled point in his own career. Severally and together, they ransack traditional genres and topoi, stretch comedy and tragedy (and most of the possible combinations) to express new ideas. Of course, other dramatists are successful and influential, even occasionally innovative. Dekker and Webster *may* have initiated city comedy's vogue, though Middleton rapidly perfected its popular form;[20] Middleton himself seems less experimental here than later, when he turns to tragedy. In this period Beaumont and Fletcher still flounder separately, though certainly a commercial failure like *The Knight of the Burning Pestle* suggests that at least Beaumont shared his seniors' interest in satiric tone and mixed forms. So few did so much, perhaps, because the artistic and intellectual maturity of a number of very (albeit variously) talented dramatists coincided with an explosive and challenging, as well as threatening, historical moment. The times incited the best and supported them financially, and in their train lesser men, even hacks, often proved inspired.

That there is a core of playwrights and plays which embodies, by whatever combination of influence and independent discovery, a distinctively Jacobean temper and a predilection for new, satiric forms comes as no surprise. We can also agree that in the years immediately following Elizabeth's death the major dramatists experience a turbulent period of increased tragic interest that is partially obscured by overlapping comedies and by a shared taste for tragicomedy. Out of this common pan they leapt into different fires: Marston soon leaves the stage; Chapman writes increasingly pessimistic tragedies; popular dramatists like Beaumont and Fletcher, Jonson, and Shakespeare (after a series of darkening tragedies) all turn to explore other possibilities.

A period of intellectual questioning and formal experiment marked by such "modern" disillusionment appeals to a twentieth-century temperament. Though only one strand of the Jacobean intellectual fabric, of course, it is an important one and ties this period to a larger, European tapestry; we can fruitfully discuss Jacobean drama as well as poetry in terms of Mannerism or the Baroque. And it is in the light of this period and these playwrights that Webster must be read, however he later ranked his own debts. His distinctive dramaturgy, its iconoclasm as well as its character-types and formal conventions, is rooted in his apprenticeship, and his own tragedies spring from that much-tossed soil. Webster did more than profit from his predecessors' experiments in theme and technique; he so absorbed their work that in his own two tragedies he developed and extended both attitudes and tragic form that are only implicit in their achievement. While his masters turned elsewhere or retired, Webster advanced in dramatic terms one aspect of that early seventeenth-century intellectual revolution, an aspect which culminates in the tragedies of his own contemporaries (and later collaborators), Middleton and Ford.

My interest in Webster's Jacobean context, then, is rather convolutedly twofold. Technically, Webster's unaided plays draw on specific dramatic developments as well as on his contemporaries' general willingness to pursue uncanonical forms. Webster's share in his models' intellectual concerns governs his choice not only of what to adapt, but also of how he will extend that heritage to express his own vision. In exploring this relation between thematic interests and formal development, I cannot specify plays which certainly influenced Webster intellectually or stylistically. Indeed, the kind of evidence uncovered by source studies or parallel-hunting suggests that, though a compulsive borrower, Webster used primarily nondramatic sources; the dramatist most frequently pillaged was William Alexander, whose plays were meant to be read, not staged, and who was hardly a major influence in matters of dramatic form.[21] And though Webster shared his taste for Montaigne with Marston, among others, common intellectual affinities would not prove even knowledge of a specific play, much less admiration. Though I have argued for pervasive cross-influence in this period, as well as Webster's personal knowledge of a number of the major dramatists, I am less interested in proving particular plays or playwrights relevant than in establishing characteristic attitudes and the theatrical responses those attitudes evoked. Most distinctively, the pressure of critical questioning pushes comedy toward satiric city comedy and tragicomedy and distorts tragedy by undermining its affirmations. Broadly speaking, there does seem to be a "natural" development, as dislocations in comic form in turn affect tragedy; but this progression is also telescoped, even simultaneous. During a brief period, for example, Shakespeare and Chapman intersperse comedy, tragicomedy, and tragedy, in no tidily logical order. What is certain is that romantic or humours comedy no longer seems satisfactory.

Demands of space and clarity limit the number of plays that can be usefully discussed. In trying to establish a context, I proceed synoptically: coherent discussion of representative plays and playwrights seems more effective than a digressive list, no matter how ample or comprehensive. Thus while mention must be made of Webster's significant debts to Middletonian city comedy and to Jonson's and Middleton's experiments in satiric tragedy,[22] I have chosen to concentrate on two more inclusive developments that I hope shed more light on Webster's art. The first is the surprising incidence of a kind of satiric and philosophical tragicomedy which may, though certainly it need not, take the form of city comedy. Of such plays, Marston's *The Dutch Courtesan*, Shakespeare's *Measure for Measure*, and Chapman's *The Widow's Tears* group themselves conveniently in the years 1604 and 1605. Of course, not all plays in these formative years, even by these authors, could be so grouped, but the fact that others—by Shakespeare, by Marston, by Jonson—could be substituted supports, I hope, the usefulness of seeing this kind of play as something new and distinctive. Second, these same authors were also drawn to tragedy, often to heroic tragedy. The same pressures which fused theoretically distinct genres create interesting, even analogous, developments in tragic form and feeling. That writers of satiric comedy or tragicomedy should produce *Sejanus* or *The Revenger's Tragedy* may seem only natural; the links between satiric tragicomedy and heroic, political tragedy in Chapman and Shakespeare (especially the late Roman tragedies) are obviously more complex and, I think, revealing. Marston's *Sophonisba* joins him to this "trend," though that play's interest may lie more in the fact that Marston wrote it, and so shortly after *The Dutch Courtesan*, than in its own internal complexity.

Such an admittedly selective approach incurs obvious dangers: its restrictions may do cursory, even summary, justice to Webster's intellectual environment; even for the dramatic traditions most important to Webster, my selection of plays is arbitrary and so may create fictitious patterns of concern or sequences of development. Yet while the period's diversity makes nonsense of tidy categories, these two developments, among others, do characterize this turning point in individual careers as well as in Elizabethan drama as a whole. If my choice of plays ultimately seems representative, it will show that the works of some very dissimilar playwrights, written for the full spectrum of the Jacobean theatrical audience, themselves suggest a shared response to new conditions. Another restriction will increase both the benefits and dangers of concentration: where possible, I will discuss experiments in tragicomedy and tragedy by the same author. Such limitation emphasizes continuity as well as change: we cannot explain what seems distinctively Jacobean as simply the product of a new generation eager to assert its difference, a young Turks' revolution against their elders' success. Further, watching one author's varied dramatic realizations as he shunts between different genres, learning from himself as well as from his contemporaries, may help distinguish the shared from the uniquely obsessive. Finally, I hope to suggest the logic, though there can be no real proof, for a kind of compressed artistic development for which we have no tangible evidence in Webster himself. Because he wrote no drama between 1605 and *The White Devil* (1611), we can only speculate as to what that development might have been, though the fact of Webster's return might suggest a continuous if vicarious interim interest. Webster himself, of course, refuses to conform to wishful schemata: after early collaborations in tragedy, chronicle-history, and city comedy, he disappears; he writes no tragicomedy before tragedy, or even concurrently; and when he does produce a tragicomedy, it is heavily tinged with the brand popularized by Beaumont and Fletcher, in defiance of his apparent thematic interests. Despite such churlish behavior toward his future critics, the fact remains that Webster's two tragedies seem to arise naturally, if not inevitably, from his contemporaries' earlier experiments. Though distinctively his own, each seems also to belong to his age.

CHAPTER I

The Art of Distance I:
Tragicomedy

IKE all art, drama reflects as well as transcends the social and intellectual conditions of its creation. The breakup of the Renaissance synthesis was accompanied by more than intellectual doubt and restlessness; economic, religious, and political changes helped to undermine the security—even questioned the theoretical form—of the social contract which comedy absorbs and, comfortingly, reflects back at its audience. More important for both comedy and tragedy is the fact that behind specific challenges to received opinion lies a fundamental alteration in consciousness. George R. Kernodle traces changes in art and science to the new sense of "a separation of man from nature, a change that required not only new philosophical concepts but new ways of feeling."[1] An acute sense of self and a need to redefine its boundaries link the period's real-life figures, its artists and scientists and politicians, with its literary creations. Though Hegel first used the term *alienation* as cultural criticism, Arnold Hauser traces the fact of estrangement from both environment and self to Renaissance economic and social conditions. He also finds Renaissance anticipations of later philosophical explanations: in Campanella's epistemology, in order to know itself, the mind must become its own object. In art the responsive style, Mannerism, expresses that "unrest, anxiety, and bewilderment generated by the process of alienation of the individual from society and the reification of the whole cultural process."[2]

In the broadest sense, alienation is the playwrights' subject, too. Jacobean drama can be seen as symptom, or product, of this fundamental shift in humanity's relation to itself and its world. Developing a historical perspective, the individual becomes both particularly conscious of what has been, a dissolution one cannot arrest, and uneasy about what might be, very differently, in the future. Sensing the dimensions of this historical process, the best dramatists explore its effects. They use stories of individual people in particular circumstances to test ways of dealing with disintegrating social and intellectual structures; they combine different generic conventions as formal analogies for, and expressions of, that need for new definitions. These plays, Mannerist if you will, do not so much dramatize a static condition or attitude as articulate responses to it.

The separation of objective from subjective alters the artist's relation both to his audience and to the fictions through which he approaches reality. In humanity's displacement from its former physical and spiritual environment Kernodle finds an explanation for those theatrical versions of scientific man, "watching the world with no feelings, no values, no human response, but only intellectual curiosity,"[3] who proved so deeply disturbing. By placing the characteristically Jacobean observer-commentator in this larger context, his intermediary position, both between author and artistic creation and between author and audience, becomes clearer. Whether as closely identified as Jonson with Horace or as distantly imaged as Shakespeare in Duke Vincentio, such figures have long been seen as authorial surrogates, dramatis personae whose control of their stage world bears analogies with the dramatist's relation to his play. Since the cool observer is often the protagonist and invites the audience's identification through his intellectual acumen and, frequently, his direct addresses to us, he serves as our surrogate, too, and allows us to share a creator-observer's distance and superiority.[4] The play's action, on one level, then becomes a test of our joint ability to establish and maintain control over the story's challenges.

In dramatizing such detachment on stage and exploring the relations between observer and observed, Jacobean playwrights apply to philosophical ends their interest in more purely literary trends. The observer-commentator's ambiguous dramatic status promises such tantalizing extensions; his attractive flexibility itself develops out of satire's transformation of both comedy and tragedy at the century's turn. Whatever its social or political roots, formal satire's adaptation to the stage put exciting pressure on both traditional genres. Satire by nature blends levity and seriousness; the satiric impulse seems to push both comedy and tragedy, from different directions, toward hybrid interpenetration: on the one hand such different admixtures as *Hamlet* and *Antonio's Revenge*, on the other a general effort to stiffen comic *dolce* with more specifically satiric *utile*. Chapman invents humours comedy; Jonson strengthens its satiric stance in his comical satires; Marston develops it within a mode of literary parody suited to his child actors. Yet Shakespeare only nodded briefly in the direction of comical satire, and Jonson's and Marston's efforts did not long survive their usefulness in the Poetomachia.

Dissatisfaction with early comical satire may reflect aesthetic distaste for a basically nondramatic action—the thesis structure of criticism/exposure/punishment which strings funny yet often discrete exposure scenes along a tenuous thread of plot "development."[5] Stasis is not the structure's only disadvantage, however. Comical satire tends to separate the just critic from his society: fools parade before him, to be judged against the standards he represents and upholds. Although drama inevitably reduces the satirist figure to a character, subject to exposure alongside his victims, satire naturally leans toward enforcing unreal extremes. Characters are divided from each other, distinguished primarily by being either judged or judge (no matter how fallible). Confrontation replaces interaction. Follies characterized by attitude, dress, and linguistic excess are funny but unthreatening; no matter how serious their implications (and Jonson especially seeks to underline potential social danger), their representatives are still fools and do not deeply challenge the satirist's judgment or the audience's complacency. The satirist's yardstick reaches toward the opposite extreme and so divides him from his audience as well as from the stage fops he castigates: his is an ideal vision of potential rectitude which no fallible individual—or society—can fully realize.

Formal satire does not, then, transfer smoothly to the stage. Indeed, satire's internal tensions alter yet intensify when it aspires to the condition of dramatic comedy.[6] Once the Old Testament voice is given a local habitation and a name—regardless of whether the satirist partakes of the vices he lashes—he becomes one member of a community moving toward a *comic* resolution. And comedy posits a norm attainable, because defined, by us all. It struggles to compel both satirist and sinner to accommodate themselves; it envisions and enforces social salvation and leaves spiritual matters to higher, nondramatic, authority. Both the satirist's standards and his person, his jealously maintained distance from other characters, pull against comedy's goal—a workable community.

Of course, comedy does not disregard the soul's health, nor does it ignore the connections between moral discovery and social regenera-

tion. Romantic comedy, especially Shakespeare's, had always emphasized personal moral and psychological transformation; even comical
satire prefers exposure leading to self-knowledge and reformation, though
it provides final judgment scenes and a firm moral authority as society's
safeguard. Yet neither inner change nor group regeneration are necessary products of the comic action. In *Love's Labor's Lost* the wom-
en may refuse their still adolescent lovers, but the human couples in
A Midsummer Night's Dream sail to a marriageable conclusion untouched, except in the most superficial way, by their experiences. Jaques
absents himself from *As You Like It*'s communal felicity; but as far as
society is concerned, if he is willing to dance its measures his private
attitudes are his own business. Mature Middletonian city comedy is a
good instance of satiric comedy that dispenses with satirist and judg-
mental finale alike. Satiric exposure is delegated to an exciting (as well
as humorous) intrigue plot. Final social harmony is achieved, usually,
by external readjustments rather than internal transformation, and what
few scenes of moral self-recognition and comment Middleton does include are often seen as blots on an otherwise admirably pristine ironic
effect.

We do not demand moral or psychological transformation unless we
have been led to expect it. Varying these conventional expectations,
determining what we will demand of a work, is an option increasingly
explored in the Jacobean hybrids. The way to make comedy deal with
serious communal problems, with the individual's relationship to and
responsibility for that community, did not lie in the addition of a satirist
and an ending which upheld his judgments. Satiric set speeches and
even commentators crop up in all kinds of Jacobean plays; they reflect
the age's temper rather than any especial generic affinity. Serious social
criticism turned instead to experimentally combining comedy and tragedy in order to intensify—to make problematic and crucial—the relation between character and society and between audience and play. The
intrusion of generically contradictory perspectives on action or protagonist is not new in the seventeenth century, of course. Many recent
studies, especially in tragedy, have explored Elizabethan as well as Jacobean "perspectivism." For comedy, we need only recall that in *Love's
Labor's Lost,* for example, the young women do not reject the lords
simply because the young men have not matured; they refuse marriage
because Marcade's news has exploded the kind of comic world Na-

varre's park initially represented, destroyed the "comic contract" whereby a discovered preference for marital union over studious celibacy would have validated the young men's eligibility. Yet however effectively such intrusions qualify our simplistic response, they do not (with a few exceptions, like *The Jew of Malta*) destroy our sense that we know what genus we are responding to, or undermine totally our acquiescence in the play's final ordering. Something radically different, and far more confusing, happens in the experimental tragicomedies of 1603 to 1605.

Many of these plays grow out of and then feed back into their author's private tragic vision. Each author's personal development here intersects with the common preoccupations of his historical moment as well as with his peers' artistic influence. Interestingly, despite *The Malcontent*'s quotations from Guarini's *Il Pastor Fido* (translated 1602), Marston's play and its contemporary tragicomedies exhibit few connections with Italian theory and practice. G. K. Hunter may be correct in arguing that Marston is here attempting "to reconstruct this genre in English," but, as he goes on to say, Marston's play bears small relation in structure or mood to Guarini's pastoral mode.[7] And Marston turns to a different blend, as well as to a city comedy setting, in *The Dutch Courtesan*.

Some distinctions might help clarify these differences. As recently analyzed by Arthur C. Kirsch, romance tragicomedy slowly perfected a drama imaging the Christian paradox, *felix culpa*. Such tragicomedy, following Guarini's authoritative defense as well as his pastoral example, reaches completion in Shakespeare's late romances, though its development is actually dominated by Beaumont and Fletcher. These plays all reveal a self-conscious interest in style and dramatic effect; in structure, the plot's shifting oppositions finally resolve themselves organically to transform the initial confusion and malice into a harmonious resolution undreamt of in the opening acts, yet also dependent upon the very sufferings which had then seemed insurmountable.[8] Shakespeare did indeed return at the end of his career to a tragicomic blend, to develop themes he had earlier touched on in plays like *All's Well That Ends Well*. His way to that spacious vision lay through tragedy, however, and only in hindsight—and with the inestimable benefit of having the late romances before us—can we call this return inevitable, or even "natural." If *Coriolanus* or *Timon of Athens* were the last Shakespearean play we possessed, who could posit on the basis of *All's Well* (still less, of *Measure for Measure*) a lost *Winter's Tale* or *Tempest*? We would see the middle tragicomedies as simply the last guttering of the genial spirit which provided us with *As You Like It* and *Twelfth Night* before entering a long Danish night.

The fascinating earlier hybrids—Shakespeare's *All's Well* and *Measure* as well as Marston's *Malcontent* and *Dutch Courtesan,* Jonson's *Volpone,* and Chapman's *The Widow's Tears*—all offer pauses in their authors' very different careers, testing points whose proximity alone suggests their debt to each other rather than to romance tragicomedy's separate development. While each creates a self-conscious and theatrical relationship with its audience, what I will call (for lack of a better phrase) ironic tragicomedy refuses fully to resolve and transcend the human sufferings and contradictions it explores. Though such plays may culminate in scenes of recognition which turn bad fortune to happy reunion, the plot's resolution fails to solve (indeed, bypasses rather than transcends) difficulties the play has itself raised. Tragedy does not dissolve into comedy; it faces comedy across a gap which the plot only pretends to span. Instead of entering a new, higher, and more desirable social plateau, we seem not to have advanced in any essential way; despite altered alignments and proclaimed harmony, the audience feels it has been returned, frustrated, to its own point of departure. The plays are ironic in the most fundamental way: they tell us one thing but mean something else.

What distinguishes these plays from later romance tragicomedy is their deliberate exploration of difficulties they cannot fully resolve. They allow and exploit generic dissonance. Their variously blended comic and tragic conventions serve this end, not any programmatic fulfillment of a new genre's prescriptions, such as the inclusion of different ranks and rhetorical levels or the final averting of threatened deaths.[9] Princes and commoners mingle in some, but others restrict themselves to court or city types; some bring certain characters near death, but in others we would be hard pressed to find near-fatality used as a means of gaining "tragic" seriousness. Rather, the pressure of serious subject matter (perhaps inherent in the source story, but often forced upon it) requires philosophical arguments, situations, and characterization that subvert the comic plot and its "natural" perspective.

Comedy begins to explore variants of tragic themes; typically comic characters and situations are given more weight than they can easily bear. Relocated in our quotidian world and in characters whose Herculean self-conceptions are quickly betrayed by their goals and their surroundings, tragic aspiration dwindles into simple narcissism. Where tragedy sees the human will grandly reshaping the world in its own image, in a lesser setting that same ambition decays into our common desire both to make others gratify our own wishes and to see our self-image reflected in others' admiration and envy. At its least threatening, this desire blossoms in self-delusions and affected posturing, follies typified by the fops and court ladies aboard that ship of fools which sails through so many satiric comedies, in all ages. The spectrum of ambition, however, is continuous, and this fact began to press sharply against conventional artistic distinctions. Pushed to contain disruptive will in both domestic and civic realms, the comic order totters. In an earlier play, *The Merchant of Venice* for instance, the comic world is so securely established, its values and assumptions so firmly held by the majority of its characters, that it can handle Shylock's intrusive passion, outwit him at his own game, and self-righteously discard him when he refuses its terms. In ironic tragicomedy the comic order may triumph, but the anarchic passions are no longer alien, exorcisable intruders. Neither singular nor harmlessly eccentric, egotistic ambition threatens the community from within. The comic conclusion—that image of the reasserted social contract in which we recognize and submit to the behavioral norms which allow communal living—is gained by wit but held together by no more than dramatic convention. No whole, greater than the sum of its parts and harmoniously attuned to its physical universe, has been formed; individuals remain discrete units, temporarily cowed or outwitted but incapable of fully relinquishing the proud selfhood that subverts an enduring union.

In such a world the individual is pulled in opposite, equally unsatisfactory, directions. He may retreat into himself and become trapped in his own fantasied self-image; he is also enmeshed in a society that limits his actions while refusing to allow passivity or withdrawal. Critical, resisting comic integration, seeking ways to preserve his autonomy and even dominate his hostile environment, he is in any case separate from his peers, detached from that community in which he must dwell. In such a protagonist and such a milieu, literary, social, and philosophical trends merge. Our discussion comes full circle, for the Jacobean sense of displacement helps explain why ironic tragicomedy developed the same concerns as were prominent in satiric comedy and revenge tragedy in about 1600. What unites such different forms is not so much their inclusion of satiric speeches and topoi as their preoccupation with the ideal of disengagement—as philosophic goal, as social indictment, as psychological retreat, but also as a means of dealing with the problem of action in a newly impersonal world. Through the theatrically useful observer-commentator figure dramatists could explore the ideal of detachment he conventionally represented.

Absolute detachment, the absence of human feelings or response, is of course impossible, at least in drama, but even the attempt to gain an emotional distance consonant with one's sense of displacement is repeatedly smashed by the intensely personal demands of family or duty. The most apparently self-sufficient satirist is forced by his own rage to descend to the fools' arena; the retreat to philosophic acceptance is pierced by the exhortations of a father's ghost, a murdered son's body. More interesting than detachment's predictable failure in the face of immediate iniquity or blood debts is the protagonist's changing motivation: increasingly, detachment is sought as practical means rather than as philosophic end in itself. *The Malcontent* crystalizes the shift: victim becomes aggressor, displacement hones control. The aim is not true, dispassionate objectivity but the more Baconian goal of knowledge as power. Man disengages himself from his world, yet, by virtue of the understanding that noninvolvement brings, he also becomes engineer of that environment. Emotional distance permits manipulation; objectivity is enlisted in the service of the ultimately subjective, desiring ego.[10]

Nor should this odd coupling surprise us. Solipsism arises naturally from acutely felt displacement: a sense of alienation may produce compensatory fantasies of self-sufficiency as often as despair. Narcissism can be an active condition. Disengagement's aim, then, is twofold and affects internal as well as external economies. It is self-protective, offering the psychological comforts promised by the stoics' philosophical renunciation: by refusing commitment to Fortune's world of mutable people and things, one guards against disillusion. Yet the rewards of noncommitment extend beyond self-defense to self-realization, even self-assertion. Removing oneself from the game of life suggests superiority to its rules, the possibility of maneuvering the depersonalized objects of existence into configurations which satisfy and confirm one's sense of omnipotent selfhood. Disengagement can, paradoxically, feed hopes of bending the world's shows to the will's desires.

Generically, the move toward tragicomedy is a natural one: finding a successful stance *should,* it is hoped, turn disaster into social as well as personal unity. *The Malcontent* bends the revenge form to a wholly new issue: retaining the serious implications of usurpation and its passionate violence, it must shape character as well as structure so that disaster can be averted and some evil passions be transformed, not just contained. Malevole, of course, provides the major solution. As stoic satirist he has achieved the distance necessary to see his world in perspective and penetrate its evils; his great *de contemptu* speeches both reveal this personal discovery and operate persuasively on at least some of his enemies.[11] An intelligent intriguer, he both frames and contains the threat of evil, for his adopted role of malcontent tool-villain allows him the knowledge and manipulative control that assure us he will not long remain a victim.

Malevole-Altofront is a brilliant dramatic solution as well as an influential "type" character, but he provokes questions about identity and role, philosophic vision and worldly action, which this tragicomedy does not wish to pursue. The extent to which Malevole is a separable mask, a projection of Altofront's self, or some combination of the two, is debatable; the question may remain academic because the play dissolves into epilogue at "the very point at which Malevole becomes Altofront again."[12] A rapid transformation of persona into character into actor neatly closes the play with an image of man as role-player and a suggestion that social control is proportionate to one's facility in practicing this art. It precludes much real worry about Malevole's delight in disguise and manipulation, in folly itself. Nor need we preoccupy ourselves with contradictions between his philosophic vision of earth as mere grave and Golgotha, his satiric comments on the court's vicious passions (many of whose representatives remain unchanged at play's end), or his deft maneuvering to regain the worldly power he has so disprized to Pietro.

Perhaps such implicit contradictions explain some of the central figure's power, the impression he gives of complexity in a world of stereotypes. Certainly, in transforming the revenge play into an inverted, tragicomic, pattern Marston discovers a character who continues to fascinate. Disguise and deception hint revelatory significance: they may realize the disguiser's hidden nature, release unsuspected drives which the known social identity kept in check. In the malcontent's confrontation with a conventional (though not very bright) Machiavel we glimpse an analogous delight in deceit and manipulation for their own sake, a similar will to power. The witty Vice of the Interlude, the tricky Roman slave, and the moral critic merge in an effort to control a world populated by aggressors and victims, users and used. Here, where the satirist slides into the self-seeking intriguer, Malevole may claim to influence later, more clearly villainous malcontents. In a more positive light, he is the normally good man maneuvering through the temptations of disguise and manipulation toward normally good ends, a composite figure who provides the opportunity to explore human nature more fully. Mixing qualities usually segregated into black or white stereotypes, he combines the satirist's traditional moral security and distance from evil with the allure of practical competence and witty vitality; as "white" Machiavel he offers a potential ideal, a viable, even desirable, new mediation between self and environment.[13] In such a figure the age confronts itself, its new world, its aspirations.

Malevole-Altofront may not, of course, have proved such a catalyst, or for no one besides Marston, but such a fanciful reconstruction at least helps explain why such a figure should suddenly proliferate. His nature invites exploration in itself. Dramatically, it offers a unifying structure for intrigue comedy which is not necessarily (or primarily) amatory and which lacks romantic comedy's genial vision of communal harmony. If the world of Marston's early tragedy and tragicomedy moves away from traditional decorum's high demands—including as it does many characters who would be at home in his comical satires—we have seen comedy itself seek a structure and, more importantly, a world view answerable to its own increasingly jaundiced vision. Easily a satirist, the observer-intriguer is also readily assimilable to the witty gamester's function and to the intrigue-structure of New Comedy, to which comic dramatists in general were turning.

Despite obvious differences, the possibilities and attractions of this character's pragmatic mastery link *Measure for Measure* with Marston's *Dutch Courtesan* and Chapman's *Widow's Tears*. Superficially at least, each play also uses the discovery of irrepressible human sexuality to reexamine individual and social identity; each dramatist distorts traditional comic patterns to explore individual responses to that fundamental human nature which his earlier satiric work had begun to redefine. The critical focus becomes more individual and psychological than in

The Malcontent, but all three dramatists link their individual studies to larger, communal problems. In each, tested characters must recognize the new self which passion has revealed, and then readapt to and be redefined by their society. At the same time, each play also examines the apparently dispassionate and self-possessed observer whose lesson in practical efficiency seems to offer such attractively benevolent solutions.

These particular plays hold, then, a double interest: the problems of distance which seem central to the period's philosophic unease find formal as well as thematic expression, and these tragicomic blends reveal similar solutions to new theatrical problems. Dramatic technique reaches for new effects by altering the audience's response to traditional materials and generic cues; manipulating aesthetic distance becomes a major structural and investigative tool. That such vacillating cues and often startling juxtapositions are not always successful is less significant here than the fact of their obviously careful construction: traditional English tonal shifts between subplot and main plot give way to subversion of one by the other, or to interpenetration as old patterns are forced to yield a new form and a new response. Formal experiments in distancing complement thematic ones. The plays all maintain a final comic order, for each ends with judicial proceedings that dissolve into marriage celebrations; yet generic variations and contradictions have undermined the assumptions on which these festive conclusions depend. Such subversive ambiguities also qualify the stature of the smug, self-styled, benevolent intriguer.

Intentions, if not success, are clear. While it might be easy to account for such endings simply as witty parodies of earlier, "old-fashioned," romantic comedies, the temptation—overly indulged in explaining coterie drama written for the children's companies—should be resisted. Two at least of these dramatists had recently written elegant and witty comedies whole-heartedly celebrating ideals of courtship and romantic intrigue; indeed, both *As You Like It* and *The Gentleman Usher* validate love's transforming and ordering "natural miracles" with the supernatural sanctions of Hymen's masque and Benevemus's mystic cure for Marguerite's disfigurement. Reexamination seems more likely than satiric self-parody. Poised between comic and tragic practice, they reassess men's ability to fulfill romantic comedy's ideals—an ability that not only guarantees the final marriages' efficacy as symbols of restored natural and human order, but also allows an uncritical use of the court-ship-marriage structure in plays by much less inquiring or accomplished dramatists. Yet whatever disturbing qualities they exhibit, these plays call themselves comedies. Changes in source material reveal each play-wright's insistence on a comic frame—the disguised intriguer whose presence precludes disaster, the nuptial resolution that, by implication at least, provides a cure for those disorders of sensibility the plays have exposed. Marston alters his source's theme from friendship to love, turns the Freevill-Beatrice relationship into an idealized courtship which seeks its natural consummation in virtuous marriage, and adds Cris-pinella and Tysefew to provide another example of harmonious, socially sanctionable love.[14] Shakespeare expands his sources' changes in the basic "corrupt magistrate" story, endows Angelo with an amatory past and a "blameless" tryst, and in the denouement provides mates for nearly everyone on stage.[15] Although the source for Chapman's main plot, the Widow of Ephesus story, more directly challenges this convention and its implications, he makes Cynthia's seducer her own disguised hus-band. More important, he frames the test of married love with a sub-plot whose witty courtship ends as it "ought," with a wedding masque and dancing, and he carefully provides a couple whose love-at-first-sight longings can be fulfilled at play's end by another wedding.

Such over-provision of partners, especially in *Measure for Measure* and *The Widow's Tears,* may mark these dramatists' amused nod at their own previous successes as well as the professional comedian's knowledge that multiplication is inherently humorous. Romantic self-discovery, the wonder of self-transcendence, becomes farcical when such essentially private experience fades into a general pattern. We sense the play's artificiality as it machine-stamps a matrimonial image on every nubile countenance. These plays offer unequivocal comic cures, but for a new kind of laughter. The new genre does not really blend comedy and tragedy, though there are threatened and even real deaths. Rather, it confounds one kind of comedy with another. Romance confronts farce throughout, and its final victory is only apparent. It cannot wholly transcend or absorb the anarchy that farce reveals. Indeed, contrasting romance elements actually emphasize the tragic potential of farce's seem-ingly harmless pranks and carefree attitude.

This use of farce is subtle. Its disturbance remains implicit, while, superficially at least, the farcical subplots help ensure the predominantly light tone appropriate to the romantic plots' comic resolution. Further, the witty intriguer holds us apart from the play's ostensible problems. His intermediary status and apparent control minimize the very threats he has fabricated. We share his intelligent, amused, condescending detachment. Whether physically disguised or simply a master of rhetorical poses, he has been a staple of farce since Plautus, and though *Measure for Measure* modifies the pattern, both Tharsalio and Freevill are blood brothers to those carefree, cynical, self-indulgent young men on the make who people the Latin model's Renaissance descendants. *The Dutch Courtesan* and *The Widow's Tears* handle their subplots differently, but both use their opening type-characterizations to establish a tone and a set of attitudes and responses appropriate to that generic model. Initial scenes provide the first part of a comic frame that brackets all subsequent disturbances and conflicting appeals.

Although he waits until act 4 to set up the plot which tricks as well as tests his friend, Freevill opens *The Dutch Courtesan* entertaining his drinking companions with an almost mock-heroic account of Cocledemoy's first assault on the Mulligrub possessions. The open appreciation of Cocledemoy's wit and genial mocking of Mulligrub's Puritan cant reveal a tolerant, lighthearted view of crime: greed is natural, cheating the norm of daily life, and Mulligrub's deceptions below stairs deserve his customer's retaliation. Wit—and its practical application in intelligent maneuvering—are prime virtues in a world defined by self-interest. We admire the man who does best what everyone attempts. Freevill and his fellows accept Mulligrub's disproportionate passion for revenge as easily as they accept the necessity for brothels; they all inhabit not a mutually supportive society but one of winners and losers. Mary Faugh cuts through distinctions of class or sex when she reminds Cocledemoy that "we all eat of the forbidden fruit";[16] Freevill quips to Malheureux, "Youth and appetite are above the club of Hercules" (1.i.67). Cocledemoy may not appear until 1.ii, but his spirit, at once cynical and festive, dominates from the beginning. His world, and the generic biases which demand that we admire his increasingly witty thefts, establish the play's tone. The opening scene thus associates the main plot's gentlemen lovers with both the subplot's cynical values and its carefree pursuit of personal pleasure.

Character analogies and juxtapositions further establish both generic and thematic similarities, and although Marston handles Cocledemoy's actual penetration of the main plot rather mechanically, he quite deftly establishes and maintains the parallels between Cocledemoy and Free-vill as witty—and ultimately benevolent—tricksters.[17] The plots alternate effectively, and the subplot's increasing hilarity spills over into adjacent scenes: it reenforces Freevill's gleeful enjoyment of his practical joke on Malheureux and helps control our response to the main plot's threat-ened disasters. Cocledemoy's felonious impersonation of a journeyman barber well illustrates this technique. The subplot's preparations for the joke (II.i), and then the dry-shaving itself (II.iii), bracket Franceschina's bargain to sleep with Malheureux if he will kill his friend and give her Beatrice's ring. The farcical framing distances us from Malheureux's temptation and fall and encourages our appreciation of its humorous aspects. Moreover, Franceschina's hilariously accented fury topples her impersonation of Senecan revengeress—and Malheureux's inappropri-ate pose of courtly lover—into parody. Later the two plots come to-gether as attempts to catch Cocledemoy and Malheureux overlap. Eco-nomically, the same set of constables makes both arrests; in each case the disguised Cocledemoy and Freevill stand by to watch how their manipulated appearances wrongly convict their victims, Mulligrub and Malheureux. Even when not yet a disguised observer-plotter, Freevill's amusement stands between us and any involvement in Malheureux's painful self-discovery. Freevill's eavesdropping (I.ii) transforms Mal-heureux's soliloquies into comic posturing. In echoing Cocledemoy's cry of delight at a cony caught, Freevill directs our response: "Wha, ha, ho! Come, bird, come! Stand, peace!" and, a few lines later, "By the Lord, he's caught! Laughter eternal!" (I.ii. 128, 137). Freevill shows no more sympathy when he steps forward to confront his friend personally. Mocking repetitions of the poor sinner's tortured rationalizations en-sure Malheureux's continued status as comic butt.

Throughout, parallels between Malheureux and Mulligrub comple-ment and enforce those between Freevill and Cocledemoy and suggest Marston's determination to distance his main plot's potentially tragic self-discovery. Parroting moral clichés from the start, Malheureux un-wittingly echoes the hypocritical Mulligrub; he is just the self-deluded, smug, and untested Puritan whom we expect such young men to ex-pose. In hounding Freevill's pleasures Malheureux even seeks his own fate, and Freevill voices our delight, rather than sympathetic pity, at the busybody's comeuppance. Repeatedly, such parallels and comic "business" break our sympathetic involvement. They undercut his characters' expressions of romantic idealism as well as their serious discussions of man's ability to unify and control his divided nature.

The comic elements have more than local effect, of course; as we saw, Marston uses his farce's generic cues as a kind of theatrical shorthand. The tavern shared initially by the men of both plots stands for a whole world where rampant egotism challenges the values the romantic plot assumes and on which the harmony of the "happy" ending is predicated. Such a world refuses to honor those cultural ideals of brotherly love and self-sacrificing behavior which stand between the individual and his personal desires. It inverts those norms, and in its topsy-turvydom lies its appeal.[18] Like tendentious wit in Freud's analysis, though on a larger scale, the psychological dynamics of farce allow us to circumvent culture's prohibitions and to liberate fundamental, amoral, sources of pleasure.[19] Within the safely circumscribed and distanced theatrical occasion, such inversion offers the fantasy of permissible self-gratification, the vicarious enjoyment of our basic, ineradicable, acquisitive and aggressive drives.[20] This fantasied world, where the ego may "rightfully" possess whatever it can win by craft or force, pits the individual against society: he must trick or coerce it into satisfying his private desires. Understanding in himself and others the primacy of these basic motives confers manipulative power, yet accepting such a world also raises personal antagonism to the level of philosophic principle and challenges traditionally sanctioned self-abnegation. Thus in order for us to identify with his superiority and control, and so share his subversive attack on public morality and repressive authority, we must be reassured of our impulses' essential harmlessness. Here, the generic cues which set up the intrigue plot also provide the festive spirit and stereotypical characters that promise safe, guiltless indulgence in aggression.[21]

Marston provides all the signals. We enjoy Freevill and Cocledemoy for the same reasons; as regards Malheureux and Mulligrub, the two tricksters double each other. What the two actions set up in act 1 do not prepare us for is the Beatrice-Freevill courtship. The romantic themes introduced in II.i do not suit the Freevill we have seen: the young rake who coolly assessed Malheureux's aptness for the "cast garment," Franceschina, and then mockingly defended the naturalness of his friend's new "love." Beatrice embodies virtues nowhere else apparent in this world: she is sentimental, trusting, naïve, guileless. As such, she is caught between the confidence man's delight in deception and the two trick-sters' demonstration of the mechanical operation of the passions. After such release, what credence in the superior attractions of this repre-sentative of all her culture's ideals? After Malheureux's self-abandonment and Freevill's defense of the body's needs—because "philosophy and nature are all one" (II.i.116)—what belief in Freevill's transformation into dedicated courtly lover? The play's *Argumentum* has assured us that we will learn the difference between "the love of a courtesan and a wife." But does the action itself assure us of what the marriages must presume: man's ability not only to perceive this difference but also to evaluate and control his passions so that he may love virtuously that purity's embodiment once he has recognized it?

Although Chapman develops his plots sequentially, and economically uses the same humorous observer-trickster in each, *The Widow's Tears* opens with generic signals remarkably like Marston's. Despite the po-tentially pastoral Cyprian setting and reiterated dedication to his fam-ily's honor, Tharsalio is just another such carefree young wastrel as Freevill. The degrading view of human nature attributed by his family to excessive Italian travel and riotous living does not in fact dominate his characterization. He is a satirist by inclination, not profession; his cynicism is witty repartee rather than railing. Primarily, Tharsalio is vital, fun-loving, and daring—indeed, he sparkles beside his brother's cautionary moralism and lumpish attempts at bawdy badinage.[22] Although a younger son more economically desperate than either Freevill or Coc-ledemoy, he treats the Middletonian solution to his problems with the same casual interest they gave their practical jokes. Initially at least, he sees wooing Eudora as a challenge that will entertain others as well as himself ("You'll promise me to laugh at it, for without your applause, I'll none"), a profitable joke whose failure he is prepared to tolerate.[23] Indeed, even before the first scene's witty banter, Tharsalio's transfer of allegiance from Fortune to Confidence sets the tone. The opening solil-oquy unexpectedly inverts its satiric diatribe against a world ruled by Fortune; instead, it promises that Fortune's challenges can be met by human ingenuity.[24]

Chapman's opening scene, like that of *The Dutch Courtesan*, displays both a festive spirit and a delight in exercising one's intelligence. Its generic cues suggest the kind of world where straightforward (however exaggerated) courtly wooing can turn into an intrigue plot based on exploiting human weakness. Tharsalio bribes his way to success. Money and promises of future favor gain him the bawd, the maids, and Argus. Tharsalio trusts in a most unromantic world where the same principles govern all, "dogs and cats . . . and men and women" (I.iii.35–36). The bawd Arsace supports his belief that social repression can only inflame, not quench, desire: she reports that Eudora's prim lectures were given "with such an affected zeal, as my mind gave me, she had a kind of secret titillation to grace my poor house sometimes" (II.iii.19–22). Still, Tharsalio is not all devil's advocate. His cynical reductionism frequently modulates into acceptably healthy comic wisdom: female coyness is a "moral disguise" because it denies the fact that we are all "poor naked sinners" (III.i.97). Dressing home truths in earthy wit, Tharsalio sounds not unlike Lavatch, the wise, often bitter clown of *All's Well That Ends Well*. It is no accident that, on the verge of the main plot's shattering revelations of frailty, Ero echoes comedy's fundamental wisdom in her promise to make Cynthia turn "flesh and blood, / And learn to live as other mortals do" (IV.ii.176–177).

Whether more disillusioned than Marston, or more serious in challenging romance conventions, or simply more theatrically accomplished and aware of his plot's implications, Chapman uses bold structural and thematic variations on his source to draw the issues more sharply and economically than Marston. Marston made questions of love, rather than friendship, his major subject, but his general focus is blurred and his main plot remains bifurcated. One of its actions involves Malheureux's discovery of lust and Freevill's educative practical joke; the other is rather loosely organized around Freevill's wooing (and testing) of the already-won Beatrice, and perhaps around his parallel "discovery" of true love and its utter dissimilarity to the casual attachment he had formed with his courtesan. To this second strand of the main plot is spliced the brief courtship between Beatrice's sister and Freevill's friend, thematically important if somewhat diffuse. The brilliant comedy of the Cocledemoy subplot bears a typically loose, Elizabethan, thematic connection to the Freevill-Malheureux action, for it extends the exploration of human passion and hypocrisy into the citizen's realm. The underplot's most interesting contribution to the play's stated subject, however, lies in the pressure that the Cocledemoy-Freevill parallels exert on the main plot's handling of love.

Chapman eliminates the social distinctions as well as the variety of action and character a subplot usually offers. Instead, by uniting all the characters via blood or marriage and allowing them to argue openly, in effect, about the subplot's significance, Chapman concentrates our attention, clarifies the opposing parties' beliefs, and encourages us to share the characters' conviction that each test proves the same proposition about female inconstancy. In order most dramatically to shock us with what are in fact crucial differences, Chapman must first make certain we share Tharsalio's carefree attitude and approve his spirited pursuit of personal desire. The diptych structure which juxtaposes the two nearly separate actions is Chapman's major solution, though within the farcical first plot he also uses local devices—juxtapositions, character stereotypes, and parallels—to distance Lysander's passion and its hints of future danger. Thus Tharsalio's instantly successful provocation of his brother's jealous doubt is framed by outrageous comedy: by the mock heroics of Tharsalio's first wooing, with its backdrop of stereotypical fops and servants (I.ii), and by the equally low comedy of his exchange with Arsace at the end of I.iii. More important, the inception of Lysander's plot and Lycus's serious warnings of disaster in III.i are also set off and isolated: preceded by the hilarious "Petrarchan" second wooing (with its exit to the bedchamber) and followed by Tharsalio's triumphant return and his offer of general nuptial festivities to celebrate a private sexual success.

The wedding masque itself forms an important happy interlude as well as the conventional and symbolic conclusion to what is essentially a courtship-and-marriage plot. Eudora now demonstrates a healthy, sensible affection, and we are reminded that she has in fact gained an intelligent, witty, vital young man who both Lycus and Lysander agree is far preferable to the diseased mannequins offered by polite society. In a perhaps uncharacteristically humane and straightforward moment, Tharsalio has himself defended Eudora against society's unnatural prohibitions: of her remarriage he asked, "What shame is due to 't? Or what congruence doth it carry, that a young lady, gallant, vigorous, full of spirit and complexion . . . be confined to the speculation of a death's head?" (III.i.162–166). The staged wedding celebration in III.ii helps confirm this wisdom. Its promise of young love and yet another marriage, between Tharsalio's nephew and Eudora's daughter, places the final social (and generic) seal of approval on Tharsalio's witty deception. Chapman has gone out of his way to soften the effects of Tharsalio's verbal cynicism and harsh generalizations;[25] in finding Tharsalio's trick, and our laughter, acceptable, we are prepared for more fun to follow in Lysander's own carefully staged "play." We are encouraged by Lysander's earlier reference to his intended test of Cynthia as "some strain of wit" (II.i.81) and inclined to join Tharsalio in dismissing Lycus's concern: "No matter, let it work; I did but pay him in's own coin" (II.iii.44).

Lysander's assumption of his brother's "part"—first as tester, then as wooer—seems merely a rather silly exercise in impertinent curiosity. He deserves what he gets. Character types and parallels enforce these expectations. Establishment moralists in I.i, Lysander and Cynthia are both associated with Eudora's proud hypocrisy by their response to her "fall." In assuming their own purity, they set themselves up as candidates for the same benevolent education in human frailty from which Eudora has profited. The plot and character parallels are smoothly deceptive; we do not immediately realize how an analogous discovery might affect their marriage. Thus however differently deployed in Marston and Chapman, similar techniques of structure and characterization prevent any disturbing emotional involvement and encourage us to share the values, as well as viewpoint, of the witty observer-trickster in all his exploits. These generic signals are elaborated from the start, and acceptance of them ensures our later discomfort when the denouement juxtaposes farce with private anguish.

Chapman's fifth-act additions to Petronius—the Watch and the Governor—suggest the care with which he sought such a final conflation. Having used up his comic subplot in the play's first half, he provides a farcical bridge between the husband's bitter success and the last lines' turn to reintegration and celebration. A wise and just Governor, benignly untying the knots woven by multiple deceptions, would ensure an immediate happy ending; he would also introduce a harmonious social order encouraging mutual benevolence. In a "pure" comedy, the victims' new self-knowledge would be absorbed into a wise and merciful society, one whose judicial authority understands and corrects its members' frailty. Such a Governor would, in short, cancel out Tharsalio. He would suggest that Lysander's acceptance of his brother's reductive beliefs—his self-transformation into Tharsalio—was an ugly but temporary aberration rather than a revelation of deeply human egoism and aggression. Instead, Chapman maintains the play's tension by introducing a conscientious Watch, good men concerned with the topsy-turvy world of perverted relationships which they must guard, and a gubernatorial buffoon who hilariously parodies Tharsalio's own confidence. The Governor tramples justice, preens himself at others' expense, and generally implies that his world, the one to which all must return, does not support ideal behavior or foster human potential. Such fools in high places justify rather than negate Tharsalio's attitudes, and fittingly, Tharsalio (with his newly sensible wife) engineers the plot's actual resolution.

Shakespeare in this period shares his contemporaries' concerns, even subject matter; the similarity between Angelo's and Malheureux's "education" is striking. Yet *Measure for Measure* differs in its handling of generic clashes. Given the prince-in-disguise frame, adapted from contemporary plays like Middleton's *Phoenix* or elaborated from his own earlier use of the motif with *Henry V*,[26] decorum as well as heavier expository requirements might explain the weighty, sentential opening scene. Duke Vincentio's public persona is defined, then bestowed like a mantle upon the hesitant Angelo, whose private virtues must now be exercised for the common weal. The centrality of questions of identity is hinted, but no more, by the Duke's somewhat suspect distaste for "staging himself" and by disturbing implications in the language which allows him to depart, yet leave himself behind. For a scene so ostentatiously expository, however, Angelo, Escalus, and the audience are left surprisingly ill-informed. Details of the Duke's destination and motives, however conflicting when they come, are deferred to the conversation in I.iii with Friar Thomas. The play thus begins again in I.ii, where its ostensible plot is launched with a typical Shakespearean tragedy's walking-gentlemen exposition. And from the burr of these dissolute young men and their brothel acquaintances neither the play nor the Duke ever quite shake themselves free.

If its first scene acts as a prologue, then *Measure for Measure*'s opening is not so unlike that of *The Dutch Courtesan* or *The Widow's Tears*. The play proper does start with witty banter. Although lower in rank and linguistic decorum, this group, too, accepts the pursuit of private needs and pleasures as natural; it finds only amusement in either denying the flesh or failing to circumvent public prohibitions successfully. Intelligence's primary function becomes the satisfaction of appetite. Throughout the play Lucio and Pompey remind us that human nature may itself oppose the ideal conduct which society tries to persuade us is natural as well as reasonable. They acknowledge no moral imperative for self-control in the interests of others' welfare. What society calls offense, they call natural.[27]

Such assumptions about human nature and the law's arbitrariness question the terms in which the main plot couches and fights its battles. The low-life characters do not recognize love, or, if Lucio's refusal to help Pompey is any indication, much of anything in the way of friendship. Sex is as natural, as necessary, as eating or sleeping—and of as little moral significance. It may be imaged in the natural beauty which distinguishes Lucio's description of Juliet's pregnancy (i.iv), but their characteristic attitude is more aptly expressed in allusions to trout-filled rivers and empty tundishes. In word and deed they challenge any faith in the ultimate convergence of private and public interest, any hope for that ideally integrated man apparently represented by the Duke in i.i and reembodied in Angelo when Vincentio gives his private "character" public scope.[28]

Shakespeare even sharpens this underworld's potential for disturbing commentary. Although Mistress Overdone and Pompey were probably suggested by one of his sources, Shakespeare, contrary to his usual practice, declines Whetstone's offer of a full low-life plot to substantiate these characters' presence. Technically, there is no subplot in *Measure for Measure*.[29] The brothel characters and his newly minted Lucio exist to provide a particular viewpoint which radically affects our response both to the Angelo-Isabella story and, just as importantly and far more intriguingly, to the peripheral story of the prince's departure, disguised lurking, and final curative return to his realm. That is, Shakespeare has created a subplot with no separate narrative life of its own, and a double main plot in which the framing disguised-prince action sets up and contains a test that had stood largely alone in his source.

Despite the lack of a full subplot, Shakespeare employs techniques of structure and characterization analogous to Marston's and Chapman's—and to similar ends. As we noticed, the underplot characters in i.ii suggest a world and a set of values against which the main plot must play itself out and which its protagonists would like to deny (if necessary, as Lucio points out later to the Duke, by extirpation). Yet the return of the repressed is everywhere apparent. That sexuality which is the life of the subplot pervades the language of aristocratic conversation; an assumption or fear of its ubiquitous claims seems to prompt Vincentio's repeated assertions of the purity of his own intentions. Thematically, of course, Angelo falls to the same passion from which Pompey and his mistress make their living, but the subplot provides more than simply analogous relevance: its very lack of narrative structure allows its characters free movement. The main plot is in fact defined by its intercourse with the brothel world, and vice versa. However virtuous his intentions toward Juliet, Claudio is well known to Lucio and Overdone; Lucio invades the convent's precincts on his friend's mission. Later he moves easily from the prison, where sin levels all classes, to become the unwilling Friar's conversational companion; in the denouement, irrepressible as the lust he has defended, he steals the Friar-Duke's carefully staged "big scene" until squashed by naked authority. Pompey, too, moves easily in any company. Wittily adaptable to all environments, he yet remains obdurately unchanged. He has a good line in fawning insubordination with Elbow and Abhorson and proves a match for Escalus and the Friar in witty argument, if not in power.

These characters' easy cynicism also helps control our emotional involvement in the main plot's confrontations and agonizing personal decisions. However affecting Isabella's assault on the man-of-snow's humanity, Shakespeare's interposed audience of Lucio and the Provost provides a barrier between us and the emotions we witness. Their commentary treats the passionate contention as a picture to be viewed, not felt, and the arguments as a series of rhetorical cues to be interpreted as personal revelations rather than considered as philosophic positions.[30] Lucio's comments in particular, of course, also work to deflect us from the argument's content to the sexual nature of this apparently abstract and verbal struggle—the physical effect of impassioned female on coldly dismissive male. In addition, the first interview as a whole is contrasted with Pompey's hilarious triumph over Elbow and, temporarily, over Escalus. As a representative of justice who becomes indistinguishable from iniquity, Elbow undercuts the court's dignity; as a symbol of society's ability to know its individual members' hearts or deeds, he makes ridiculous the idea of justly administering the law. Pompey makes a shambles of both justice and mercy; he turns potentially serious matters into an arena for exercising his own wit. In more general terms, the Pompey-Elbow comic interlude in ii.i, like Lucio's interventions in ii.ii, reflects a characteristic use of farcical interruption to puncture serious abstractions and to focus us on personal issues. Here the play's technique for dealing with social problems, like Pompey's, provides no mean introduction for Vincentio himself.

If Pompey's antics and Lucio's comments qualify our response to Angelo's and Isabella's high seriousness, Vincentio's return in ii.iii reassures us. The safety catch we glimpsed in i.iii is on. Our psychological interest in the characters' response to external demands and their own self-discoveries remains absorbing, may even be intensified, yet our reaction cannot be the same when we suspect that passion's consequences need not be suffered.[31] The slight detachment of our observer's position in ii.ii is reenforced in ii.iv: we watch the second interview as if looking over Vincentio's shoulder (as we indeed do for the prison interview between brother and sister). Our interest shifts to confrontation's substance—how Angelo will respond to his "fall," how Isabella will respond to the deputy's proposition—and our lessened involvement is rewarded. Expectations raised by the first interview draw us into the scene; yet our sympathy, encouraged by Lucio's absence, is crossed by the comedy of Isabella's misprision and Angelo's frustrated attempts to turn forensic debate to private ends. We have been made sociologists; we share the position theoretically conferred on Vincentio by his friar's robes.[32]

While we have become the ideal observers, a separate theater audience yet also identified with the disguised duke and committed to his search for the seemer's real face, Vincentio partly relinquishes his objectivity to try to alter the course of events. Like Freevill, Tharsalio, and the Lysander who assumed his brother's role, Vincentio seeks to become playwright-director. Superior knowledge will allow him to refashion life as art, though the new didactic plot's structure is suspiciously close to that of a practical joke.[33] But as with Marston's and Chapman's manipulators, the attempt to supersede one's dramatic role only more firmly reminds us of Vincentio's position within the play and ours outside it: he can control events only by being at the same time part of them. He is a dramatic character, and the attempt to transcend that fictive status is itself a characterizing act. In each play we are encouraged to adopt a particular kind of detached and amused attitude, one established by the subplot but embodied in the main-plot character most in control of himself and his environment. Our response, generally dependent on its distance from the characters' plights, is here keyed to our identification with the protagonist. We share his detachment; we are predisposed to accept his other attitudes. In each, we retain this attitude (or try to) even as the generic signals shift and our surrogate moves into the play's action, becoming as much an object as his manipulated peers. Yet though the character may recede until finally absorbed into the tableau of conventional couples, his approach to us has changed our relation to him and to that conclusion.

Through the witty intriguer, the playwrights con us. They extend in a new way our theatrical involvement, for in judging him we must judge ourselves. We must recognize the effect of the very qualities which seemed so admirably and engagingly to make him master of his world. The intriguer has sought and gained our approval in two ways. His iconoclastic wit and vigorous, pragmatic plotting offer the liberating pleasures of festive rebellion: through him we can briefly mock our own ideals, safe in a comic structure which ensures that their spokesmen are hypocrites who will actually benefit from exposure. In this we are rewarded for sharing the protagonist's distance from moral quandaries and the human pain they give rise to. (Verbally unwitty, Vincentio is, of course, a slightly different and more complicated problem: however, his friar's disguise does remove him from immediate involvement or intense moral commitment; as the play changes shape in act 3, his delight in constructing stratagems and his apparent ubiquity allow us to join him in treating the play's "life" as a game.) These protagonists are more than simply observers who suggest a congenial, undemanding point of view; they also practice what they preach. Although their public responsibilities vary, once in action they all seem subtle, flexible, apparently self-possessed and uncommitted. Such a man can more successfully deal with the play's declared problems than any of its other characters. Both engaging and efficacious, he personally reenforces our predisposition to side with the smart over the stupid, the witty over the dull, the successful over the failed.[34] He offers us fun; he makes the play, his play, a comedy, and we should be grateful. Yet we are not wholly satisfied with our hero and his solution; the nuptial resolution he engineers fails to meet the potentially tragic dilemmas which have been the play's subject.

What has been frequently observed of *Measure for Measure* is true for all these ironic tragicomedies: problem and solution remain on different planes. Alongside other, unresolved problems, each play accepts the fact of human sexuality and tries, like a romantic comedy, to define social man's natural virtue. But channeling anarchic passion into socially acceptable love and marriage proves less than satisfactory, despite the final scenes' image of harmonious integration. Surprised to discover their animal appetites, the plays' moral absolutists are shattered when they realize their apparent helplessness before their bodies' demands. (Even Malheureux, who resists his initial impulse to kill his friend, still feels he "must" possess the courtesan he now despises.) "Blood" rules. Before its importunities God's prohibitions, and man's, fall. Sexuality has been, at one level at least, simply the loose thread which has unraveled a whole ideal of humanness. At this level marriage is, of course, no solution—or no more a solution than was Gertrude's legal union with Claudius.

For a number of illuminating reasons, Marston's denouement is perhaps the most satisfactory. He minimizes any disturbance of his predominantly farcical tone by distancing Malheureux's anguished self-discovery in i.ii and ii.i; he refuses to provide Malheureux with a last-minute marriage partner. Further, at the end he blurs Freevill's disquieting likeness to Cocledemoy. Cocledemoy is paired with Malheureux, as bachelors, and our sense of Freevill's and Cocledemoy's twinship is further diminished by Cocledemoy's disappearance into the subplot. He finally seems separated from the main-plot characters, no longer the gentleman "of much money, some wit, but less honesty" who parried Freevill's classical allusions and scatological witticisms. In *The Dutch Courtesan* the trickster's manipulations are also unrelated to securing the final marriages, so we are less likely to wonder whether attitudes manifested in one activity might not be fatal to the other. At least in Marston's ending, farce and romance are kept separate.

Farce can satisfactorily end in marriage, of course, as it does in many Middletonian city comedies and in Chapman's Tharsalio-Eudora plot. As long as beneath the gaiety everyone assumes a Hobbesian human nature and acts on the same aggressive and acquisitive principles, the young man who wins the girl and the money is by definition the most deserving; paradoxically, his selfish manipulations actually benefit her (and society) by putting society's prizes in the hands of the most able. In an intricately structured game where we care nothing about individuals, but only their sexual or economic status, we enjoy our temporary liberation and accept the final marriages as reward and closure, the cheese at the maze's end. In such a world, substitution is the swindler's master stroke, whether it be in the dark, where one woman takes the place of another, or in the daylight, where a courtesan may be passed off as a desirably wealthy niece or widow.

The intriguer actively tries to turn "his" play into such a world. Though the degree of subversion varies, each dramatist undermines his character's efforts; he uses his intriguer to explore, not resolve, his play's most fundamental concerns. The observer-trickster's role is dual, then. As both solution and problem, he is crucial to the play's tragicomic effect. Whether or not he initiates the central imbroglio, his presence and active participation ensure a technically comic issue. Yet while responsible for much of the play's hilarity, he also causes our final discomfort, our sense of betrayal. Freevill, Tharsalio, and Vincentio view their work with triumphant self-satisfaction; they remain unchanged, but our partial identification has been shattered. We are suddenly outside, judging ourselves as well as them and their works. The expected festive release—enhanced by the last scenes' almost hysterical confusion and speeded-up revelations—is finally punctured; we are left looking at comedy's tableau but feeling some of the guilty complicity associated with tragedy's spectator. Of conventional tragedy, however, there is no evidence. Death has never really threatened seriously, for we saw that by chance or stratagem someone always knew of vile intents in time; however marginally of tragic stature Duke Vincentio might be, his half of *Measure for Measure* is the most farcical, and in it dignified verse and action virtually dissolve. The dramatists have pitted romance against farce in a losing battle and encouraged our identification with the farceur himself. Our delighted adoption of his carefree egotism makes us, too, destroyers of the values from which we wanted only temporary release.

Since Marston most fully preserves his city comedy's formal integrity and effect, his qualification of Freevill interests precisely because it so evidently disturbs the otherwise uniform focus of his two farcical gulling plots. Removing Freevill from the tavern world which he and Cocledemoy so easily master, Marston chooses to explore Freevill's relation to Beatrice's world of civilized values and romantic commitment. We witness wooing and testing scenes; we watch his friend court Beatrice's sister. The play's erotic pairings have often been seen in hierarchic terms: ideal love represented by Beatrice and Freevill, normal and natural love by Crispinella and Tysefew, and abnormal physicality by Malheureux and Franceschina. But although his centrality suggests that Freevill's union should represent the ideal, Marston has countered this expectation by placing at his play's center a definition of natural virtue and an example of admirable love which limit Freevill's claims. Crispinella defends truth, not social form, as virtue's best guarantor and virtue itself as "a free, pleasant, buxom quality" (III.i.48). Her criticism of crabbed self-righteousness attaches itself to Malheureux and his concern with social reputation, of course, for he exhibits the most dangerous effects of hypocrisy and repression. In context, however, she is criticizing her sister's capitulation to society's demands for "severe modesty," especially in marriageable young women. The standard she voices also measures whatever virtue Freevill displays in the trap that both educates his friend and tests his bride. Crispinella gets the most telling of Montaigne's remarks on the evils of Custom; like the Beatrice of *Much Ado About Nothing* from whom she is probably copied, her common-sense truths about the relations between men and women cut across the illusions supporting both other attachments. Malheureux founders because he cannot reconcile the accepted cultural ideal of love and "good" women with the fact of a whore's powerful attractiveness; Freevill hopes to be saved from a world of whores by the good woman's love which his cynicism suggests he had despaired of finding. Though all urge marriage on Crispinella, she sensibly recognizes the danger in assuming that two fallible people's union will be an absolute panacea. Since "there is no more affinity betwixt virtue and marriage than betwixt a man and his horse," she would "rather prove a wag than a fool" (III.i.80–83).

It is Crispinella and Tysefew who understand that a true marriage requires mutual support and offers mutual satisfaction.[35] Their courtship, like their characters, remains undeveloped; yet when Tysefew assures Crispinella that "if you will be mine, you shall be your own" (IV.i.76), he at least hints at that discovery of self through commitment to another which we commonly associate with Shakespeare's mature ideal. (Malheureux, of course, cannot be himself and Franceschina's; the pressures of disgust and desire split his psyche.) Grounded in their willingness to drop defenses and declare honest desire, the real affection cementing the Crispinella-Tysefew union blossoms at the very moment Freevill deserts his bride to play tricks on Malheureux. Beatrice seems never to have taken on the reality for Freevill that would allow her presence either to create or destroy him. She remains a symbol, an embodiment of the virtues and way of life Freevill now wishes to possess, and he readily seizes the opportunity his disguise affords to test that symbol's constancy. Test her he does, and Marston allows her suffering to dominate two scenes (iv.iv and v.ii). Here Freevill's observing presence and self-satisfaction, emphasized by his gloating soliloquy, do not distance her pain; they make it grotesque and remind us it is unwarranted as well as unnecessary. Freevill is pleased with Beatrice's "patient, yet oppressed kindness" and confident that, when he decides "she has wept enough," her torment will only endear him to her (iv.iv.88; v.i.104). Yet surely Crispinella voices the appropriate response (and directs us away from any "Patient Grissel" acceptance): "Brother, I must be plain with you; you have wrong'd us" (v.ii.58).

Beneath Freevill's easy cruelty runs the untransformed egotism which depersonalizes friends and lovers alike. What seems an appropriate attitude toward the stuffy, hypocritical friend becomes disturbingly calculating and exploitative toward the sincere and defenseless fiancée. In their first scene together, Beatrice repeatedly mentions her want of "wit" and "skill," the credulous simplicity which should keep him from distrusting or deceiving her. The roué's wisdom mixes oddly but revealingly with his romantic hyperbole: "And would to God only to me you might / Seem only fair! Let others disesteem / Your matchless graces, so might I safer seem. . . . He that is wise pants on a private breast" (ii.i.32–37). She offers a refuge, a retreat from the world of thieves, tricksters, and whores; her ignorance and simplicity are precious because they are "the only possible guarantee that she is free of the corruption which surrounds her."[36] We remain unconvinced of their love's reality (or mutuality) because Freevill's feet stay firmly planted in the tavern world he shares with Cocledemoy. He *enjoys* his mastery there, however much he at times recognizes that its valued qualities oppose the virtues he admires in Beatrice.

Freevill could well say with Cocledemoy, "Conscience does not repine" (iii.ii.33), but Marston has taken him out of the world that justifies such an attitude. Cocledemoy remains with the bawds and petty thieves. We can enjoy him there; his values do not threaten. He even lets us share the artist's disinterested mastery, for when we are told that for him the witty stratagem is its own reward we also see that it has harmed no one else. In Freevill, Marston unobtrusively describes a kind of detachment that easily justifies aggression's pleasures, "the end being good" (IV.ii.47). *The Dutch Courtesan* reveals little about God's motives, but much about what contents the impure virtue of Freevill and Cocledemoy. By doubling the tests to which Freevill's disguise is put, Marston shows him accepting and forgiving his faults with excessive alacrity: the Montaignian recognition of our nature's mingled good and ill, which justifies gleefully submitting Malheureux to the "vildest of dangers" for his own good (IV.ii.35ff.), sounds much less laudably realistic when it also absolves Freevill of gratuitous unkindness to Beatrice.

Freevill does not change fundamentally, but Marston forces no absolute condemnation. Freevill may give up Franceschina, but he is allowed to have Beatrice *and* his fun. Beatrice's absolute purity and undemanding love assure his safety there; he need come to no marital agreement, for she will never restrict his self-indulgence. Disguised, he notes with satisfaction that neither disgrace nor contempt "once stir [her] faith" (IV.iv. 83–84). He can afford to indulge his love of trickery, of playing puppet master, with Beatrice as well as with Malheureux; both her unnecessary tears and Malheureux's final gratitude satisfy his ego. Freevill attains his goals. In a world where nearly everyone wants his "will," Freevill simply manages to be top dog. With the exception of Crispinella's brief rebuke, we are not reminded of his cruelty; he goes his way unaware of, and untroubled by, his contradictory desires. Evidence of the adolescent selfishness he shares with Cocledemoy fades before the finale's high spirits and Mulligrub's forgiveness. We are left with only a visual reminder of Freevill's distance from the more civilized world he gains by marriage: the partially doffed costume in which he watches Cocledemoy conclude the play. Disguised as a pander (one of Cocledemoy's many roles), Freevill had chosen a mask which discovered as much as it concealed.

Tharsalio dons no disguise and tortures no loved one by pretending death, yet Chapman's play more insistently confronts us with the amoral ego's disturbing potential. He intensifies the extremes which the play's denouement must pretend to reconcile. As we saw, the signals for permissible aggression associated primarily with Cocledemoy and only secondarily with Freevill are in *The Widow's Tears* concentrated in Tharsalio and his plot. Though initiating Lysander's doubts suggests an unbrotherly spite, a desire to inflict retaliatory pain, aggression is

largely submerged in comic fun. Even Cynthia's expected fall fits Tharsalio's larger aim to protect and advance his "house." We share Tharsalio's urge to puncture the kill-joy's smug condescension; we agree that
pride and dotage need comedy's educative cure. The first plot's outcome
ensures our identification with Tharsalio and rewards our participation
in his uninhibited activities; the second plot's heightened sense of play
then glosses its changed circumstances. Such an elaborate masquerade
promises to outdo Arsace's, and even sober Lycus enjoys adding theatrical flourishes to his role as the murdered man's friend. The characters'
concentration on intrigue, on technique over content, encourages our
own amused distance.

Lysander changes the script, however. Like Freevill, he finds in disguise a tempting liberation from his known social identity and its responsibilities. What had been only suggested in Freevill's toying with
Beatrice or Tharsalio's determination to prove Eudora hypocritical becomes painfully explicit in the humorless Lysander: aggressive, competitive drives are no longer balanced by the witty self-knowledge and implied self-control that allowed us, too, to treat life as play. In working
out another set of consequences for his brother's confident narcissism,
Lysander exposes Tharsalio by becoming his double. Despite the brothers' apparent opposition in act 1, Chapman prepares us to accept a
fundamental likeness when each enters "with a glass in . . . hand";
"splitting" Tharsalio now forces us into a new relationship with those
aspects which, combined in him, we had so enjoyed.

True "Confidence" reduces others to minor actors in the ego's private
drama. Though such minor characters merit no real consideration, they
are still important in validating the egoist's beliefs and self-image. Thus
Eudora had to surrender in order to prove Tharsalio's philosophy and
justify him before his mocking family. Tharsalio allows the trial of
Cynthia to continue because he refuses to "despair but she may prove a
woman" (IV.i.136–137); when she fails, he is euphoric. Despite the fact
that total emulation of his brother's sexual success will destroy rather
than create a marriage, Lysander's need for immediate personal confirmation requires Cynthia's capitulation to the wooing soldier's charms.
His persistence grotesquely mimics his brother's earlier determination to
"retrieve the game once again" (II.iii.13). Now it is no longer a game,
and changed circumstances expose the desperate need to "win" which
also underlay Tharsalio's fun. Lysander cannot accept Cynthia's ap-

parent success in winning her husband's wager, for he has effectively relinquished that identity; as an anonymous soldier he must undermine the very abstinence he should find flattering: "All these attractions take no hold of her; / No, not to take refection; 't *must* not be thus" (IV.ii.162–163, my italics). The "moral imperative" in both cases is that of the narcissistic ego. Largely stripped of the wit, high spirits, and happy outcome of the first wooing, the second test reveals the disastrous potential inherent in its demands. Neither brother will admit failure; implicit in Lysander's paean to her purity (IV.ii.181–188) and Tharsalio's willingness to "let the trial run on" (IV.i.137) is the necessity for Cynthia to die in order to prove her constancy. Should she prove inconstant, of course, Lysander has vowed to "split her weasand" (III.i.227).

Cynthia lives, but hardly to prove the logic-chopping conclusion that "happy events make good the worst attempts" (III.i.91–92). No beneficial access of self-knowledge, no acceptance of human frailty instead of impossible aspirations, can balance the discovery of mutual betrayal. Surprisingly, in a play whose comic reversals both seem dependent on traditional antifeminist comedy, the emphasis has shifted to larger questions of identity, responsibility, and community. The graveyard, its "tomb, within sight of so many deaths" (V.ii.36), proves an apt locale. The complacent Lysander of I.i is destroyed, and not merely because the wife in whose renowned loyalty he took "special glory" has proved a woman (II.iii.51). In falsifying his death to test his wife's vowed constancy, Lysander inverts the husband's protective duty and so denies his role; with a good deal of truth he later tells Cynthia "I am he that slew thy husband" (V.iii.27). In assuming the soldier's guise and his brother's personality, he loses his own identity. Disillusioned, Lysander turns his murderous anger on his wife and calls his disguise his "trustiest friend," for it "in truest shape hast let me see / That which my truer self hath hid from me" (V.v.2–4). Chapman does not allow the ironic self-application to remain implicit, for he is ultimately concerned with broken bonds, not female inconstancy. Cynthia turns back her husband's projected guilt and remarks on his loss as well as her own: she calls him "a transformed monster" who "hath lost the shape of man" (V.v. 81, 83). Lysander has lost himself, his wife, and his marriage. Both he and Cynthia join that paranoid world of deceit and betrayal which Tharsalio's confident belief in human frailty assumed.

Lysander lacks his brother's ability to stand alone and uncommitted. He thus more clearly displays the egotist's dangerous and contradictory emotions. Dependent on his wife and ignorant of himself, Lysander's doubt breeds fear and hatred; the self resents, even denies, its own needs as well as its social bonds and responsibilities. In extending his brother's behavior, Lysander displays the same delight in manipulation, the same desire to toy with and judge others; he will willingly test and punish this "other," even though he is publicly sworn to support her and she is necessary to his own private self-fulfillment.

The blind aggression of such confused and destructive drives can be seen, in retrospect, to underlie Tharsalio's more acceptably witty be-·havior. In order to revenge his wounded pride—to pay "veny for veny" (I.iii.132)—he has sacrificed his sister and destroyed his brother's happiness along with his illusions. The family Tharsalio had wished to advance he has also in some sense annihilated. Certainly his belated intervention in Lysander's plot cannot mend a shattered relationship; warning Cynthia merely allows her the revenge of "cross-capers." The assault on Cynthia's *post-mortem* fidelity has exposed truth but also turned mutual dependency into warfare. Such revelations cannot be wholly erased by the comic fitness of Cynthia's retaliation, though they can soon be swamped by the comedy of the Watch and the Governor.

Plot and character parallels are for Chapman, as for Marston, very sophisticated elucidative techniques. Instead of simply extending thematic relevance or furthering characterization through foil personalities, the doubled intriguers and echoes between sub- and main plots work to undercut the protagonist's assumptions and displace him from the play's moral center. Marston suggests, and Chapman insists on, a final dislocation between our view and the unchanged and triumphant intriguer's view of himself and his play. Both ensure distance as well as identification by reminding us of the very values the farceur's "play" ignores. Marston's theme leads him to add a loving couple whose commentary bars us from accepting Freevill's courtship as ideal. Concerned with more general family bonds, Chapman introduces the moderate, humane Lycus, confidant to both brothers. Rational persuasion cannot prevail against their stubborn willfulness, but Lycus's attempts emphasize the cruelty and unnaturalness resulting from both brothers' depersonalization of their closest relationships. Having failed tactfully to moderate Lysander's inhuman expectations of his wife (II.i.58–76),

Lycus later questions his friend's plan in harsher terms: "Would any heart of adamant, for satisfaction of an ungrounded humour, rack a poor lady's innocency as you intend to do?" (iii.i.1–3). Lycus further compares Lysander's "curiosity" with Nero's desire to inspect his mother's womb.

Lycus alone can deal with human complexity, accept human imperfection. He understands that Cynthia's inability to live up to her proud and foolish vows need not cancel her love's sincerity; his response to her real suffering, however fictitious its cause, shows both brothers to be employing her as a puppet in their private, self-justificatory fantasies. Such compassion openly challenges Tharsalio's casual disregard of consequences and feelings, for Lycus enforces the very discriminations between seriousness and play which Tharsalio refuses to make: "You may jest; men hunt hares to death for their sports, but the poor beasts die in earnest" (iv.i.35–36). Although Lycus's advice goes unheeded, he has pierced the insulation shielding this world from moral judgment. Momentarily we see that attitudes as well as events have become grotesque.

Implicated by our enjoyment, uneasy with an ending we distrust, we are encouraged to reconsider the witty intriguer and the direction in which our vicarious freedom has led us. While Marston blunts this effect by finally concentrating on Cocledemoy and wit's harmless, even beneficial exuberance, Chapman's return to farce does not soften the contradictions. Tharsalio and his values seem to rule everywhere in Cyprus, yet their triumph sours the very festive conclusion they provide. Vicariously, we have mocked our ideals, laughed at humanity's ability to distort and evade its aspirations. Yet the psychological depth with which Chapman has treated Petronius's fable ultimately exposes the consequences of transferring apparently playful attitudes beyond farce's protective frame. Tharsalio's refusal to commit himself elevates the subjective will to the status of moral standard and denies the emotions out of which communal bonds are forged. Judging others by oneself means no one can be trusted; Cynthia must "act" her despair because Tharsalio himself always plays a part. True affection and trust are unthinkable; happiness in social dealings depends on blind ignorance (Tharsalio's first advice to his brother) or achieving a protective detachment similar to his own. He sees as gullible stupidity the kind of creative faith to which Cynthia, too late, looks back: "Love's resolute, and . . . runs blindfold through an army of misdoubts / And interposing fears" (v.v.45–48). Tharsalio ends the play stating the necessity of open-eyed accommodation to an unsatisfactory reality, but his "humorous" solution requires a retreat into subjectivity beyond Lysander's, or the audience's, capacity.[37] Tharsalio, however pleased with himself and his stratagems, is not a fully persuasive recommendation for his own advice: he seems cut off and self-absorbed, a man dramatizing himself before mirrors.

Our initial assent to Tharsalio's claims has been eroded. Not only have the results of unleashed "Confidence" proved disastrous to his family, but Tharsalio himself proves rather less admirably flexible and imaginative than when surrounded only by comic plodders. In the last scenes' return to the comic order, Chapman also implies the wider social consequences of Tharsalian attitudes. In a world where "near-allied trust is but a bridge for treason," soldiers of the Watch may well worry that "friendship and bosom-kindness are but made covers for mischief, means to compass ill" (v.iv.33–35). Society's justicer reveals no such mundane concern. In a hilarious, fun-house distortion, the Governor's blind justice mirrors in the public realm Tharsalio's attempts to make others justify his own beliefs. The Governor's willingness to condemn without proof, because "for my part, I am satisfied it is so; that's enough for thee" (v.v.193–194), echoes the Lysandri's ruling principle in sublime parody. We laugh at a caricature of the narcissist's ideal: the man who legally *can* define reality to fit his imagination. Totally detached from the facts and people around him, the Governor floats free of reality's limiting demands in a final, fantastic comment on Tharsalio's self-image.

Chapman's refusal to synthesize comic surface and revealed anarchy, his substitution of witty rearrangements for true resolution, recalls the discordant strains of *Measure for Measure*. Judicial endings are of course appropriate for any play whose action repeatedly puts individuals on trial. Yet just as the embittered Cynthia and Lysander remain mute witnesses to their comic resolution's inadequacy, so Isabella's silence provokes similar doubts about the efficacy of manipulated alliances.[38] Moreover, though Shakespeare's Tharsalian duke gets to be his own Governor, this identification of the intriguer with his society's social and legal head does not make *Measure for Measure* markedly more political: with the disguised duke's return, unromantic questions of governance and ethics lose their significance as well as their urgency. Indeed, criticisms of Vincentio's playing god with his subjects, of that delight in intrigue for its own sake which leads to the hilarious prolonging of act 5's "suspense," sound remarkably like the objections invited by his unducal peers in Chapman and Marston.

Vincentio zealously evades governmental problems, both in leaving rigorous enforcement to Angelo in act 1 and in extending nearly universal pardon (as well as marriage) in act 5. Part of our dissatisfaction with the play stems from its obvious failure to provide the expected princely education. The Duke remains apparently untouched, except in his amour propre, by his contact with humility's base-string: he returns Vienna to the condition of license his stratagem aimed to cure. As a private man, too, Vincentio apparently misses that lesson in self-knowledge and compassion which he imposes on other self-righteous absolutists: he demonstrates the same "indifference to human feeling" with Angelo and Isabella in act 5 that he had earlier shown with Juliet.[39] Public and private "solutions"—pardon and marriage—seem at once pragmatic and beside the point; both stem from a character who has himself become a focus of Shakespeare's interest. Whatever Shakespeare had in mind when he wrote acts 1 and 2, when Vincentio takes over the play in act 3 *Measure for Measure* also becomes a study of the observer-intriguer. For this reason Vincentio, in many ways so unlike Freevill and Tharsalio, bears some rather surprising resemblances to those witty, roguish precursors of Webster's Flamineo and Bosola.

Vincentio's political and social eminence, as well as the intriguer's plot centrality, suggest his mediation of the play's oppositions. We expect him to embody, or discover, the desperately needed mean between justice and mercy, between abstinence (with its concomitant sexual revulsion) and ungovernable lust. Instead, we find a familiar dislocation, a refusal to support our expectations or his claims. The humane Escalus seems alone in realizing or being willing to shoulder the burden of fitting the law's spirit to individual circumstances. About love, little is said. Juliet remains a generally silent symbol, and we are offered no description or exemplar for that ideal integration of individual and social needs which the Duke's final marriage arrangements seem to propose as cure-all. Vincentio's conclusion ignores Pompey's and Lucio's remarks as well as the disturbing implications of Angelo's helplessness before his body's amoral demands. We are not in a world where human intentions or vows can be trusted to govern behavior: the "life" we have been shown, in court and brothel, simply will not shape itself to Vincentio's dramatic art.

The larger play exposes the manipulator's presumption and limitations. Like Freevill and Tharsalio, Vincentio offers educative intentions to excuse his deceptions; in each case, therapeutic goals cannot compensate for a failure to perceive others sympathetically, and hence to grasp the real situation that must be dealt with. Vincentio's actions reveal a familiar, if unacknowledged need to see others justify his own views. Himself a "complete bosom" above the "aims and ends / Of burning youth," he yet distrusts Angelo's and Isabella's similar claims. He expects, almost wills, Angelo's fall, and his description of Angelo to Friar Thomas in I.iii sounds remarkably like Lucio's mockery in the succeeding scene. He neither understands nor sympathizes with Mariana's irrational "continuance of her first affection" (III.i.240), though he will happily use her love to scale the deputy and free Claudio. Surprisingly, though neither Angelo nor Barnardine acts according to Vincentio's predictions, their unexpected responses never move him to question either his premises or the feasibility of the end toward which he works them all. Substitute heads carry the same significance as substitute women, for in the Duke's play role is identity, personality is subsumed in function.

In all such qualities he resembles city comedy's private intriguers. In context, the extraordinary spite with which he responds to Lucio suggests less the ruler's concern with his subject's slander than the private individual's anger when others refuse to mirror the desired self-image. We laugh at the man caught in his own disguise, forced against his will to provide his own puffery. Lucio's portrait of the Duke is intriguing because it so contradicts the image Vincentio assiduously cultivates; it forces us to see how much the Duke's ideal self-image resembles Angelo's. Lucio's observations may not strike us as likely to be true, yet it is not Lucio's veracity but Vincentio's stuffy, defensive response that is the interchange's point. The final distribution of parts does create the mirror of his mastery that Vincentio desires, but its artificiality hints its status as successfully imposed, yet still self-justificatory fantasy.

Although Shakespeare displaces his princely intriguer from the play's moral center, he does not associate him directly with the brothel world's acceptance of—even delight in—human animality. The Duke would seem immune to the reductionist assumptions that challenge his final romantic arrangements and pardons. Yet, beyond his isolating self-absorption, Vincentio's behavior does suggest further, subterranean connections with the libertine world he as Duke condemns. However humorless he appears, Vincentio shares his subjects' desire to play, to turn his back on responsibility and amuse himself with the game of life. When the Duke sheds his public persona in i.i, he substitutes Angelo for himself in more than merely the political sense.[40] Oddly perhaps, we never see a simply private Vincentio; instead of appropriating Angelo's identity as private citizen, he assumes a disguise more congenial to his self-image: the friar's spiritual and physical purity. Yet Shakespeare betrays his duke. Vincentio chooses one counterpart; Shakespeare provides him with another—Lucio. Chapman explored Tharsalio's dark side through his humorless double, Lysander; Shakespeare examines repression's effects by objectifying the "splitting" that society demands of its idealists. Of course, Pompey, Lucio, Overdone, and the rest of the underworld characters represent in general that animal nature which the absolutists deny in themselves, and it has often been remarked that the aristocrats seem to have banished warmth and affection, as well as grubby sexuality, to the stews. Yet Lucio is particularly, insistently, associated with Vincentio. In the first two acts, Lucio in fact fills in for him while Vincentio gets his disguise together; he later refuses to be dismissed from the fastidious new friar's presence.[41]

Together, Friar Lodowick and Lucio make up man. They image not simply those warring spiritual and appetitive demands reflected in Angelo's slide between extremes, but also Vienna's opposition between seriousness and play. The "fantastical duke" of Lucio's description may seem a far cry from the pompous ruler of i.i, but Lucio, himself designated "a Fantastic" in the Folio's dramatis personae, knows whereof he speaks.[42] This sportive fellow lurked all along beneath the robes of office; liberated by holiday anonymity, he stands before us, a fantastic friar. Lucio suspects royal duplicity from the start (i.iv.54–55); though he probably errs in projecting his own indiscriminate sexuality, the man he "slanders" certainly displays a propensity to answer dark deeds darkly. In the last scene Vincentio enjoys insulting authority and toying with Escalus and Isabella as well as Angelo. He may lack the fantastic's verbal wit, but despite his tedious moralizing, the Duke exhibits a similar playful delight in surfaces which his plots try translating into witty action. We react against Lucio's final punishment partly because we sense in its rigor Vincentio's final condemnation of the unacknowledged "fantastic" in himself, his recommitment to the stuffy and hypocritical sobriety of Viennese public life.

Lucio's presence calls attention to a refreshingly exuberant liveliness almost smothered beneath Vincentio's prim denials and friar's habit; it also suggests a more damaging similarity in operative ethics that separates them, in a fundamental way, from the true idealists. Lucio plays aristocratic bawd for Isabella in act 2, but hardly more can be said for the Duke's later services for Mariana. Both pragmatists concern themselves with means, not ends. Vincentio's manipulations, his casual substitutions, his inadequate response to individual suffering, all associate him with Lucio's cynicism and that detachment from others in the interests of the self-protective ego which seems to bar Lucio from love or friendship. If Lucio's witty smuttiness relies on "sex intellectualized . . . stripped of emotion and therefore debased," Vincentio's stratagems may suggest a similar though less pernicious depersonalization.[43] Evading the pain of involvement, Vincentio reduces act 2's emotional clash of principles and personalities to the superficiality of an intrigue game of wits, a "question of one shyster out-tricking the other."[44] In making puppets out of Angelo and Isabella he also removes them from the arena of moral choice. The Duke seems to "intellectualize" both political and personal solutions throughout. Mary Lascelles is surely right to say that he communicates ideas but not "feeling"; he fails to give "the impression that he is deeply engaged."[45]

Lack of engagement, a protective detachment and isolation of the self, has been the focus of my interest in Chapman and Marston. Though partially obscured by the decorum of princely rank, it is at least a peripheral interest in *Measure for Measure*. The Duke may enter into a token commitment with Isabella and so seem to rejoin the characters he had condescendingly manipulated, but his proposal seems even more inadequate than Freevill's dedication to his wife's naïve virtues. Shakespeare further dampens our concern, of course, by turning his play toward outrageous farce halfway through: the increasingly unbelievable substitutions, the hysterical tempo at which Vincentio runs his subjects through their paces in act 5 (himself unable to stop the game or throw off his disguise), the final pairings' apparent moral tidiness, all aim at papering over "metaphysical disorder" with technical smartness.[46]

At some level, however, we sense a connection between Lucio's mocking devaluation and the attitudes implied by the Duke's intriguing, and that intuition colors our response to the play's superficial cheer. Lucio reduces personal and social ideals to fodder for smutty jokes because in his opinion aspiration is unrealistic. Men are creatures of appetite, governable only by arbitrary external force. To claim otherwise is to lie, and both self-delusion and hypocrisy are subjects for laughter. But the other side of Lucio's acceptance of sex *and* venereal disease, of a human nature shaped by its appetites and committed to self-preservation, is the Duke's "Be absolute for death" speech. When one can no longer joke about disillusionment, no longer preen oneself on superior mastery of an essentially meaningless game, life itself becomes simply a burden. This speech—and the prison to which all Vienna comes—lies at the heart of *Measure for Measure*. It may be controversial as a friar's Christian consolation, but through its visionary despair Shakespeare allows his intriguer to see the consequences of those attitudes he elsewhere seems to share.[47] The bleak hopelessness to which Vincentio asks Claudio's accommodation stems from the individual's isolation. Helpless before nature's physical determinism, we seem cut off from any creative alliance with our universe; unable to transcend our own envy and greed, we betray the ties of blood and friendship which should link us to our human community.

"Be absolute for death" is like a tiny window onto the world Lysander discovers when he tries practicing Tharsalio's "virtues" outside the safe parameters of farce. Shakespeare finds in human nature less free-floating aggression than do Chapman, Marston, and the other writers of city comedy. Yet through Lucio and, by implication, the Duke, he too seems to trace both personal cynicism and the fragmentation of communal life to the self-protective disengagement prompted by a "realistic," reductionist philosophy. Detachment, our defense against disillusionment, severs those commitments to reality that make life meaningful. Paradoxically, it even threatens the very self it was enlisted to protect. Distance gives way to active participation, but the intriguer's involvement takes the form of deception and manipulation; significantly, he tends to lose himself in disguise, abandoning his social identity for the pleasures of anonymous omnipotence. Such retreat cannot be prolonged, though in these plays we are mostly spared the horrors of illusory control broken on the rocks of others' willfulness and of chance. Only Lysander pays the full price of his experiment with godhead.

Such discoveries are, of course, largely implicit. With varying success, they are absorbed by the plays' concentration on wit and intrigue rather than the suffering it causes, on stock comic characters who will not ruffle the intriguer's surface manipulations, and on the maneuvering's traditional, happy outcome. Destructive and self-destructive impulses are, by and large, balanced or canceled out altogether. We have been shown enough, however, to sense that the plays undermine their own endings, and this uneasiness places us at an ironic distance from the final unions and their smug engineers. At least in Marston and Shakespeare, the intriguer's proposed nuptials can be seen as desperate attempts to escape from the subplot's world of aggression and materialism into romance's charmed rewards. Certainly the intriguers have carried with them from the subplot (with its safely less distinguished sensibilities) values that challenge romance's promises. Caught between genres, we cannot fully credit the individual transformations or celebrate the capacity for education to virtue and charity and affection that the marriages and reconciliations should symbolize.

By endowing the detached observer with authorial aspirations and allowing him to take over the play's direction, the dramatists attach our discontent to the intriguer and *his* play rather than to their own. To accept the intriguer's manipulated conclusion we must see comic plotting as an adequate moral solution. To accept him as ideal (that is, at his own valuation) and identify with his victory we must not only grant the reductionist assumptions that underlie his plotting and his wit but also applaud enthusiastically the external adherence to society's rules that he achieves by a combination of trickery and force. We enjoyed the intriguer's wit and rambunctious vigor; his pranks even made avoiding disaster possible. But instead of consistently offering release from the burden of difficult individual and social ideals, his success denies the very values it attempts to ensure. His final answer to the recalcitrant is authority; his solution for the idealist is accommodation, the acceptance of things as they are.[48] The hypocritical absolutists who have been the butts of all three educative tricks learn that they proposed higher standards for themselves, and others, than they could fulfill; more devastatingly, the trickster's claim to moral as well as situational mastery also suggests they should renounce the aspiration itself as ridiculous and untenable. The spiritual code may be comically impossible to uphold, but the plays' voiced or implied moral norms make unsatisfactory and inadequate the solutions offered by wit or a purely social code. The observer-intriguer manifestly fails the test of creating a satisfactory conclusion to his "play." The ending's inadequacy and the trickster's self-infatuation become the final comment on the limits of his philosophy: it cannot admit the needs it fails to satisfy.

CHAPTER II

The Art of Distance II:
Tragedy

 H E world of ironic tragicomedy and of the satiric comedy whose assumptions it seems to share no longer answers, even potentially, the heart's desires. It is petty,
often spiteful, occasionally grotesque, largely unreform-
able. It is also, of course, very funny. It offers temporary relief from trying to be better than we are, but only by present-
ing such aspiration as ridiculous and rewarding those who refuse to
take its issues seriously. Such plays accept, explore, and make comic
capital out of a world where tricks—even successful ones—cannot certainly change human nature, and where trust, compassion, and charity
exist only to be violated. The characters' wishes for the best do not
persuade us it is so. Worse yet, a trusting or confident generosity can
prove pernicious as well as laughably naïve. A limited mastery is possible: the extent to which human effort brings about the final image of
personal and social harmony depends upon recognizing imperfection
and working through it toward rearranging errant people or desires.
Idealists and absolutists lack knowledge of self as well as others. They
are often comic butts, hypocrites who betray themselves almost as readily as they abandon those who trust them.

Apparently, the loss of ideals is the beginning of wisdom. Jacobean
cynicism appears in many comic forms, and by combining the satiric
observer-commentator with farce's active manipulator, some of the most
interesting plays explore this "wisdom's" potentially efficacious and benevolent aspects. Yet while such moral realism may save circumstances
threatened by hypocrisy and self-deception, situational solutions can
offer only qualified success: the "solution" to perverted ideals seems
often to require tacit denial of the ideal itself. We are dissatisfied because we have glimpsed the personal and social cost of assuming endemic human folly and lack of self-control. Comedy's triumph, in making hypocrites "turn flesh and blood, / And learn to live as other mortals

do," has revealed a fairly nasty idea of how mere mortals subsist together. Education in these plays means adjusting to what the detached observer-intriguer has known or suspected from the start: we must accept what is, because, to paraphrase Marston's prologue to *Antonio's Revenge*, men are what they must be. Such accommodation is the price both characters and audiences must pay for the comic ending, the final "happy" tableau. Ironic tragicomedy's world, then, if not its denouement, resembles tragedy's.

The genre into which ironic tragicomedy's manipulator organizes his story materials proves unsatisfactory, sabotaged by the author whose surrogate he seemed. Yet the trickster himself still dominates his play's ending: he wants approval for his wit, he demands acceptance of his world. Focusing on the intriguer and his solutions, the playwrights investigate a "generic" world view and not just a specifiable set of topics, such as marriage or heterosexual love. Using issues of governance, friendship, and familial bonds as their medium, the plays openly explore this view's effect on how people live together in various social relationships. Finally, and especially through their complex attitude toward their comic manipulators, these "problem" plays suggest that perhaps the denouement's price is too high and the final happiness, like Cynthia's dead husband and apparent adultery, "a *deceptio visus*, a mere blandation."

Whatever his comic lineage, the trickster's aggressive plotting and reductionist values ally him both with sixteenth-century villain protagonists and with the ambitious politicians against whom later tragic heroes struggle. Observers as well as manipulators of the political scene, they accept a limited yet satisfactorily malleable world and seek its prizes as their right. Iago's roots can be traced back to Richard III and beyond, as well as to the rich, creative soil which produced Duke Vincentio. Yet the Jacobean intriguers, however embellished with mysteriously metaphysical evil or stereotyped Machiavellianism, seem more at home in their world, and this representative quality can sustain powerful critical effects. Satiric tragedies like *Sejanus* and *The Revenger's Tragedy* offer no convincing opposition to the trickster and his vision; even his defeat suggests no hopeful alternative to his cynical perspective, discovers no saving wisdom in the face of destruction and loss. *The Revenger's Tragedy*, especially, may descend from Marston's innovative work in the *Antonio* plays and *The Malcontent*;[1] it creates an intriguer—

and a world—locked into Malevole's "dreams." With Vindice, we sink deeper and deeper into a nightmare of caricatured evil. Farce's aggression is unsoftened and unchallenged; its fast-paced mechanism becomes an infernal machine.[2]

Yet Jacobean tragedy often seeks transcendence through its protagonists. At the opposite extreme from satiric indictments, equally simplified but now affirmative, lie tragic melodramas like *Sophonisba* and *The Second Maiden's Tragedy*. Given the plays' authorship—Marston's last unaided tragedy and, probably, Middleton's second—we might predict the comic type-characters and satiric spirit marking both court's and subplot's alliance with city comedy and tragicomedy. Less predictable is the lack of complexity or urgency, the nostalgic stylization, apparent in both plays' central conflicts. Sharing satiric tragedy's firm moral scheme, these plays, too, create generalized political and moral *exempla*. Male revengers, half in love with easy vice, give place to transparently virtuous women. Marston, particularly, surprises us with his simplicity. The depth and hinted ambiguities toward which his tragicomedies had turned now seem to evaporate. Altofront's ability to merge successfully with a world that denies his values, Freevill's richly ambivalent attraction to Beatrice, fade before tragedy's mortal resistance to oppression. Idealized heroines face a world that offers no temptations, only the vile demands of a hated tyrant's lust; in each case, while all around her cede their maidenheads with alacrity, the lady in question simply and unwaveringly chooses death before dishonor. Martyred innocence offers the easiest, least ambiguous answer to the cynic's assumption that everyone, no matter what his boasts, can and should be forced to inhabit the same plane "as other mortals do." The secular saint's life contracts larger issues into questions of female chastity; it simplifies response to yea or nay.[3] If such plays seem to retreat from the complexity and engagement of earlier work, we might remember that Marston soon moved beyond theatrical consolations, and Middleton turned later—perhaps influenced by the Websterian tragedies he admired[4]—to the searching psychological studies for which he is best known. Webster may have toyed with such a melodramatic conception of tragic greatness and helped Heywood recast the ever-popular Appius and Virginia story; fortunately, the most apparent influences on his tragic dramaturgy were those of Shakespeare and Chapman.[5]

While Marston's caustic distancing looked forward to the adult companies' satiric tragedy as well as to private-theater experimental comedy, Shakespeare's *Measure for Measure* presaged a kind of tragedy where inner response holds more interest than the play's dramatization of social oppression or decay. G. K. Hunter notes that for Shakespeare's absolutists "knowledge of the corruption of the world is less important than their discovery of their own corruption or incapacity."[6] This interest in self-discovery, in responding to one's own fallibility as well as to the world's evil, also marks *The Widow's Tears*. Although Marston may have felt compelled in *Sophonisba* to "answer" his own earlier indictment of human nature, both Shakespeare and Chapman continued to explore that tension between desire and the world's offered satisfactions, between glorious self-definition and becoming the deed's creature, which lends such power as well as psychological realism to their tragicomedy. Quite probably Chapman wrote *Bussy D'Ambois* before *The Widow's Tears*, just as Shakespeare finished his first "Jacobean" tragedy before producing his "problem plays," but each dramatist exhibits a similar general movement from romantic comedy to the psychological studies that distinguish his later tragedies. And if *Hamlet* shares satiric tragedy's nostalgia for a time of simple moral certainties, the vanished heroic world of Hamlet's father, the prince is forced to meet Claudius under new rules of politics and diplomacy. He must adapt his ideals to a world in which his ethical standards seem irrelevant.

Of course, the clash between the old and new moralities itself constitutes the obsessive subject for much Jacobean tragedy, but in Chapman's and Shakespeare's heroic tragedies, characters espousing the "new" ethics and its political order become separated from the context of pure villainy by which revenge plots or strong morality structures had contained their energies. The struggle—a historical one and thus appropriately refought in contemporary France and ancient Rome—lies beyond simple moral categories. In Chapman's *Bussy D'Ambois* (and the *Byron* plays) and Shakespeare's late Roman tragedies the flexible man, perfectly adjusted to his times, faces a self-proclaimed hero whose moral as well as physical virtues belong to another era.[7] The same tension that animates ironic tragicomedy clearly provides the dialectic for some of the most interesting Jacobean tragedies: the observer-intriguer reappears as antagonist.

Ironic tragicomedy's concern with the morality of detachment complements its practical experiments in the dramatic uses of distancing. If the farceur's success mocked the idealist's belief in self-transcendence, so too the Machiavel's reductionist assumptions challenge the heroic image by which tragic protagonists try to shape their conduct. More desperately ambitious, the political realist still shares the trickster's cool pragmatism and willingness to be whatever the occasion demands; manipulative abilities derive from calculating observation, but also from healthy common sense. The trickster-Machiavel is no longer simply a villainous stereotype; he absorbs the authority as well as the practical success of those historical figures on whom he is modeled.[8] Though sometimes decked in the trappings of standard Machiavellianism, like Bussy's Monsieur, at base his challenge is both more mundane and more insistently unanswerable. He embodies that prudent flexibility by which the individual mirrors and masters society's own adaptability amid changing historical conditions. In him, and in those who choose his world, is heard that "deflating accent," that "suppler outlook," that Maynard Mack discovers in the worldly wisdom of the tragic hero's foil.[9]

The most radical change, of course, lies neither in the Machiavel nor the issues' expanded political scope but in the absolutist tragic hero himself, and hence in the conditions under which we accept or reject the realist's pragmatic accommodation. The distance enforced between us and the tragicomedies' trickster "hero" suggested the dramatists' own hesitation before a protagonist whose virtues lay so completely in the interpretation of his time. Qualifications that undermine an easy identification with tragedy's heroes reveal almost equally debilitating doubts about the possibility of frail humanity's self-transcendence. Our tragicomic perspective on these plays may clarify just how much of that distancing is comic, and how much at the tragic hero's expense; equally clearly, however, the tragic protagonist is no more a simple comic butt than a martyr-hero. The absolutist takes on the same ambiguous complexity formerly displayed by the benevolent manipulator: now the engaged character moves forward and offers substantial opposition to the farceur's metaphysical, if not his practical, triumph. Not only does the tragic protagonist refuse to accept the realist's world; by his misunderstood death he confirms that vision's inadequacy and substantiates the doubts implicit in ironic tragicomedy's denouement.

Webster's seedy Italian courts may seem unrelated to heroic tragedy's military worlds and soldier protagonists. Certainly, his observer-intriguers suggest a more obvious lineage, back through *The Revenger's Tragedy* to common forebears in city comedy and tragicomedy. Yet Webster does not write satiric tragedy—nor, despite his works' generic complexity, merely sophisticated parody.[10] Even in *The White Devil*, satire's cartoon characters and grotesques are joined by more representative men. Far as his plays seem from the "old-fashioned" heroic tradition explored by Chapman and Shakespeare, Webster does in fact play out that dying mode. He shares his colleagues' interest in technical experiment, in developing tragic meaning out of conflicting generic perspectives; he pursues their concern with detachment's moral consequences. However inimical to grandeur his dramatic world appears, however vigorously it denies the possibility of moral greatness, everything works toward the cynic's final grudging and futile recantation. In the end, Webster's plays explode the egotist's carefully restricted sphere of commitment, destroy the terms on which he had thought to negotiate a safe career. The antihero finally acknowledges his double's existence. In spite of himself, he too must suffer the search for subjective, humane values to balance the impersonal knowledge and protective double-dealing that life had seemed to demand. Thus, despite Webster's obvious debt to the witty, self-conscious intriguers of contemporary tragicomedy and satiric tragedy, the context that best clarifies his tragic dramaturgy must include those explorations of loss and affirmation, of private destruction and self-discovery, undertaken by Shakespeare's and Chapman's dying heroes.

It has been remarked of Shakespeare's late tragedies both that they are great psychological studies and that, since their protagonists offer far fewer revelatory soliloquies than their predecessors, the spectator identifies much less fully with their heroes.[11] The same features mark Chapman's *Bussy D'Ambois*. These plays lack a focal, morally determining act, an eloquently introspective hero, a tightly structured plot. Instead, they diffuse character interest and gain dramatic tension from local juxtapositions, which explore the ambiguous protagonist's heroism itself, as well as from his interaction with the society that challenges his absolute values.

Private moments are devoted not so much to ruminating on the promptings of desire and the consequences of action as to formal, quasi-objective attempts to define the external situation and by that definition establish an appropriate course of action. Bussy at the outset assessing "the state of things," Antony pondering the significance of Fulvia's death, Coriolanus summing up his exemplary fate before Antium—in such moments the protagonists seem consciously to strive for distance on themselves in order to understand how they fit into the world they see about them. However inaccurate the hero's sense of this condition, the generalizing, self-objectifying tendency is itself characteristic. Acutely aware of his unique individuality and demands, each protagonist also shares society's view of him as exemplar and upholder of quasi-external heroic standards. Thus a distinguishing feature of these men is their initial self-confidence. Revaluing their definition of honor, discovering the capacity to suffer for it meaningfully, comes hard precisely because these men are already complete heroes, defined by past deeds as society's bravest and best. Although variously successful politically, they seem even to their critics to need only sufficient scope in which to practice virtues they have already attained. Instead, they must discover in themselves the basis for a different, untraditional kind of heroism and uphold values for which their society offers neither guide nor exemplar. Introspection is not a soldier's occupation, however; we are not made privy to rich internal debate. Change or self-discovery happens in silences, between scenes, or by sudden instinctive choice. Results are enacted, not process.

Lack of inwardness or conscious self-analysis is not, of course, the sole reason for our distance from these colossal figures. Ironic tragicomedy's methods persist in heroic tragedy's search for affirmation. Most obviously, the disquieting shifts of perspective so characteristic of Shakespeare's late Roman tragedies extend the earlier plays' fascination with distancing techniques. While Chapman and Shakespeare employ this structural principle for manifold effects, such perspectivism also emphasizes those generic contrasts which allow farce to question the human freedom and dignity that romance assumes. Something close to the farceur's point of view repeatedly distances us from the tragic hero and undercuts his self-proclaimed stature. Bussy, Antony, and Coriolanus frequently appear as thrasonical braggarts or petulant children; indeed, the extent to which comic perspectives threaten all three is well illustrated by critical interpretations which, taking the part for the whole, insist on satiric exposure as the plays' only goal. By and large, we have come to see the deflating juxtapositions, the comic framing of character and incident, as integral parts of a dialectical structure which allows the hero's antagonist his due and will not forget the disparity between a heroic self-image and the diminished nature that action all too often demonstrates. Tragic stature is something attained late, only under pressure, and with great difficulty.

The frequency of derogatory comment and the amount of comic undercutting do not by themselves explain the nature of the aesthetic distance established. Scattered generic switches confuse rather than complicate. In these tragedies, however, a particular critical perspective is established early; it is also coherently rooted in a philosophy which itself challenges the protagonist's self-image. That is, the play's introduction to its tragic issues includes a point of view which, if true, negates those issues' significance and reduces the hero's suffering to an amply deserved reward for his inability to understand, let alone master, the world in which he tries to act. Subsequent generic juxtapositions then form a pattern through which the play seems to debate its own meaning.[12] Here the tragicomedies' first scenes, establishing the tone and expectations appropriate to a farcical exposure plot, suggest a model: attitudes demanded by the initial scene frame the main plot's romantic action and qualify the seriousness with which we take its dilemmas. The tragedies' openings, too, encourage a distanced, analytic attitude toward their own heroes. Lacking subplots, like *Measure for Measure* they use perspective shifts and different sets of characters who frankly place the same central action in different interpretive frames.

Bussy D'Ambois offers this introductory critical perspective in most concentrated form. In many ways a companion piece to *The Widow's Tears,* it allows its protagonist a self-defining prologue-soliloquy, then moves to confront him with irreconcilably opposed interpretations of his own significance. Bussy's initial assumption of the stoic satirist's role, bitterly lamenting the plight of Reason and Merit in his green retreat, is immediately questioned by his future patron, who expounds an equally abstract but opposite evaluation of Fortune's rule and the present "state of things."[13] Monsieur wears the rhetorical as well as philosophical trappings of the traditional Machiavel and at once declares his allegiance to Fortune and its rewards: power and rank. In him the egotism underlying Tharsalio's worldly wisdom finds its political scope. Like Tharsalio, Monsieur typifies an opportunist's way of looking at the world, one which accepts honor's neglect, assumes human corruptibility, and depends on using others' blind self-interest to effect his own dream of power. Tharsalio's "wisdom" seemed, finally, substantiated by his play's events, his witty egotism the only defense against trust's inevitable disappointment. Events prove Monsieur's practical competence: Monsieur knows and manipulates his brother's court; he presides as interpretive tragic chorus over the execution arranged for his fractious tool. Bussy's tragic stature depends, in part, upon disproving his patron's metaphysical assessments.

Monsieur challenges Bussy's stature in two ways. Clearly contrasted with Bussy in wealth and position, Monsieur's philosophical espousal of *Realpolitik* marks him as Bussy's complement and antithesis. Interestingly, however, Monsieur also sees Bussy as his double, a man now "discontent with his neglected worth" but "young and haughty, apt to take / Fire at advancement" (1.i.47–50). In part, Monsieur's reductionist philosophy requires interpreting Bussy's satiric railing as hypocrisy: "None loathes the world so much, nor loves to scoff it, / But gold and grace will make him surfeit of it" (1.i.52–53). Bussy's "enchanted glass" speech is his answer: in conventional satiric terms he condemns as morally decadent and trivial the court Monsieur represents. Yet Monsieur counters Bussy's smug rhetorical question with an unexpectedly cynical reply: "No, thou need'st not learn [corruption], / Thou hast the theory, now go there and practise" (1.i.104–105). Questioning the satirist's easy judgments as well as the sincerity of his virtuous retreat, Monsieur touches the play's underlying struggle. He believes he can use Bussy for his own ends by tempting him with gold and advancement; Bussy sees through the temptation but thinks he can use Monsieur's mistake to "rise in Court with virtue."[14]

Bussy's rise in fact elevates him to parallel status with the king's brother. As Henry's eagle and Tamyra's lover he threatens Monsieur's courtly preeminence; by act 3 both Bussy and Monsieur seem to agree that they represent equal but opposite moral and political forces. Yet Monsieur's initial belief in human corruptibility not only sets up the play's dominant pattern of statement-counterstatement, it also characterizes Bussy's subsequent actions as those of a knave or a fool. Such a challenge to the satirist's asserted moral purity focuses our interest not on Bussy's ability to transform Henry's court (for on this count Monsieur's cynicism seems amply justified), but on Bussy's ability to resist its contamination and suit his actions to the moral standard he professes in 1.i.[15]

In initially pegging Bussy for a fool or a hypocrite, Monsieur suggests the outline of a potentially comic, self-deluded absolutist, an outline that Bussy all too often fulfills. Chapman immediately provides a setting to tempt Bussy's potential as courtier and buffoon. Henry's court, where all dance a "continual Hay" and real evil goes unchecked, proves irremediably trivial and self-satisfied. Monsieur's errand-boy Maffé represents at its most superficial the arena in which Bussy plans heroic deeds. Maffé's world ensures Monsieur's survival and triumph; in it heroes must appear fools, and in its eyes Bussy, as he admits, has "no merit." Yet such knowledge does not temper this moralist's behavior. With Maffé, and then the court's gentlemen, Bussy is reduced to the level of physical rebuffs. Bussy also seems to know the court form, can become "a Courtier at first sight" (1.ii.81). The gusto with which he adopts his new role, his vulgar banter with the ladies and defiant insolence to the Guise, partly deserve the mockery of Barrisor and his friends. Like Maffé, they judge by externals; to them Bussy's behavior merely suggests "what a metamorphosis a brave suit can work" (1.ii.118). The proud defiance with which Bussy countered Monsieur in 1.i translates into the public actions of a self-important bully, a "dunghill cock" (1.ii.149–150). Bussy may disdain them as "perfumed musk-cats," but they insist on the similarity, not difference, of this "perfumed Ass" whose fancy clothes make him "imagin[e] himself a Lion" (1.ii. 209, 187–188). The conflict of mighty opposites begins to seem rather one-sided, and Bussy's initial behavior anticipates a progressive exposure for this self-deluded "slave of his passions."[16]

Comic exposure is heaviest in act 1, where Bussy's attempts to defy the court in its own terms produce laughter or scorn instead of admiration or heroic action. Although Bussy sees himself as a Herculean moralist, "for honest actions, not for great" (1.i.124), his nobility and goodness are largely a matter of words. His deeds define another, potentially comic stereotype. Chapman does not desert his protagonist here, of course. Bussy is not alone in thinking himself above the court's trivial corruption, the sole upholder of a moral ideal of "man in his native noblesse" (III.ii.91). Yet neither does Chapman let us forget Bussy's unheroic, even antiheroic aspects. Chapman's usual technique is juxtaposition, not merely of word and deed but of several often conflicting interpretations of the same situation. Typical is the confrontation between Bussy and Monsieur in 1.i, where contrasting rhetorical stances imply competing philosophies and moral assumptions, and Bussy's continued fascination and ambiguity stem from these "big scenes" where differing perspectives are juxtaposed, not from Chapman's rather untidily developed plot. Even as Bussy comes to impress the court with his valor and virtue, Chapman takes care to counterpoise heroic potential with reductionist interpretations that echo Monsieur and mock the hero's grandiose self-image. In II.i the Nuntius's glamorizing report contrasts both with the courtiers' departure for the duelling field (I.i) and with the Guise's interpretation of the epic combat as "piteous and horrid murder" (II.i.105). Though Bussy may not here seem a fool, we are reminded that, in one view at least, he is an egotist and an outlaw who brings chaos and bloodshed rather than moral reform. As Guise later says, "D'Ambois is pardon'd: where's a King? Where law?" (II.ii.24).

Bussy's martial courage in battle remains ambiguous. His greatness in love is similarly hedged with qualification. Tamyra's refusal of Monsieur's tawdry proposition, her disgust with her ambitious husband's excuse for royal corruption—those princes are virtuous who "will entreat a vice, and not command" (II.ii.125)—should win our sympathy. Monsieur's smutty devaluation of Tamyra's "honor" and the grossness of his later wit-duel with Pero and the maids (III.ii) further define Bussy's relationship with Tamyra as something beyond the court's debased idea of love. Yet in one sense Tamyra has succeeded where Monsieur failed. Monsieur discovers he cannot bend Bussy to his will or use him to "effect" his own "ambitious end" (III.i.107). Tamyra's sexual seduction does more than offer Monsieur a lever with which to topple his rival; it implicates Bussy in the court's hypocrisy and deceit. Tamyra is both different from the court world—refusing its easy corruption, in love with its challenger—and part of it. Bussy's mysterious greatness draws her beyond the confines and hence the protection of the recognized social order; his affair with her leads him to adopt that world's pragmatic values. Her shame and concern with reputation require his hypocrisy in both personal and public spheres. Eagerly he accepts the Friar's counsels in "this our set and cunning world of Love" (II.ii.195); urged by Tamyra, the Friar, and Behemoth, Bussy finally agrees to "curb his rage, with policy" and fight Monsieur with his own weapons (IV.ii.138). The rope of pearl Monsieur offered in exchange for Tamyra's virtue reappears, tellingly, around Bussy's neck.

Bussy's unhesitating submission to Tamyra's needs also helps qualify his one opportunity to play moral reformer, his "hawking" for the king. Bussy assumes the role of virtuous satirist when he has just come from adultery, and we are reminded of his new duplicity by Monsieur's gloating discovery of Bussy's "venery" as soon as the scourger leaves the stage. Yet such effects are less significant than the whole attack's futility: Bussy's final "rise in Court with virtue" is an illusory victory at best. Chapman's use of the satiric set speech against the standard topics (flatterers, great men, corrupt clergymen, and iniquitous lawyers) is highly ironic: the subjects may have relevance to the earlier general discussion of England and France and serve to extend our sense of present corruption, but they are, in immediate terms, pitifully irrelevant. Bussy's stature is further qualified by Henry's use of him: Bussy remains a pawn in greater men's political struggles, only now Henry tries "to convert / The point of Monsieur's aim on his own breast" (iii.i.109–110). A good but weak king, Henry is interested in the political, not moral effect of Bussy's attack. Beyond its challenge to Monsieur's power, the "hawking" is only a rhetorical gratification for Henry, who thinks he can flee Envy and avoid cleansing his court by uniting satirized and satirist in a peaceful handshake. Though Bussy sweeps out on Henry's arm, this long scene does not close on his triumph, nor even on the low comedy of the lords' and maids' riddling exchange. Bussy returns for the "flyting," that grotesque parody of friendship's honest exchange in which Bussy must accept as many telling insults as he inflicts. Monsieur likens Bussy's valor to mad Ajax's; he admits "strange gifts in nature" while denying Bussy a "soul / Diffus'd quite through to make them of a piece" (iii.ii.349–350).

Although act 3 does not dwell on Tamyra, she is the means of exposing Bussy's naked human frailties to the court and finally to Bussy himself. Such knowledge promises to negate the threat a virtuous Bussy poses to Monsieur's whole materialist philosophy. Monsieur hopes to find that the "spirit rais'd without a circle" who so "awes my throat" will prove merely a "royal beast of chase," a hart who may be taken where "he breaks his gall, and rutteth with his hind" (iii.ii. 297–300, 152–156). The lovers' affair joins them to Monsieur's fallen world; it removes both exceptions to his "rules" and seems to reconfirm his intellectual mastery. Monsieur's glee is like Tharsalio's at discovering Cynthia's "fall": "Why this was the happiest shot that ever flew! the just plague of hypocrisy levelled it! . . . I thought I could not be so slighted, if she had not her freight besides" (III.ii.199–204). We may not concur with Monsieur's devaluation, for it is biased by his need to disbelieve in any love but lust, but Chapman does not spare us this possibility or its implications for hyperbolic expressions of romantic idealism. Bussy's capitulation to politic advice further emphasizes just how far love has led him from the resolve to set a new court "fashion" for virtue.

Bussy's final ludicrous and futile conversion to "policy" in act 4 brings to fruition I.i's latent possibilities and threatens his stature in a new way. Monsieur's initial assumption of human corruptibility led him to interpret Bussy's defiant idealism as hypocrisy, fine rhetoric cloaking real political ambition. An impoverished courtier and soldier "on the make," Bussy as a would-be Monsieur has simply chosen a different mask under which to pursue his worldly goals. Though late in the play and at Tamyra's urging, Bussy's decision to become his knavish patron's equal recalls to us the possibility that Monsieur is not Bussy's antithesis but his alter ego. The parallels were suggested as early as I.ii, when Bussy entered in his new dress, an instant courtier. He seemed to have put on more than an external costume, and his bawdy exchange with the ladies was echoed, disturbingly, in the sexual language defining Monsieur's relationship with his new protégé: Bussy was Monsieur's "own sweet heart" whom Henry urged his brother to "wear," since he had been "woo'd and won" (I.ii. 56, 69).[17] In dismissing Bussy's pretentious swaggering, Barrisor assumed that Bussy, in "Monsieur's cast suit, imagines himself to be the Monsieur" (I.ii.159–160). Monsieur later, calming a threatening Bussy with no doubt hypocritical sweetness, nominates him "my Love's glory: heir to all I have" (IV.i.93). Such attraction, even identity, gains concrete realization when Bussy finally decides to turn politician and fight his battle for court goods with courtly deception.

Bussy seems to have lost himself in his courtier's role, allowed Monsieur to be his "maker" in the very sense he initially vowed to resist. The conscious choice to become Monsieur is Bussy's low point, an implicit denial of everything he has stood for, which brands him heroic only in the extent of his self-deception. To attain tragic stature Bussy must prove himself different from Monsieur, unable finally to become this alter ego. He must also prove that difference admirable and convince us that it is not the limiting stupidity of a man rapt with his own flattering image, incapable of greatness or even elementary self-knowledge.

Although nominally Fortune's darling, "triple pillar of the world" and proven conqueror, Shakespeare's Antony, too, suffers an immediate challenge to his heroic self-image. During his Egyptian sojourn both Antony and the world he mastered have changed, but *Antony and Cleopatra* delays introducing the hero's mighty opposite or the new Rome his virtues will govern. Instead, the play characterizes its protagonist by framing his declaration of value—in which his "space" is Egypt and "the nobleness of life" lies in the embraces of a "peerless" and "mutual pair"—with his soldiers' disgust that "plated Mars" has been "transformed / Into a strumpet's fool."[18] There is here no question of hypocrisy, only of folly. To the Roman soldiers the new Antony "is not Antony" at all (1.i.57); the general they loyally served has been replaced by an infatuated lover whose dotage corrupts his manhood. *Antony and Cleopatra* at first promises to follow a dramatic tradition portraying conquerors in disastrous relationships with women.[19] It suggests that Antony has made the wrong choice and denied the heroic past he still claims to represent; Philo's view is later seconded by Caesar and Lepidus (1.iv) and by Pompey (11.i). This tradition sees Antony as a fallen hero who must prove his ability to crown his claims with deeds; he fulfills the role of magnanimous warrior-hero only when he leaves sensual love and Egypt behind.

In *Antony and Cleopatra* separate sets of characters repeatedly provide particular viewpoints affecting our response to the main action. Yet while its characters appeal to our emotional involvement and commitment, the play at the same time forces us to observe with some detachment.[20] The dramatic structure by which Shakespeare continually opposes Rome and Egypt—both within scenes, through "Roman" commentary, and by careful scenic juxtaposition—economically allows two important developments. Demonstrating the incompatible values defining these antithetical "empires" lets us realize long before Antony that his soldiers are right: he cannot be both Rome's and Cleopatra's. Such a structure also allows Shakespeare to dramatize the distance between Antony's proclaimed identity and the self-deluded, impulsive fool his actions define.

Such deheroizing arises from more than the hostile interpretations framing the lovers' declarations. Antony and his queen themselves illustrate the rigid, conventional, and fundamentally comic characterizations supplied by the Roman commentary. Shakespeare does not later deny this demeaning first impression. Antony is always in danger of fulfilling his critics' stereotype of an old philanderer no longer capable of nobility or valor, and Cleopatra's dramatized "variety" continually flirts with the ridiculous. So, too, a tendency to self-delusion, a belief in their own heroic hyperbole, remains a part of both characters. *Antony and Cleopatra* is studded with scenes in which the reductive lens of low comedy transforms the central characters' grandeur and makes a farceur's attitude appropriate.[21] The Egyptian queen turns jealous shrew and hales Rome's messenger by the hair (II.v); she later exhibits a ludicrous concern with Octavia's physical appearance (III.iii). The party on Pompey's barge extends the comic devaluations of Menas, Agrippa, and Enorbarbus to the whole Roman alliance: the glamorous world-shakers are but drunken men, at the mercy of their servants' comments and plots. In such scenes, as in *Bussy*, comic pressure qualifies the very form of tragedy and suggests that the hero's justifiable pride may be its comic counterpart, the boundless vanity of the fool who believes his own fustian.

Antony's own "variety," of course, encompasses all views of his Egyptian conduct, but the decision to break his "fetters" and recover the Roman Antony does not restore his lost dignity. Philo and Demetrius might approve, but Antony remains fair game to friends and lovers alike. Cleopatra mocks the departing Antony's vows as hypocrisy, "excellent dissembling" which futilely tries to "look / Like perfect honour," and she ridicules his anger as "Herculean . . . chafe" (I.iii. 79–80, 84–85). Disbelieving the sincerity of Antony's conversion by "a Roman thought," Enobarbus answers with bawdy jokes both Antony's sorrow at Fulvia's death and his rededication to Roman "business" instead of Cleopatra's. Enobarbus's mocking reductionism is even-handed: it touches Cleopatra, who is dubbed both a "new petticoat" and a "wonderful piece of work" worth the traveler's sight (I.ii. 167, 151–153); it also extends to all the world-conquerors in Rome, not just Antony. Enobarbus must be a "considerate stone" because his cynical truths threaten the delicate renegotiation of Antony's and Octavius's relationship (II.ii.103–110). In II.vi his exchange with Menas mimics the proud egotism with which Antony and his future brother-in-law had jockeyed for precedence, each speaking "as loud as Mars" to maintain his dignity (II.ii.6).

Shakespeare's devaluation of his heroic protagonist is thus progressive. If Antony at first stood condemned for having forsaken Rome and its values for wanton idleness, in acts 2 and 3 he seems equally compromised when he suits his actions to a Roman setting. Like Bussy, Antony is caught in a double bind of which he remains unaware. Both Antony's reputation and his self-image rest on a Herculean idea of the hero—the defiant exponent of a golden age of self-sufficient warriors.[22] Caesar's awed description of the retreat from Modena vividly pictures for us that traditional Roman ideal. Yet the warrior-hero seeking personal honor through combat is now ludicrously out of place. What Monsieur tells us at the outset of *Bussy D'Ambois* reveals itself only gradually in *Antony and Cleopatra*. This world is won not by martial virtues but by tactics, that politic abandoning of "mouth-made vows" when one's opponent is at a disadvantage which Enobarbus and Eros discuss in III.v. Dreaming of his past, Antony's "valour preys on reason" and corrupts his military judgment (III.xiii.199). He fights at sea on a dare; finally he comes full circle, back to the stereotype of I.i, when he follows his love like a "doting mallard" (III.x.20). Antony has again lost himself, temporarily but fatally. As "sworder" and "old ruffian," he is mocked by both sides.

In the new world, then, power is honor, the world's prizes the only acknowledged goal. Antony's spiritual rededication to life "by the rule" and attempt to wed Roman virtue by marrying Caesar's sister do not signal the prodigal son's renewal. Instead, Shakespeare uses Antony's return to initiate a revaluation of the Roman virtue that in I.i was so casually assumed to be a standard of value. Both Enobarbus's comic debunking and the barge scene—displaying two drunkards, a primly self-conscious puritan, and a hypocrite too cowardly to act upon his own ambition—are part of that reexamination. Further challenges range from Ventidius's disclosure of the conquerors' tawdry jealousy and borrowed glory (III.i) to Enobarbus's and Agrippa's denial of heroic hyperbole as they parody Lepidus flattering both Antony and Caesar (III.ii). Roman honor is proved hollow; military virtues, even when Antony can demonstrate them, are useless against Caesar's political sophistication. To the extent that Antony tries to join the new Roman world, seeking empire at any price, he must suffer the same exposure. Octavius may become the "universal landlord," but in the middle acts Shakespeare strips his possession of grandeur.

Antony's attempt to become Caesar is, of course, short lived. Octavius sees that in marrying Octavia Antony takes "from me a great part of myself; / Use me well in 't" (iii.ii.24–25), but symbolic acts cannot purchase the virtues necessary for political dominance. Antony returns to "his Egyptian dish" and, too often, to his old ways. Unlike Bussy, Antony does not threaten to lose his stature, his very identity, by accepting his opponent's pragmatic philosophy. The intent is there, but his will is tied to Cleopatra. Once Antony has left Rome, protecting his love requires the martial hero's "royal occupation," not the Machiavel's deceit and disguise. Yet though Antony does not renounce his initial beliefs, he does subvert the hero that standard defined.[23] Considering Antony a fool whose corrupted judgment "restores his heart," Enobarbus joins Canidius and Hercules in desertion. In responding too fully to Cleopatra's variety, Antony loses himself; identity, like authority, melts from him, and he is left without coherence, a body unable to "hold this visible shape" (iv.xiv.14).[24]

Yet the circumstances marking the Roman Antony's nadir also force Antony to redefine himself and his goals. Against the apparent judgment of men and gods, Shakespeare sets the buoyant, self-confident Antony of the armoring scene. Necessity leads Antony to the unconscious resolution of his earlier dilemma: Cleopatra replaces Rome and its warrior gods as Antony's final end and inspiration. The boasts of i.i. and the vow to "go from hence / Thy soldier, servant" finally receive full commitment. The "delight" with which he now rises from one love to engage another "business that we love" marks the end of self-division and revitalizes an Antony who again inspires his soldiers' brave loyalty (iv.iv.20–21). As Cleopatra's knight, Antony successfully proves himself with "gests" (iv.viii.2). The lovers are no longer out of phase, and their hyperbolic self-definition gains real resonance from its mutuality. The "day o' the world" and "lord of lords" seem finally ready to take their stand together.

Antony's ideal is no longer one of heroic self-sufficiency. His new self-image depends on Cleopatra: his deeds are done for her, her response defines his worth. Having refashioned himself around an ideal of mutual dedication, Antony is annihilated by Cleopatra's apparent betrayal when her ships desert to Caesar. His sense of "Antony" must dissolve "as water is in water" if the "heart I thought I had, for she had mine" has proved only self-interested and instead beguiled him "to the very heart of loss" (IV.xiv. 11, 16; xii.29).[25] Mardian's report of Cleopatra's suicide, her decision to mingle "her fortunes . . . With thine entirely," reinstates their interdependence and allows Antony to die an honorable lover's death; he envisions himself rushing towards Cleopatra, half of a pair as peerless in the next world as in this.

Antony's stature at his death remains debatable, for his assertions build upon the sand of Cleopatra's lie. Trust is as dangerous as hyperbole in this world, and Shakespeare hedges Antony's end with doubts. Afraid even to name the deed he begs, Antony asks his servant to dispatch him; forced to become his own executioner, his botched attempt reflects the inept, dishonored soldier more than the eager bridegroom. The final repository of Antony's reputation is Cleopatra. If her "size of sorrow" is indeed "proportion'd to our cause," then her deeds will determine Antony's greatness. To accept Caesar's offer is to espouse the worldly, self-regarding "wisdom" which Thidias calls her "noblest course" and Caesar commends in the Seleucus scene. Like Caesar, such a Cleopatra "words" Antony while looking out for herself. At the end of *Bussy D'Ambois* Tamyra fades in significance. Exchanging impersonal, emblematic definitions with her husband, she is important to Bussy— and to us—primarily as this "killing spectacle: this prodigy" which prompts her dying lover to revalue himself and his life's meaning. Shakespeare's procedure in *Antony and Cleopatra* is, quite obviously, other. Daringly, he kills off his heroic protagonist early and recalls at his death the initial outline of a bumbling fool, duped by both his own fulsome rhetoric and the "mouth-made vows" of a brilliant courtesan. To a surprising extent, Shakespeare leaves Antony's significance and his play's meaning in the hands of a woman whose imagination and rhetorical splendor can rise to match her lover's, but whose past defines her kinship with the opportunistic Caesar.

Antony and Cleopatra is also a love tragedy with a dual focus, and though Antony finally accepts her as his true analogue and double, I have rather slighted Cleopatra to concentrate on Shakespeare's portrayal of his warrior protagonist. Lacking even adulterous love, *Coriolanus* offers a bleak counterpoise to *Antony and Cleopatra's* assertion of final, if limited, transcendence. Shakespeare's last tragedy ruthlessly exposes its hero's failures; he can neither adapt his virtues to the world in which he must act nor, more importantly, discover any escape from the heroic solipsism that shackles his humanity. The self-righteous absolutist flounders wihtout support in a world inimical to the very virtues it praises. While familiar structural techniques establish the perspectives that challenge the hero's worth, *Coriolanus*'s concentration on its protagonist's nature reveals possibilities implicit, or only lightly touched upon, in the earlier heroes.

To an even greater extent than with Bussy or Antony, the presentation of Coriolanus is external and reserved. The play seems designed to frustrate our sympathy or involvement with its central mystery.[26] Unintrospective, distrustful of language, taciturn or inarticulate at critical moments, Coriolanus fails to define himself. We are kept separate from a man who does not try to touch us with his rhetoric. The high degree of interposed commentary further distances the protagonist and repeatedly transforms him into a comic butt or philsophic *exemplum*. Within their plays, Bussy and Antony inspire admiration and love as well as mockery and envy; they counter initial disbelief with an ideal whose attractiveness compels even as it judges their private defalcations. Lacking the moral reformer's public ardor or a private exaltation of total emotional commitment, the positive aspects of Coriolanus's ethic remain largely implicit, buried in the furious diatribes leveled at all whose oppose his will. Extravagantly emotional in response to almost any stimulus, he also most clearly illustrates the disengaged, self-referential nature of heroic solipsism. Seeing himself as his heroic ideal, he is his own standard and all others must comply or be damned. Coriolanus enters alone; unlike Bussy and Antony, he moves progressively beyond love and friendship. As he severs himself from all ties with his community, Coriolanus could command our assent to his self-image only by convincing us of that standard's absolute value and his own embodiment of it. Shakespeare allows him to do neither.

Unlike Antony, about whose capacity for heroic action a good deal of doubt is voiced both early and late, Coriolanus suffers no detraction on the score of physical bravery. The disgruntled citizens, who see in him the "chief enemy to the people" yet acknowledge the "services he has done for his country," impugn not his courage but his motives.[27] Self-referential bravery approves itself, and though Coriolanus's pride may not exceed "the altitude of his virtue," the citizens (and later the tribunes) feel they owe nothing to a man who has already paid himself. (Interestingly, of course, Coriolanus shares his opponents' view: in I.ix he refuses the state's tribute, both praise and goods, on the grounds that such rewards are superfluous, hence lies, and can only tarnish the intrinsic honor of the deed itself.)[28] Aufidius, Roman generals, common soldiers on both sides, all agree that Coriolanus is the preeminent warrior he claims to be.

Coriolanus's irascible pride, like Bussy's, seems ludicrously inappropriate in the civil and political sphere to which he transfers his military habits. Lack of self-knowledge, combined with rigid self-righteousness, submits Coriolanus, too, to manipulation, even by those who do not fully understand him. Bussy's instinctive belligerency discharges itself in politically irrelevant confrontations, while Coriolanus's threatens the fabric of the Roman state; in both cases the automatic response and rhetorical excess are themselves demeaning. Trivial, even comic contexts transform hero into pugnacious and irrational bully. In *Coriolanus* the initial exchanges between the citizens and Menenius provide a comic background for the protagonist's furious entrance, at which point the rhetoric verges on rodomontade.[29] Coriolanus proves his superhuman, indeed reckless, bravery at Corioles; he also proves incapable of adjusting his response or vocabulary to other occasions. Again in II.iii, the citizens' good-natured joking establishes their political naïveté but also the real good will they bear the would-be consul. The mocking irony with which Coriolanus attempts to distance and negate the people's "voices" distorts the situation as much as his later wrath: he cannot acknowledge as just or reasonable the citizens' hope that the man they elect should prove "our friend" (II.iii.103). Such Bergsonian inflexibility frequently reduces him to comic status, a humour character full of easily triggered, braggadocian bombast.[30]

Coriolanus's inability to be other than one thing is apparent not only in the ease with which the tribunes treat him like a dog to set on sheep, but also in his failure to execute even those parts he himself chooses to play. He cannot put on the gown of humility in any but the most literal sense; it becomes an intolerable disguise which must be thrown off if he is to know "myself again" (II.iii.146). In IV.v the dramatic confrontation between Aufidius and Coriolanus is framed by the servingmen's low comedy, and at the scene's opening the disguised Coriolanus wishes to avoid "puny battle" with bereaved Volscian widows and children; yet he cannot bear to be treated as his mean apparel requires. A comic figure, the aristocrat caught in his own disguise, Coriolanus refuses to act his role, yet acting his "nature" in this context requires the warrior-general to turn kitchen bully and fulfill precisely the reductive posture he wished to escape. Coriolanus's efforts to master the dramatic arts are ludicrously inept. Indeed, he insists on principle that he only "play / The man I am," that other parts he will never "discharge to th' life" (III.ii. 15–16, 106). Such incompetence springs from a healthy fear of action's determining, creative power: even hypocritically performed, the body's deeds will "teach my mind / A most inherent baseness" (III.ii.122–123). Laudable in itself, Coriolanus's almost instinctive abhorrence of deceit also stems from an obsession with his own integrity which limits his action instead of freeing it.

Coriolanus compulsively reenacts his narrow self-image on others' cues, but that ideal does not quite contain his nature. Self is seen as another role, though he has been taught that it is the only honorable one and hence not to be deserted. The self Coriolanus thinks he "is" is the youth Volumnia clucked to the wars, the man whose brave deeds earned the "good report" she found sufficient "son" (I.iii.20). Her ideal of fame won through service to Rome has been internalized and authenticated by battlefield success. That Volumnia should now call him "too absolute" and demand he play a part "of no allowance to your bosom's truth" surprises him, since he believes his aggressive absoluteness enacts his mother's Roman ideal (III.ii. 39, 57). Yet Coriolanus has filled her narrow martial ideal with his own, in some ways even narrower, self-referential meaning, and the language that sees the self as a separable role hints what events soon demonstrate: his "nature" and the self he thinks he is are at odds.[31]

Through deceit Coriolanus may win a peacetime garland, or so Volumnia claims. Coriolanus's stubborn intransigence forces us to see that her methods are morally corrosive as well as tawdry. The honor and policy which to her son are antithetical collapse into alternate aspects of the same nobility: in trying circumstances dissembling with his nature can be done "in honour" (III.ii.62–64). Volumnia is right that "in this" she is "these senators, the nobles" (III.ii.64–65); in justifying politic deception she also speaks for the tribunes and Aufidius. Her methods would surely destroy both her son and the "Roman" principle of truth he serves (as Aufidius's willingness to "potch" at Coriolanus with "wrath or craft" negates the honor he tries to appropriate). For the absolutist, stretching words to cover their opposites provides no answer; without Coriolanus, the struggle over who rules Rome—nobles, plebeian representatives, Volscians—becomes one of politics, not principle.

Coriolanus is tempted only briefly to become the successful soldier-politician his mother desires.[32] Like Bussy and Antony, Coriolanus too faces his politic double, and the play, unlike North's translation of Plutarch, takes care to establish Aufidius as both antithesis and alter ego. Aufidius and Coriolanus, each his city's "very heart of hope," envy each other's nobility (I.vi.55); both have difficulty fitting themselves to their country's conditions. Coriolanus, seeing the Volscian general as his only peer, proclaims that "were I anything but what I am, / I would wish me only he," and mighty opposites threaten to merge when Coriolanus, like a "wife . . . fallen out with her husband," seeks Aufidius's love in Antium (I.i.230–231; IV.iii.32–33). In this play of strained familial relationships, love thrives most prominently on the battlefield. Still, the sexual overtones framing the revenge pact are particularly insistent and recall Bussy's and Monsieur's perverse courtship. Coriolanus predicts that they may "interjoin their issues," and at his proffered service Aufidius's "rapt heart" dances more excitedly than on his wedding night (IV.iv.22; IV.v.117–119). In the servingmen's coarse translation, Aufidius "makes a mistress of him, sanctifies himself with 's hand, and turns up the white o' th' eye to his discourse" (IV.v.200–202). But if Aufidius is the man Volumnia asks her son to play, Coriolanus's declared affinity belongs to his mistaken sense of self. In fact, his path throughout has been toward a final, solipsistic singularity. The Aufidius/ Coriolanus parallels remain thematically significant but dramatically unpersuasive.

Although in a limited sense he serves as a moral yardstick, Coriolanus is of course no exemplar of transcendent integrity, no unmoved mover securely indifferent to fickle opinion or the world's dispraise. Immediate challenges to assert his integrity fuel an underlying necessity to play himself, continually, in order to know himself. Constant re-creation requires opponents, and Coriolanus uses words as weapons, bludgeoning his gainsayers with curses and reductive epithets; he clings desperately to his confused ideal and tries to firm its outline by courting both the plebs' hatred and his mother's praise. Instinctively he pushes toward the physical confrontation by which he could enforce his definition of himself, of nobility, of Rome. Yet insecurity blinds him to his own potential as well as to the situation's real demands, and in playing the man he thinks he is, he overacts. Ironically, Volumnia is right: "You might have been enough the man you are, / With striving less to be so" (III.ii.19–20). If Antony's self dissolves in the movement toward infinite variety, Coriolanus's self-dramatization constricts without satisfactorily defining him. Coriolanus is in danger of becoming his own statue, a mechanical man programmed to act in one, limited fashion.

More than Bussy or Antony, then, Coriolanus seems even to himself to demonstrate a psychological determinism which, at least implicitly, substantiates his opponents' materialism and denies him mastery of either faults or virtues. Lepidus had insisted that Antony's flaws were not only "spots of heaven" but ineradicably "hereditary, . . . what he cannot change, [not] what he chooses," but Octavius called this excuse "too indulgent." In *Coriolanus,* Second Citizen protests that they ought not to "account a vice" what Coriolanus "cannot help in his nature," and for much of the play Coriolanus's lack of freedom is assumed (I.i.40–41). As he soliloquizes before Antium, Coriolanus wonders at how the world's "slippery turns" have apparently transformed him, though unchanged, into his opposite (IV.iv.12–26). Others do not share his view of himself as innocent victim, yet all sides agree that he acts compulsively, agent of an irascible nature which may or may not be "too noble for the world" (III.i.253). If he is unfree, Coriolanus is also not responsible for his acts in any real moral sense. He becomes the exponent of his own instinctive aggression—since wrath repeatedly o'erwhelms his best intentions—or the tool of stronger, craftier wills who are themselves accountable for what they engineer.

As either the tribunes' stalking horse or the will-less masculine extension of Volumnia's ambition, Coriolanus appears less than a hero, indeed, less than a man. A proclaimed moral exemplar, his self-perpetuating rages define rather a helpless, irrational child, and parallels linking Coriolanus with the citizens he so despises substantiate this diminished stature. A shared political naïveté makes them docile pupils of Rome's real contenders. In context, some of Coriolanus's accusations come rather amusingly home to roost: complaining he has "had children's voices," he warns the nobles not to "live with such as cannot rule, / Nor ever will be rul'd" (III.i. 29, 39–40). He denies the plebs citizenship in his Rome; he belittles their humanity with animal epithets and the grotesque reification of their tongues and voices. But the tribunes find that Coriolanus can be manipulated as easily as their "herd," the plebeians, and that he exhibits the same diminished humanity he attributes to others.

Though expected between enemies, such depersonalization pervades all forms of social interaction, even the closest relationships. Its prevalence contributes to our sense of this world's coldness and human inadequacy. To his mother, Coriolanus and his fame are interchangeable "sons"; she picks and chooses which of his qualities are hers, then appropriates his valiance to her own credit. In II.i, the surrogate father, Menenius, joins Volumnia in reducing Coriolanus to the number and quality of his wounds. Cominius, whom Coriolanus clipped "in arms as sound as when I woo'd," can also see his friend as the untamed sea, a planet, a "thing of blood, whose every motion / Was tim'd with dying cries" (I.vi.30; II.ii.109–110). Indeed, savage dehumanization marks all descriptions of Coriolanus on the battlefield. He himself accepts this status: to the soldiers who lift him in I.vi he cries, "Make you a sword of me?"; [33] in IV.v he offers himself and his hatred to Aufidius's "use." As "mechanical warrior, a man turned into an instrument of war," Coriolanus becomes a wind-up toy, pointed at the enemy and released;[34] his brave deeds are not his own, the imagery suggests, but simply reflex actions. Mechanical exaggeration, so laughable in the council chambers of civilian life, on the battlefield creates a pitiless human caricature of the grim reaper.

Instead of submitting to Volumnia or Aufidius, then, Coriolanus finally loses himself in his admirers' grotesque deification, believes he is "a thing / Made by some other deity than nature, / That shapes man better" (IV.vi.91–93). The dehumanizing battlefield imagery lends disturbing power to his assumption of godhead. In seeking to "depopulate the city and / Be every man himself," Coriolanus becomes no man: the enacted self is now a "thing," a "lonely dragon" (III.i.262–263; IV.i.30). He denies "all bond and privilege of nature," to himself as well as his family, and claims to "stand / As if a man were author of himself / And knew no other kin" (V.iii. 25, 35–37).[35] The less than human asserts its superhuman prerogatives; the soulless giant whose only harvest is death tries to re-create the world in his own image.

Coriolanus is made far less sympathetic than either Bussy or Antony. Shakespeare does not merely probe the self-declared hero to find a fool, a fallible man striving desperately to filter tawdry acts through the prism of heroic rhetoric. To a surprising extent, Coriolanus lacks mediating admirers. He severs rather than forges emotional bonds. Antony and Bussy become progressively more fully human, albeit politically impotent; Coriolanus has, momentarily, the ability to transform a child's spite into nightmare reality. Despite the powerful shock of Coriolanus's grotesque self-apotheosis, however, in v.vi he dwindles again to the stature of political puppet. In his isolation more awesomely distanced than Bussy or Antony, Coriolanus has suffered the same kind, if not degree, of comic exposure. In each case we have been encouraged to see the hero as comedy's absolutist, foolishly deceived about himself as well as about the world he cannot subdue. Generic cues which repeatedly disengage us from the protagonist's plight, from his unique and significant suffering, also align us with his society's demand for reasonableness and practical efficiency. To the extent that we share the detached, even amused perspective of the hero's critics, we implicitly adopt the realist's standards and accept his mundane world. Denying the hero's claims, we are implicated in his destruction, and, more important, in his critics' repudiation of heroic possibility. Our attitudes, and the plays' perspectives, are not so one-sided, of course, but we are distanced from the hero's ideal by his own inadequacy. To renew our belief in tragic potential, and with it the value of metaphysical aspiration (despite our knowledge of frailty), the dramatist must restore his protagonist's stature and balance distance with commitment.

Some techniques enhance the hero's stature while keeping him remote, both from his peers and from us. Commentary can assert as well as demean the protagonist's significance. Instead of making him too easily explicable, it can reaffirm his mysterious superiority: conflicting assertions suggest that the qualities driving the hero to folly and self-destruction also define his greatness. Often while the hero is mocked for failing to embody his ideal, he is paradoxically seen as representing it. Thus our sense of Bussy D'Ambois's grandeur rests not merely on his own claims or the Nuntius's translation of duel into epic combat. Even as the onlookers' jibes stress Bussy's vulgarity in "courting" the Duchess, the cynical Monsieur voices his first tribute to Bussy's greatness of spirit: magnificent, untamable, "his great heart will not down, 'tis like the sea" (1.ii.138–146). Bussy is both ridiculous and awe-inspiring. The man who thought to use him and will successfully engineer his death is also cowed by one who transcends human categories and manipulation, a "spirit rais'd without a circle" (III.ii.300). Even in his most demeaning acts, Bussy affords lesser men a glimpse of heroic spirit.[36]

So too Antony, even in the early acts of *Antony and Cleopatra*, elicits more than laments or mockery. Though everyone else assumes Antony's present incapacity, for Cleopatra he remains the "demi-Atlas of this earth, the arm / And burgonet of men" (I.v.23–24). What others see as a vitiating and unstable "variety" she calls a "heavenly mingle," for the violence of his moods expresses her own. Qualities that adulterate the military ideal "serve to round out the heroic figure in the mind of Cleopatra."[37] Even a defeated Antony, image of the strumpet's fool, inspires his soldiers' love and loyalty. Enobarbus, that wittily cynical voice of Roman realism, prudently leaves to make his fortunes with Caesar; yet he discovers that he cannot find "honor with . . . safety" in Caesar's camp and that the discretion which prolongs life does not in itself confer value. His rededication to Antony as a "fall'n lord" and not a fool prefigures Cleopatra's—but also Eros's, Charmian's and Iris's. An apparent failure as hero and general, Antony remained the man who, as Decretas tells Caesar, "best was worthy / Best to be serv'd" (V.i.6–7); his soldiers' apocalyptic cries at discovering their wounded general balance Caesar's cool acceptance. Cleopatra's "Emperor Antony" bears little resemblance to the man we have watched for four acts, yet that man has inspired more than a lover's imagination. The dream recalls the man's inadequacies, yet is at the same time the measure of his greatness.[38]

Coriolanus all too consistently pursues his frightening absoluteness; dream and man coincide. Yet while the imagery of battlefield mechanization challenges that ideal's attractiveness, it also asserts Coriolanus's separateness and superiority—he is a thing, but shaped better than other men. He awes even those who would have him different if they could. As Coriolanus pushes Rome toward internecine war, Menenius eulogizes a nature "too noble for the world," and later a jealous Aufidius acknowledges Coriolanus's "sovereignty of nature" and the "merit" that chokes detraction. Even Coriolanus, most subject to mockery and manipulation, is repeatedly accorded the superhuman stature he claims.

A tendency to objectify the protagonist and grant him the mysterious greatness of natural phenomena marks all these plays and exalts the hero as belonging to a different order of being. He is also felt to be representative, the subject of a larger struggle which transcends his personal follies. He stands for a whole heroic way of life, and his nature and fate are seen, even by those who destroy him, as immensely significant. The heroic code itself is being tested, and despite his personal failings, the protagonist is seen, finally, as embodying its values. His fate determines the moral nature of the world he leaves behind. In confronting him, his political opponents test that code's assumptions against their own reductionist beliefs; his defeat confirms their cynical view of human nature and justifies their possession of a value-less historical world.

Bussy D'Ambois most ostentatiously debates its protagonist's significance and his fate's meaning, and Chapman provides the competing philosophies with extremely self-conscious and articulate spokesmen. Bussy enters pondering his situation in abstract terms, and Monsieur shares his protégé's urge to translate immediate events into the terms of his own metaphysical system.[39] King Henry, too, likes philosophic abstraction; he later defends Bussy as the type of "man in his native noblesse," sole survivor of a prepolitical golden age (III.ii.88–110). Monsieur finally joins Henry and the Guise in accepting Bussy as the "absolute" hero he claims to be; as one of "Fate's ministers" Monsieur no longer believes Bussy to be a self-deluded soldier of fortune or slave to passionate ambition. Monsieur's self-interested philosophizing is matched and countered by the Guise, and in act 5 they frame Bussy's end with opposite interpretations of its meaning. Monsieur's allegiance to policy assumes a world of manipulable men, endorsed by a nature either unresponsive ("stark blind") or inimical to worth (a "courtier" nature which gives "that which we call merit to a man . . . that effects his ruin"); his philosophy is best substantiated if Bussy—"young, learned, valiant, virtuous, and full mann'd"—is all virtue, ruined (v.iii. 18–20, 38). The Guise insists on a higher morality and maintains that nature's own decorum defines Bussy's worth: if he suffers a shameful fate he must lack virtue, for nature deals in proportioned ends. Carefully, the debaters elevate and distance their subject. Each theorist loses the man in the interpretation; each explains away Bussy's death by fitting it to an impersonal pattern that both justifies the society these men control and frees them from personal responsibility for Bussy's "fate."[40] Insulating themselves against the suffering individual's claim to sympathy, they also stand between us and Bussy and offer their own concentration on externals, their own judgment of worth by its worldly achievement.

Neither of Shakespeare's late tragedies argues the meaning of its protagonist's fate so self-consciously. Though both share *Bussy*'s obsessive concern with defining nobility in general and the hero's nobility in particular, Shakespeare's warriors are neither so alarmingly self-objectifying nor so frequently drawn to metaphysical speculation. Chapman's moral theorists reflect both personal taste and his theater's predilections; they also lend weight to a story lacking intrinsic moral resonance. Antony's and Coriolanus's lives, so crucial to turning points in classical history, carry their own significant implication in ways that a relatively obscure sixteenth-century French courtier's could not, and we are continually reminded that Rome's fate is entwined with the protagonists'. To some extent, Shakespeare's soldiers, too, become heroic types as well as individuals. All agree that Antony, at least in the past, embodied Rome's virtues and enjoyed divine patronage; and if "valour is the chiefest virtue," then no one doubts Coriolanus is "most dignifie[d]" in its possession.

Though Caesar pays lip service to the honor whose loss Antony laments, he quite clearly sees himself as Antony's opposite. Like Monsieur and Aufidius, he finds that policy succeeds in obtaining his goals— power and empire—in ways that honor and reputation cannot guarantee. Intangibles can be useful with fickle mobs and foolish soldier-politicians, but value inheres in physical effects. Ambition to be "sole sir o' the world" and "universal landlord" need not begrudge Antony his metaphoric status as "sun and moon," or even "lord of lords." In his eulogy for his dead rival, Caesar's skillful political rhetoric appropriates Antony's virtues and thus shares Antony's nobility in the only meaningful, because practical, sense. Caesar seeks a distanced command of all events. He declares himself the high gods' minister to "do justice" for Octavia (III.vi.88); he frequently exits to a press conference where he will explain his actions. In II.iv his counselors find he has already put in motion the propaganda machine he asks them to recommend. In fact, he is surprised and pleased to discover that nature forbears comment or tribute at Antony's death: although "the breaking of so great a thing should make / A greater crack," it does not (V.i.14–15). So too Aufidius, pondering Coriolanus's situation and his own intended advancement, adopts the mutable world and its demonstrable favors as moral standard: the only meaningful virtues "lie in th' interpretation of the time" (IV.vii.50).

As his critics dignify the protagonist, avowing both his superhuman stature and his symbolic significance, they also more clearly define themselves and the world their pragmatic realism accepts and thereby creates. Initially, despite his stirring rhetoric, the protagonist's deeds encouraged our assent to others' scepticism. Yet while the protagonist acquires mystery and complexity, the "reasonable" standards by which he has been judged become less attractive as well as less adequate. The world that mocks the hero's behavior itself becomes less acceptable as an arena in which to test human worth.

A self-confessed Machiavel, Monsieur would seem an unlikely moral yardstick for a man of virtue as well as courage. Yet he is initially an engagingly witty and forthright cynic who sounds more like comedy's knave than true villain. His practical shrewdness seems confirmed by Bussy's entrance into court: as fool or knave, Bussy certainly appears the proud mushrump who thinks clothes make the man. Monsieur is also the first to recognize Bussy's great heart, and his obvious astuteness lends special power to his final, "choric," view of his protégé's defeat. Yet while Chapman gains Bussy our sympathy, primarily through the affair with Tamyra and his at least verbal disdain of courtly corruption, he also undercuts Monsieur's stature and qualifies the court's ability to represent reasonable social judgment. Henry is content to let virtue rust in isolation, "avoid" the envy that rules his court, and flee the "dim ostents of Tragedy," whose gathering he will not oppose. His is a trivial court, given over to bawdy courtship and adultery. Although Monsieur can play upon its passions, he is very much a part of it; he recedes into the social web of the net he wove to catch a Mars. The vulgar riddling with the court maids, the confident debasement of love to bestial attraction, the ready use of a jealous dolt to effect his own revenge and eradicate the spirit he cannot control, all demean Monsieur and transform a potentially compelling spokesman for political realities into the cowardly backstairs manipulator who so fittingly defends a courtier nature.

With the exception of Aufidius, Shakespeare's late politicians are less clearly villainous than Monsieur. Neither are their goals inherently unworthy. Octavius ruthlessly pursues political hegemony, but his ambition is only more extreme and possessive than the other triumvirs'; once he has his way, the peace and prosperity he promises will indeed distinguish his reign. His "wisdom" realistically "dare[s] but what it can," and such cautious ambition, not surprisingly, masters the "time" and "fortune" Antony and Cleopatra so frequently scorn (III.xiii.79–80).[41] His cool exploitation of others' weaknesses, his apparently total emotional detachment, earn neither his soldiers' nor our affection, but his rise to power incurs none of the moral opprobrium of Claudius's or Macbeth's.

Realist politicians are more widely distributed, and more unappealing, in *Coriolanus*. Distinguished by cowardice, deviousness, and a spiteful disdain for their constituents as well as Coriolanus, the humorless tribunes are particularly repellent, but the aristocracy is equally self-interested and only marginally more sympathetic. Menenius's fable adumbrates the ideal of harmonious cooperation of all classes, but the man himself displays no real compassion for the citizens' plight, refuses to acknowledge any patrician responsibility, and in his language and smug complacency suggests he is indeed a "perfecter giber for the table than a necessary bencher in the Capitol" (II.i.80–82). Loving Coriolanus as a father, Menenius seconds Volumnia's demand that her son join policy with honor and make his words bastards to his heart's truth. In the end, Volumnia does exchange her son for the "good report" and fame to which she would have sacrificed his integrity. Yet Shakespeare gives these politicians their due, however unlovely their ethics in practice. Like Octavius on Antony, their observations about Coriolanus are true, if incomplete. Though their patriotism rests largely on class loyalties, they do want to save Rome. In both acts 3 and 5 they argue sensibly that one man's private truth cannot justify depopulating the city. Like Octavius, they identify themselves with Rome: the ease with which they sacrifice truth and loved ones can, in some sense, be said to be disinterested. Unquestionably, and historically, Rome is stronger for their pragmatic compromise with absolutes.

All gain their limited objectives, but in the process the world they win has been remade in their image. Martial courage is largely irrelevant; magnanimity wins hearts but leaves one naked to the prudently acquisitive. We discover with the hero the world he tries to dominate: Henry's envious and frivolous court; the unheroic "empire" defined by the triumvirs' military and political maneuvering; a Rome of squab-

bling, blame-shifting nobles, tribunes, and plebs, or an equally petty
Antium, whose citizens look for war's "stirring times" and tangible
spoils. There is no world elsewhere. Everywhere "our virtues / Lie in th'
interpretation of the time," and mastering the time requires adopting
whatever virtues further that goal.

The heroic ideal for which the protagonist speaks and which others
glimpse through his valor functions in complex ways. On the one hand,
in failing to fulfill his ideal's claims, the protagonist seems both to
substantiate the cynic's belief in endemic self-deception and to establish
this mundane world as the only credible one. The heroic ideal boils
down to, in Monsieur's terms, "ridiculous and vainglorious" valor, and
the protagonist's self-betrayal, more than his final destruction, proves
him no simple, great-souled hero brought down by nasty, scheming
Machiavels. On the other hand, he holds out an image of human potential that both shames and inspires. The tragic hero's inability to master
policy, to merge fully with a world he cannot change, marks his greatness as well as his folly. The political world must finally eliminate what
it cannot control, but after destroying him his critics pay tribute to a
grandeur of spirit they do not fully comprehend. Defeated, each protagonist is called "noble" and eulogized as the heroic figure he claimed
to be. The epic realm of godlike and fearless men, glimpsed through the
hero's valor, thus measures both the hero and the world that defeats
him.

Despite the closing elegiac strain, these heroes are not suddenly transformed into nostalgia's monument to a golden military past. Through
their protagonists Shakespeare and Chapman examine the idea of the
heroic as well as its fallible devotees. The comic pressure which bears so
tellingly on the hero's stature threatens to make his ideal as well as his
acts ridiculous. The traditional ideal may at times seem comically inappropriate; stripped of its glamor, it can also take on disturbing new
dimensions. In his paradoxical isolation and dependence, Coriolanus
most clearly illustrates both extremes. Largely deprived of mediating
admirers, Coriolanus is in some ways most distanced from us and from
his ideal. Repeatedly seen as less than human, his acts define an insecure
adolescent who seeks by altercation to reconfirm a second-hand identity. Turning within to find a new, more fitting self, he discovers a role
that brings him frighteningly closer to the valorous hero's traditional
absoluteness: he can be "a god to punish, not / A man of their in-

firmity" (III.i.80–81). Through ill-judged emotional entanglements and inadequate assertions of valor, Bussy and Antony fail to master such occasions as the new political world offers. They gain some sympathy as lovers and underdogs, and a steady descent from their initial claims further obscures the egotistic isolation which supports the hero's defining valor and which Coriolanus's apparent worldly success releases in grotesque apotheosis.

The hero's essential narcissism drives him toward opposite but related extremes. In varying degrees each protagonist is tempted to adopt his rival's pragmatic ethics and use craft as well as wrath to ensure his own preeminence. (*Coriolanus* merely varies the pattern by splitting the hero's politic opposite into three—Volumnia, the tribunes, and Aufidius.) Deed-achieving honor may also become divorced from its justifying social sanctions and free the hero to redefine the world so as to provide the deed's occasion. Coriolanus jokes about his loyalty to Rome when he suggests that, were the world at stake and Aufidius "upon my party, I'd revolt to make / Only my wars with him" (I.i.233–234). His reversal later illustrates not the world's slippery turns but Coriolanus's complete redefinition of his world's components when they no longer validate his superiority. Valor enforces essentially private judgments; the self performs before mirrors.[42] Despite Bussy's continued loyalty to both King Henry and Tamyra, his proud contrariness lends more than a grain of truth to Monsieur's accusation: Bussy would dare anything "to feed / The ravenous wolf of thy most Cannibal valour / (Rather than not employ it)" (III.ii.338–340). Antony need not seek occasions in which to exercise his valor, since circumstances demand that he be "himself." Yet however he disprizes to Cleopatra the world's goods and Roman honor, the extent to which brave deeds define him is evident in his flight from Cleopatra, undertaken lest he "lose" himself in trivial sport, and in his later switched allegiances. World dominion is important, since playing with half the world partly expresses his ideal of the "nobleness of life," but it is the royal occupation itself that most satisfyingly defines him. His most devastating betrayal is of an absolute, almost private standard of soldierly valor, and he doesn't truly lose his way until he "offend[s] reputation" and deserts himself.

Cannibal valor both depends on others for its confirmation and denies their inherent worth. Essentially detached from the communal life, however its acts may incidentally defend or reform it, its self-referential

meanings tend inevitably toward isolation and self-deification. Coriolanus's self-conscious denial of his own humanity, his refusal of instinct
and nature itself, is only the most extreme example. Initially "alone / To
answer all the city" in Corioles, he ends alone against the world, trying
to create new meaning for the "kind of nothing" to which he has
reduced himself. Dehumanization is here complete, but in pursuing his
solitary ideal each protagonist "loses himself" in some fashion and is
forced to discover a new self and relation to his world. Humanness is
established in acknowledged bonds and in love, as *Coriolanus* makes
clear. Through action prompted by such acknowledgments the protagonist approaches, however briefly, a new identity different in kind both
from his own initial self-image and from the symbol of antique virtue
others finally declare him. Such revaluation can be no less profound or
moving for being unexamined in any explicit way, or even for its apparent irrelevance to the play's historical action.

Antony and Cleopatra of course offers the most stirring, complete,
and self-conscious challenge to the egoism of Antony's martial spirit as
well as to Caesar's material obsession. Still, though Antony from the
beginning asserts an amatory as well as military heroism beyond his
soldiers' narrow ideal, the lovers' initial exchanges suggest rather two
uncommitted egoists playing at transcendent passion. They use each
other as mirror and measure of their own greatness and, through the
other's display, find their own sense of self gratifyingly dramatized.[43] Only
when Antony has lost both himself and his patron Hercules does he
fashion an identity with Cleopatra's love as its core. The extent to
which his sense of himself is now defined by another is clear when he
thinks Cleopatra has "sold" him to ensure her safety: he is unmanned,
without a visible shape. Not until after Antony's death does Cleopatra
finally decide he is her man of men and that her sense of self is bound
up with his fate. She is "again for Cydnus" because she can recapture
her own magic, the splendor of Enobarbus's speech, only with Antony
as the goal of her journey. Her greatness does finally require new heaven,
new earth, and she divorces herself from a world in which self-interest
will always justify the token commitment of "mouth-made vows, /
Which break themselves in swearing" (I.iii.30–31). Tardily but "entirely," she mingles her fortunes with Antony's and makes Mardian's lie
truth.[44]

Though narcissistic and absorbed with the public effect of their suicides as much as the private meaning, each has also widened the sphere of his commitment and must finally prove himself worthy of another and of an ideal that cannot be singly maintained. Their love is narrow, intense, founded on sexual abandon and incapable of duration; the final glorious dedication rests on worldly defeat and arbitrary, private assertions of value. Yet the responses of Enobarbus, Eros, Decretas, Iras, and Charmian forbid our dismissing it as simply an *égoisme à deux* vainly claiming wishes as fact. Antony's grace and bounty have expanded the idea of magnanimity to Jovian proportions, and the lovers inspire such devotion because their mutual dream, the commitment in which they could not live but into which they die, encompasses more than private martial or erotic ideals.

In *Bussy,* too, sexual passion determines the hero's worldly fate and also provides the impetus for his final revaluation. Tamyra is, of course, no Cleopatra. She lacks heroic presence and courage; she cannot inspire the dual transcendence of a love tragedy. When she insists that Bussy practice deception, she allies them both with Monsieur's world, where virtue need only appear, not be. In Tamyra's love there is little defiance or intimacy, no exaltation. She tries to protect Bussy and, when this fails, she asks his forgiveness; she cannot join him. Bound by the same social codes as her husband and like him chained to "the course I must run for mine honour sake" (v.i.21), she watches Bussy die alone. Yet despite Tamyra's retreat, her adulterous love offers more than a convenient and theatrical denouement or simply another instance of man's inability to be his own virtuous standard. Although finally a source of despair rather than inspiration, Tamyra's love, too, shatters the hero's initially self-referential world. Tamyra has bound Bussy's life to hers, and his declarations sound the note of heroic extravagance: to deny Tamyra, though she lead him to destruction, would deny his spiritual life (v.ii.68–72). She has become his motive. Faced with his murderers, Bussy undertakes to defend Tamyra's "spotless name" alone, "me against the world" (v.iii.105–106).

In the last scene's context, however, Bussy's asserted commitment seems more verbal than real. Despite the ringing declarations, Bussy appears detached, grandiloquently protesting Tamyra's innocence to suit his vanity and to afford him a needed heroic stance. Absorbed in his own effect and desperately concerned to ensure that his "fame / Live in despite of murder," Bussy self-consciously tries out roles for a dying tragic hero.[45] He rails bitterly at his "worthless fall" and at a soul too weak to confer immortality or prove life anything "but a Courtier's breath"; he props himself on his sword "like a Roman statue." The restrictive narcissism of this particular sterotype recalls the image of colossic statuary with which Bussy spurned great men in i.i, and he soon turns inward to concentrate on himself and his sword's "inherent valour." Only when the sight of suffering Tamyra, imploring personal forgiveness, pierces his self-protective egotism does Bussy's accent change. Refusing deterministic explanations, Bussy accepts responsibility for "this killing spectacle: this prodigy" and turns his attention to his life's meaning, for himself and others. He sees finally how frail was the condition of his "strength, valour, virtue," how he might have "shook the firmament" but didn't. Acknowledging his failure to live up to his own values and intentions, he characterizes himself as a "warning fire," a "falling star."

Bussy's despairing estimate is not the play's last word. The Friar's ghost closes the 1607 quarto with a tribute that redefines Bussy's significance: it emphasizes not Bussy's failure but the lasting value of his great spirit, "new sparks of old humanity" now made a "star." Bussy's own searching revaluation provides emotional support for the ghost's assertion of transcendence. Although until his final moments he had refused to recognize his participation in humanity's fallen nature, at his death Bussy at least partly demonstrates the goodness and greatness he had eulogized as twin aspects of his heroic ideal. He had insisted on man's responsibility for his physical and moral life, the right and obligation to be a law to himself in a corrupt society. Finally holding himself accountable for his personal failure, he redeems that vision for us and hints an ideal of compassionate humanity for which his world offers little example.

Through Tamyra and her love's demands on Bussy's humanity, Chapman gives some specificity to the idea of virtue so vaguely adumbrated in the opening soliloquy's homey fisherman: he suggests a new dimension to the Marlovian greatness Bussy admired and pursued. In Bussy as well as in Antony, private and illicit love finally provokes self-discovery along with political defeat. The protagonist faces the inadequacy of his heroism in more than simply practical terms; he also discovers a transforming and ennobling value in the commitments that make him so desperately human. Love creates a new, vulnerable self. It explodes the hero's splendid but self-protective isolation; it also challenges the politician's reductionist philosophy and manipulative detachment. Only hinted in Bussy, commitment's implications are felt more strongly in Antony and Cleopatra, of course, for against the exclusively material empire that Caesar wins, the lovers' great speeches poise a world of emotional richness and depth he loses. And though their apotheosis must be private and exclusive, as characters their persuasive attractiveness reaches beyond the asserted glory of erotic passion. The ease and spontaneity of their servants' final dedication testifies not merely to the protagonists' personal charisma but to the existence and power of love itself in the widest sense. These unnecessary yet unbegrudged deaths are the strongest possible symbols of love's effect on the self-protective ego. Through love and the most personal commitments Chapman and Shakespeare suggest our potential—and need—for the kinds of relationships so conspicuously absent in the plays' surviving communities.

Lacking any romantic complications of its heroic ideal and the inspiration of intense, transforming, personal devotion, Coriolanus is both more public in its focus and more self-consciously attuned to social as well as private meanings. Disavowing kinship and leaving his "remission . . . in Volscian breasts," Coriolanus's concentration on revenge makes him an almost pure expression of the ego's impulse to self-justification. If Coriolanus exemplifies most fully the disturbing isolation and inhumanity toward which heroic self-protection tends, he is also called upon most clearly to reevaluate himself and his career in larger, communal terms. As a private individual he must "know" again wife, mother, child; as a public figure he must acknowledge the social bonds of a countryman; as superhuman conqueror he must recognize that assuming divine rectitude and correctional power yet leaves him a god lacking more than merely "eternity, and a heaven to throne in" (v.iv.24–25).

Volumnia appeals to her son on all these grounds before disowning him, though Coriolanus's silence prevents our learning the motives behind his submission.[46] Volumnia's emphasis falls on private, familial violations and on the conversion of good report to infamy, and Coriolanus may respond to these most personal and immediate appeals. Yet Volumnia also suggests, surprisingly, a new dimension to that honor which would imitate the gods: the mercy that creates peace. That Volumnia here espouses a sense of honor convenient to Rome but not heretofore part of her son's education seems likely: she has before combined policy with honor and earlier had envisioned him rather treading his enemy's neck than exercising forgiveness. Volumnia's sincerity is less important than her argument or the fact that this "unnatural scene" heals her son's self-division. It has taken "no little thing to make [his] eyes to sweat compassion" (v.iii.195–196), but Coriolanus finally takes back his remission from Volscian breasts. As an argumentative lever, Volumnia has insisted on his responsibility for his decisions—"That if you fail in our request, the blame / May hang upon your hardness" (v.iii.90–91)—not upon the world's slippery turns. Acts have always been Coriolanus's preferred eloquence, and in finally accepting what they tell him he has become, Coriolanus accepts his own fallible humanity. He does so open-eyed, at least momentarily undeluded about the mortal cost of standing by his deeds in Corioles.

Through Volumnia's often abstract appeal and Virgilia's pacific and loving presence, Shakespeare has challenged the codes by which, in their different ways, Rome and Coriolanus live and has offered instead a more comprehensive ideal of humanness. In reintegrating his divided humanity Coriolanus has also discovered man's only possible emulation of the gods' graces: though still lacking "eternity, and a heaven to throne in," Coriolanus has acquired the mercy that tempers revenge and makes communal life possible. The play seems clearly to answer negatively Cominius's rhetorical question about valor as the "chiefest virtue," but that Coriolanus pledges his life to this ideal his silence leaves unclear. Whatever Coriolanus's discovery about his proper relation to his world, once in Corioles he loses the poise that suggested full acceptance of self and the new deeds which would express it. The man who dies asserting his unique valor defends a lesser honor and seems indeed a reversion to act I, not the man who said "But let it come" in a camp outside Rome.

In these plays, society is not prepared to honor what its hero has, at great cost, become. These protagonists are "heroes" in a world that neither supports heroic action nor honors the virtues it praises. They are also mysteries to themselves and to those around them. Throughout the plays their stature remains problematic; are they knaves? fools? madmen? They are fully, not to say excessively interpreted, but we are always aware of the individual commentator's need to see the hero's nature and fate as proof and justification for his own behavior. Only in death can they safely be eulogized in terms of the outmoded ideal they claimed to represent, for in this way society reaffirms its own ethical status. To the extent that we share the raisonneur's mockery, as we share his historical and political world, we are implicated in the hero's fall. And the society meting out that fate is fully exposed as one we wish to deny having joined.

If the outlines of the political, historical world and its judgments are clear and uncompromising, our relation to that world and its challenger is not. Comic perspectives and the expectations they generate have distanced us from the protagonist and diminished our involvement with a man who so obstinately and unreasonably courts his own destruction. The protagonist is no distillation of the noble and great, no embodiment of an abstracted human potential; nor is he built wholly to the heroic scale he claims, that of a man whose rages, mistakes and frustrations are so titanic that they set him apart and above us as an object of awe and veneration. Rather, his excesses often make him a figure of fun and the target of justifiable criticism from those prudent realists who cannot understand his aspiration. Lack of introspective intensity and suggestions of physiological or psychological determinism combine to support his critics' "reasonable" assessments. Just so, ironic tragicomedy's subplots demonstrate little difference between humanity and bestiality and seem to support the intriguer's conviction that we are creatures of appetite and that our human intelligence's chief duty lies in procuring those appetites' satisfaction. Such possibilities challenge belief in the kind of moral character and freedom on which tragedy stakes its claims. As Arnold Stein has said of *Antony and Cleopatra,* such tragedy "bodies forth all the evidence against itself, against tragedy, against the life of the imagination."[47]

Ironic tragicomedy looks toward tragedy in its anatomy of broken bonds; its final reestablishment of communal peace lacks the ring of conviction. We are dissatisfied because what should be a happy ending demands accepting principles that limit rather than enhance human life. These tragicomedies also reveal that men cannot love, cannot transcend their own petty egos. Their idealists are little men who will never quite survive the self-knowledge thrust upon them. The way of romantic comedy is out of reach; there is no loss and then gaining back of an expanded self through real commitment to another.

Heroic tragedy's prevailing philosophy is cynical prudence, not stoicism. "Wisdom" is still of the possible, and the protagonist earns—even deserves—his fate. Yet manipulation of rhetorical styles and expectations also maintains the hero's ambiguity: we see and *feel* in contradictory ways about him and, through him, about the action's central issues. Now nobility and value are associated with folly and excess, with giving of oneself and even, finally, with giving one's life. These plays concern themselves with the need and cost of reestablishing those necessary bonds the ego seeks to deny. Irony has become paradox. We both condemn and admire the protagonist. We can wish him no other fate, since he can transcend his limitations only in death, yet we cannot accept the society in which that fate is "inevitable."

In earlier tragedies judgments are clearer: we know the offense when it is committed; evil is more obviously evil and does not survive the hero's death. A weakened and perhaps lesser community remains, but we do sense that something has been restored to the individual and the state. In these later plays, however, the hero's death seems to lack both moral and political resonance; the world goes on, virtually undisturbed by his passing. There is no monstrous "unnaturalness" at the action's core and no demonic or quasi-demonic counsellors. (Hercules is conspicuous by his departure, and it is remarkable how *un*ethereal Chapman's spirits are: Behemouth and his cohorts have become simply extensions of the political world, and each side has spirits who cancel out the other's efforts.) The sense of suprahuman moral imperatives is gone, and with it some of the cosmic reverberations of the heroes' actions. These men are strangely peripheral to their worlds. They are excluded before they are killed, and the final death is almost always suicide, even when nominally done by others. They do not die as payment for the wrongs they have committed (as do Hamlet, Othello, Macbeth and even Lear). Instead, they die because what they have found has no place in the world of the play's end. In this sense, the late heroes are much less than their predecessors, and their political ineffectuality marks them off sharply from the protagonists of monarchic tragedy or of an earlier generation's conqueror plays.

In fact, despite the broad, historically significant, political canvas of Shakespeare's late tragedies or the urgent topicality of Chapman's earlier ones, none of these plays is really interested in whatever specifically political solution accompanies the tragic denouement. They consider Aristotle's (and Plutarch's) man as a political animal, but, disillusioned, they go beyond politics—classical or modern—to explore the most elemental bases of human interaction, union, and decay. Man is first a social and familial animal, yet that condition is as precarious as it is fundamental. Hunter observes that in Shakespeare's last tragedies the "domestic emotions, love, loyalty, mutual comfort" have become, generally, the "prey of political ambition"; but this is because politics has become the expression of man's egotistic drive for autonomy. It is not really the political world that has taken over, though it forms the significant background for more personal interests, but a kind of grotesque and extreme individualism whose natural and only sphere is the public world. Egoism cuts through even the closest bonds and renders all men alike—equally expendable, however useful. Whether justified by an archaic heroic code or up-to-date Machiavellianism, men have retreated inward, and they play out the selves they wish to be in front of a private mirror. They lack introspection because they are *only* public men, enacting themselves, to themselves, through their manipulation of others. In Hunter's terms, along with the "sense of an immanent sustaining metaphysical order" they have lost the "domestic scene whose values of trust and repose" provided, or could provide, the protagonist "with an alternative vision of life."[48] They can believe in and trust only themselves.

Egotism destroys both ends of the spectrum that connects self with its universe; both extremes lack, or refuse, introspection. Presentation is external because these men have in a sense externalized themselves, and their plays are interested both in the private result of such psychological defensiveness and, in a larger sense, in the world such disengagement creates. The politicians' detachment offers no way out, for in accommodating themselves to tangible reality they have shrunk their hearts as well as their hopes. Though the heroic protagonists are connected with as well as crushed by the political world to whose measures they cannot march, they are finally opposed—or oppose themselves—to the "real" world of politics whose time is history. The hero instead moves toward discovering a knowledge capable of shifting the play's moral center away from the realists who claim to represent all there is.

Though Coriolanus would seem the essence of rigidity, Antony of an irresolution which rots itself with motion, and Bussy of a fatally schizophrenic alternation between the two, these men all dissolve, try to remake themselves, and are finally remade through others into a self they originally neither foresaw nor desired. As the hero moves, blindly, between competing interpretations of his world and the conduct appropriate to it, he is exposed as "hero." But the plays also expose that ideal as not merely inappropriate in peacetime or naïvely foolish in a world dominated by policy, but hollow in itself and no answer to the valueless world of farce or history. Finally, the heroic ideal is found to be as perniciously isolating and limiting as its opposite. Neither can satisfy the heart's needs. In this larger sense, the dramatists use their protagonists' initial heroic stature as they use kingship in monarchic tragedy—not as a moral standard in itself, but as a dramatic shorthand for the greatness of soul necessary if that standard is to be achieved. At his death, then, the protagonist has learned his ideal's limitations as well as the hollowness of the society that offers to shield him if he will accept its standards. Great enough finally to know himself and his responsibility for his fate, he also glimpses, however briefly, a definition of human nobility in which true greatness finds release only in overflowing the bounds of the responsible, reasonable self. To the extent that he succeeds, his death demonstrates that the most important actions are free, undetermined, and even out of character.

We have been, from the outset, justifiably dissatisfied with these heroes. Even at the end, when they have won through to values we didn't always know were missing, they still remain incapable of living the virtues they defend. Yet, though they lack Lear's final state of grace, in their dying moments they have been called upon, like him, to forge new values—or to re-create in themselves those values we as a race are forever misplacing. However they may hope or despair of the universe's posthumous confirmation, these protagonists must forge man-made meanings, for such wisdom is no longer writ large in nature's book, nor, if in God's, honored by men.[49] The demand is a heavy one. The plays redefine heroism and nobility but, with the partial exception of *Antony and Cleopatra*'s transcendent assertion, much of that redefinition remains implicit or unavailable as consolation to the suffering protagonist. The hero remains at the end unsure of his value. He learns how far short he has fallen of his own hyperbole; of the values bought with suffering he is distrustful or only dimly aware. He retreats and looks back to when men were men and he was acknowledged master. We may not know quite what we want of these men as heroes, or what new self or truths their mistakes should discover. Yet whatever their worldly and even spiritual limitations, they struggle toward, glimpse, and briefly even hold before us the old truths that make us men. Their own achievement may be wavering, inarticulate, or evanescent as their last breath, but as they learn they show, and teach, us.

CHAPTER III

"The White Devil"

HILE older ideas of epic heroism reach their fullest Jacobean development in Shakespeare's late Roman plays, Chapman's tragedies tame ancient ideals to a new vision of less superhuman aspiration and diminished scope. He brings the heroic posture "up to date": no longer the prize of conquerors and kings, the straitened world of his modern courts becomes an arena for satirists and Machiavels, a testing ground for the soul that leaves the social order untransformed. Although Webster's Italian courts superficially resemble satiric tragedy's stylized corruption, he shares Chapman's interest in bold moral challenges as well as his attraction to the hard particularities of recent, even notorious, continental intrigue. His lost play *The Guise* suggests the degree to which their interests coincided, while his extant plays pursue Shakespeare's as well as Chapman's concern with the way private relationships shape public behavior. Still, Webster's dramatic worlds lack grandeur; they are nastier, more constricting than Shakespeare's or Chapman's. Despite the possible inspiration of Nathan Field's portrayal of Bussy D'Ambois (for the play may have been revived in 1610–1611 to accompany its sequel)[1] and *The White Devil*'s obvious allusions to Antony's and Cleopatra's heroic love, Webster foregoes the sympathetic attraction of heroic male protagonists in all his plays. Even in tragedy, and particularly in *The White Devil,* he employs character types and preoccupations more readily associated with satiric city comedy and tragicomedy.[2]

It was perhaps unfortunate—at least for commercial reasons, given the Red Bull's usual fare—that for his first unaided dramatic effort Webster's models should have been closer to the private theater's offerings than the public's. Yet his method as much as his matter was ill-calculated to catch the groundlings' fancy, for in dramatic technique he was as maddeningly experimental and ambiguous as Shakespeare or Chapman. Certainly Webster refused his first audience the pleasures not merely of an easily identifiable hero, but of a secure moral framework and the predictable fulfillment of generic expectations as well. Pursuing themes of erotic love, familial bonds, and political pragmatism in his own way, he too utilizes conflicting rather than unifying dramatic techniques. And, as it does in the plays of Shakespeare and Chapman, such generic detachment supports an exploratory, forensic dramatic structure whose "action" refuses to yield clear and unchallenged moral imperatives. In undermining his play's moral framework he complicates any secure, unambivalent relation to its opposed characters. Would-be heroic lovers are refused even the stature of an Antony or a Cleopatra, much less the unclouded sympathy of a martyr's sacrifice. Indeed, all the major protagonists are victims of their own distorted ideals as well as their oppressive environment, and they are estranged from themselves as well as others. Such complications threaten conventional moral and emotional alignments, and Webster follows Chapman and Shakespeare in using the machinery of the traditional revenge play to heighten this confusion. Harold Jenkins's description of reversals in the revenge plot's usual emphasis could, considered loosely, apply to Shakespeare's late tragedies as well as *Bussy D'Ambois* and both Webster's tragedies: their protagonists "do not pursue revenge; they suffer it."[3]

In this and other ways, Webster's plays differ from *The Revenger's Tragedy*, with its superficially similar witty tool-villain and fetid Italianate atmosphere. *The Revenger's Tragedy* adopts the full revenge pattern, though it alters motivation from the political to the merely personal, and Vindice's world is theatrically heightened, made abstract and representative rather than real. Despite the similar prominence of love, even its perverse permutations, Webster's courts, like Chapman's, are political centers as well as symbolic battlegrounds on which individuals struggle for private satisfactions. Moreover, *The Revenger's Tragedy*'s witty intriguer stands from the beginning at the center of his play's grotesque action. Vindice enters as an apparently good man, a railing satirist and honorable revenger, and then loses himself wholly in his Machiavellian disguise; he gains only the most fragmentary sense of his own loss. Webster retains the psychological interest this play shares with its best contemporaries, but his tool-villains are technically peripheral figures whose intrigues boast no noble motive. They enter as would-be Machiavels, quasi-political versions not of Hamlet but of Tharsalio and Freevill or the "economic revengers" who populate Middleton's great city comedies. Inverted versions of Bussy D'Ambois, they are eager and willing to provide the service Monsieur had hoped of his protégé. Far from kicking at the traces, they want to rise in court, but already know that virtue will never be in fashion. Having reached the farceur's accommodation to man "as is," they willingly define themselves in terms of the corrupt political and personal relationships they see about them. They choose to be unresponsible, cogs in the political machine whose power they hope to share; if pressed, they use their practical knowledge of the world's ways to justify the means by which they pursue its prizes.

Yet though Webster's intriguers seek a monolithic venality which will both necessitate and reward their Tharsalian progress, they enter a world much more complex than Vindice's venomous "nest of dukes." They attempt to control as well as interpret their plays' action, but they remain peripheral figures in each plot's central confrontation, swept into the final revenge action by their own meddling intervention. Attempted domination succeeds beyond expectations based on their importance to the plots' nominal protagonists (to say nothing of their minimal significance in the nondramatic sources); yet their "voice" is only one among many. Each remains embedded in a dialectical structure moving toward a tragic recognition he neither wants nor indeed believes possible.[4] In this Webster's plays resemble Chapman's and Shakespeare's tragedies, though Webster has replaced the heroic protagonist with his apparent antithesis and strengthened, as well as demoted, the woman with whom he must share a stage. Although, unlike many critics, I find Webster's primary interest to lie with the commentator-intriguer who appears in all his works, it is not because his cynical disillusionment best expresses Webster's own despairing view of the terrifying world in which "womanish and fearful mankind" lives. The witty cynic himself seems a common thread uniting three very different dramatic efforts; yet it is his interaction with a world refusing fully to conform to his reductionist beliefs, and with characters who finally pierce his cool detachment, that forms the real core of Webster's drama. Given Webster's fondness for stories of tyrannic passion and Italianate aggression as the setting for his apparently self-sufficient individuals, the satiric accommodator can be structurally as well as thematically useful.

In *The White Devil* especially, diffuse action anatomizes numerous forms of egoistic disengagement, and the tension between idealists and amoral pragmatists seems pitiably unbalanced. Here the cynical commentator's effect on aesthetic distance becomes crucial. Indeed, although

The White Devil was less commercially successful, less optimistic, and perhaps less fully controlled than its successor, it affords not only some of Webster's most brilliant poetry but also some of his most daring theatrical experimentation. This is nowhere more apparent than in his reduplication of commentator-intriguers. The crowded first scenes offer no recognizable single protagonist, much less a hero of martial stature or idealistic ambition. Apparently lacking a hero—even one later seduced into adopting the politician's philosophy as well as his tactics—the play yet brings some close to heroism. Webster's unpromising protagonists begin at what constitutes the usual tragic hero's low point, his capitulation to the world he had opposed. In The White Devil all the major voices initially sound the same, yet those who will finally question the worldly knowledge on which they have acted must somehow be differentiated. Webster's first act is, despite its open nods to Chapman and Shakespeare, his own brilliantly original solution.[5] If Webster did have precedents for his careful use of reduplicated intriguers, they lie in the ironic tragicomedies whose tone so resembles Webster's own.

The opening of The White Devil provides a wittily acerbic prologue to the play's subsequent themes and patterns of opposition. In content, tone, and degree of abstraction, Lodovico's tirade is close to Bussy's first sketch of "the state of things" at court, where Fortune, not Reason, rules and "Reward goes backward, Honour on his head." Yet Lodovico inverts Bussy's moral stance: he laments not the absence of reason or justice but the fact that fickle Fortune, true to her nature as "a right whore," has spurned him. The tone is Bussy's, but the assumptions are Tharsalio's: if Democritus's gods do govern, then men's actions can be traced to their own instinctive pursuit of pleasure and avoidance of pain. Men are not evaluated as good or evil but as friends or enemies to the individual egoist's desires. Great men may be feared or fawned on; as intermediary agents for Fortune's arbitrary distribution of courtly reward and punishment, they certainly deserve no special respect.

However falsely righteous Lodovico's anger, it is extreme. With the logic of resentment he "proves" the iniquitous distribution of punishment and the corruption of justice: in one confused medley he cites the Duke of Bracciano's freedom to "seek to prostitute / The honour of Vittoria Corombona" and the (implied) refusal of Vittoria to purchase Lodovico's pardon with a kiss. Lodovico's rhetoric equates Bracciano's intentions with his own sins, thus emphasizing that only the powerless suffer. An emotional disproportion echoes the logical one and completes Lodovico's characterization: his brutal answer to the courtiers' stoic maxims reveals the violent core of his solipsistic world. No crimes but his have been mentioned, yet, the "logic" implies, since Vittoria did not or would not buy his pardon from Bracciano, Lodovico will "make Italian cut-works in their guts / If ever I return" (1.i.52–53).

Lodovico's interlocutors provide a neat antithesis to his righteous anger. They remind him of how richly he deserves his banishment, and their pointed moralizing further evokes a principle of order and justice by which men reap what they have sown. Yet the moral opposition is apparent, not real. An obvious deference to power ("You term those enemies / Are men of princely rank") and the grotesque yet enviously detailed catalogue of Lodovico's luxurious excesses hint similar beliefs behind the moralistic language. The carefree, knowing tone in which they mock his "tragic" stance and "doubt not" they "shall find time . . . to repeal / Your banishment" cuts across the sententious content of their stoic consolations (1.i.59–60). Like Lodovico's former followers, Gasparo and Antonelli "laugh at [Lodovico's] misery" (1.i.24); seeing through their "painted comforts," Lodovico calls attention to the mechanical triteness of their smug duet in the "well . . . with two buckets" image (1.i.28).

Antonelli and Gasparo ostensibly uphold traditional morality and so undermine Lodovico's sense of righteous indignation. Hypocritically, he turns on the system he had exploited. Yet the courtiers' laughter also echoes the self-seeking world's. The cannibalistic imagery with which they describe Lodovico's former companions, swinging helplessly between surfeit and regurgitation, suggests the same physiological regulatory mechanism which in ironic tragicomedy and heroic tragedy contradicted the declared belief in human freedom and self-control. Pat, stoic maxims do not long hide the fact that their carefree cynicism and acceptance are simply the light-hearted side of Lodovico's own ethics. Finally, they appear the suave dissemblers Lodovico takes them for, polished versions of Lodovico himself.[6] We are not wholly surprised when they reappear in the Moor's gleefully vengeful entourage and prove active participants in Lodovico's worldly sphere, where murders are of no more consequence than "flea-bitings" (1.i.32).

Gasparo and Antonelli confuse our sense of moral positions in this first scene and so enforce a satiric distance from both sides of the controversy: all the spokesmen here seem guilty, either of hatred and logical inconsistency, or of hypocrisy. The courtiers also introduce us to a typical feature of both the play's world and the abundant moralistic commentary offered on its own action. Such commentary is sudden, an unexpected intrusion into a scene of apparently assumed and accepted amorality. That stoic maxims cannot control violent passion is clear: Lodovico's murderous hatred issues in promises to kill those he blames for thwarting his will. He does not merely scorn to accept fate's blows; he is so obsessed with private revenge that he takes only minimal care to defend it as "just" punishment. The pull of context and tone against conventional, often formulaic moral wisdom also suggests that verbalization alone may be considered sufficient. Appropriate words establish the speaker's stature and allow judgment, though in fact such moral tags may cloak the same ambitious maneuvering (or willingness to enjoy the spoils) we see elsewhere more openly acknowledged.

Stripping the smug composure and condescension represented by Gasparo and Antonelli, the first scene brilliantly introduces a world where egoistic detachment allows a calm acceptance of any misfortunes but one's own and where men, like animals, helplessly yet ruthlessly pursue appetite's satisfaction. The courtiers' witty, determinedly calm and casual attitude seems to contain any threat, yet Lodovico's initial rage bares untamed, explosive depths. It is the world of farce run mad, where Plautus's *homo homini lupus* becomes Lodovico's gnomic observation on great men's use of their sheepish dependents and where passionate violence promises, even as it devalues, the murders to come. Lodovico and his moral "critics" collapse, finally, into one voice. Indeed, Lodovico so far regains his own courtly composure as to match them, maxim for maxim; he closes the scene by answering their stoic aphorisms' ideal "full man" with the actual great men they all understand, whose successful exploitation represents every individual's secret goal. More important, Lodovico's final witty *sentence* perfectly catches Flamineo's tone. As Lodovico's courtly double, Flamineo will extend into a scene of self-proclaimed heroic love both Lodovico's cynicism and the amoral, witty detachment with which this world's courtiers treat others' woes.

Bracciano's entrance changes the play's tone: threats and bitter maxims give way abruptly to the wish, "Your best of rest." The new scene—quiet, domestic, amatory—seems to promise a different, more elegant and sophisticated world. Although the whole Bracciano-Vittoria affair plays allusively against *Antony and Cleopatra*'s titanic passion, Bracciano's "quite lost Flamineo" initially stresses a chivalric, even Petrarchan love completely at odds with Lodovico's aspersion of "close pandarism" and "prostitution." Flamineo shares neither Philo's disgust nor his sense of shame, but his view of the affair immediately challenges Bracciano's courtly hyperbole; he reintroduces, now playfully, the voice of cynical detachment. Bracciano can hardly believe his good fortune in obtaining private audience with the unattainable mistress of his heart; Flamineo refuses to believe it could be otherwise, given the fact that the lover is noble, maids bribable, and the nature of women wanton. He assumes that for Vittoria's benefit Bracciano plays a role which is unnecessary when master and servant are alone together ("we may now talk freely").[7] As Lodovico had opposed Machiavellian "realism" to the courtiers' conventional and proverbial maxims, Flamineo now answers Bracciano's conventional romantic idealization with coarse devaluation.[8] Determined to explode romance's illusions, Flamineo uses his own experience to prove that love is lust, women politic, their coyness bait to make the taker mad. Flamineo knows that desire is merely physiological; his image of suitors, like thirsty drinkers pushing and shoving for a purely physical satisfaction, suggests that continence comes only with satiety. With such knowledge Flamineo rejects the sonnet-mistress of Bracciano's idealization and denigrates Vittoria to both husband and lover.

Flamineo maintains toward Bracciano's "heroic" love the light, cynical, and bantering tone which marked the courtiers' attitude toward Lodovico's "heroic" anger. In this play's opening, as in the tragedies already discussed, grand assertions are not allowed to go unchallenged. Nor is Flamineo's mocking disbelief in transcendent passion an aberrant transplant from the city comedy world he seems to inhabit, where to believe in love is indeed to be "unwisely amorous" (1.ii.39). Flamineo claims the status of interpreter and offers his infatuated master the "wisdom" of Tharsalio or Freevill; Webster amplifies our confusion by providing generic cues that support Flamineo's casual attitude. Surprisingly, Camillo fits the comic stereotype his brother-in-law satirically "presents" to Bracciano, and to us, as "an ass in 's foot-cloth" (1.ii.51). Camillo's worldly self-confidence, his pedantry and heavy wit, his smug refusal to be put off with astrological references or "perspective art" analogies, and his contribution to the *doubles entendres* highlighted by Flamineo's asides, all delineate the perfect comic butt, the man who, like Master Hairbrain in Middleton's *A Mad World, My Masters,* can be manipulated into helping to cuckold himself.[9]

The conventionally comic situation, the *doubles entendres* and the cheapness of the trick whereby Camillo begs to be imprisoned, encourage responses that contradict Bracciano's initial tone. In this new context, the situation becomes tawdry. Since the gulling of Camillo precedes Bracciano's meeting with Vittoria, our laughter at its stereotypes makes us more receptive to Flamineo's reductive commentary on the lovers. Having accepted him as trickster-commentator in one "plot," we are inclined to grant him both functions in the other. The trick is, essentially, a practical joke: using Camillo's own good opinion of his wit and sexual attractiveness to gull him, Flamineo and Vittoria even arrange their joke in the foolish butt's presence. As a comic frame it both distances Camillo's plight and undercuts the idealizing lover's return. Bracciano's Petrarchan commonplaces value the lady as a means to his soul's salvation ("for if you forego me / I am lost eternally"), but in such a city-comedy context this rhetorical posture is ludicrously inappropriate.

The comic prologue and Flamineo's adoption of a commentator's role both distance us from the lovers' interview; yet they do not ensure our full acceptance of Flamineo's proffered interpretation. In engineering both situations and attempting to control them for his own advantage, Flamineo establishes himself as an interested participant, a playwright-narrator within a larger play (of which Cornelia's appearance now reminds us). He claims the intimacy and stature of a satiric presenter, yet is himself distanced; his observations are made to Zanche, not directly to us. We are as interested in him as in the action he watches; his comments become not only interpretation, but self-revelation. He purports to strip pretense and reveal a calculating, self-interested "truth" beneath the lovers' high-minded rhetoric, but though he qualifies our acceptance of their words' face value, the only truth Flamineo can surely reveal is his own. His consistently reductionist interpretation projects the voyeur's own sterile experience: the voice remains "cold, itchy, filthily knowing."[10] Congratulating himself on his talents as intriguer and on authoring this cure for his economic straits, he admires what he assumes to be the masterful duplicity of the participants. He savors

Bracciano's *doubles entendres* and applauds as devilishly artful Vittoria's suggestion that Bracciano "make away his duchess and her husband" (1.ii.258).¹¹ Flamineo tries repeatedly to reduce the lovers to his own level and force Bracciano to recognize their kinship as worldly, selfish men; he insists that Bracciano see Vittoria as only a cunning female provided by the good servant for his master's delectation.

The lovers' polished rhetoric may mask a certain wary maneuvering, even an individual pursuit of selfish ends, but it does not unequivocally support Flamineo's debasement to smutty lust. In the courtly exchange Vittoria tests Bracciano's devotion; he gives her jewels, and in response to her ambiguous dream, promises to set her safely "above law and above scandal." Sounding rather like Shakespeare's Antony at that play's beginning, Bracciano expresses nothing so much as total infatuation. He does not lightly take a mistress; for him she will be "dukedom, health, wife, children, friends and all" (1.ii.268). Bracciano's elegant language betrays no certain hypocrisy. Though Flamineo denies the possibility of such passion, subsequent events confirm Bracciano's real and lasting commitment. Vittoria, too, eludes Flamineo's categories. However ambiguous her presentation, Vittoria remains quite independent of her brother. Flamineo's plots and comments all point toward a goal of expensive adultery, an arrangement from which he would profit as both pander and brother. Whatever her feelings for Bracciano, Vittoria plays for more and refuses to follow Flamineo's bawdy linguistic lead. Although Bracciano and Vittoria establish the alliance he plots for, they do not quite enact Flamineo's script.

Instead of continuing to play off reductionist and romantic attitudes, or allowing Flamineo the intermediary's power to shape (if not control) our response, Webster further distances the whole interview by introducing a third perspective, Cornelia's. The seduction scene becomes a series of receding groups, and this arrangement emphasizes our own position as critical spectators. We watch Cornelia watching Zanche and Flamineo watching Vittoria and Bracciano. Each group has its own viewpoint and distinctive rhetoric, and the dialogue continually changes our perspective.¹² Cornelia, too, claims to strip pretense from "truth," and she turns back upon Flamineo the moralistic language of his sometime satiric pose. Though Flamineo blesses the accord that promises him preferment ("most happy union"), in an aside Cornelia laments that her son is the agent of their house's ruin (1.ii.216–220).

She interrupts both lovers and observers just when Flamineo's goal seems won, and her reinterpretation of their behavior stands as a challenge to all three. Cornelia redefines Flamineo's "success" according to those intangible values of traditional morality that his reductionist philosophy denies. She also questions the religious implications of Bracciano's Petrarchan courtship: no longer the suppliant to whom Vittoria grants mercy and health, he is a mildew corrupting himself as well as others. His gifts bring Vittoria dishonor; further, he violates a greater responsibility than that to his own wife, for the "lives of princes should like dials move, / Whose regular example is so strong, / They make the times by them go right or wrong" (1.ii.287–289).

Such an ideal, now blasted, provides the play's moral ambiance, and characters react in various ways to traditional morality's overthrow. In using great men's crimes to justify his own, Lodovico prefigured Flamineo, while the courtiers adopted a smooth, conventionally acceptable rhetorical surface to hide their cynical acquiescence in the real "state of things." Cornelia holds the ideal, not fact, as moral yardstick. Cursing conjugal dishonor, she tries to shock her daughter back to the paths of righteousness. Cornelia's words touch Vittoria, who flees in shame or fear ("O me accurst"); but the reclamation is isolated and apparently brief. They do not sway Bracciano, for powerful princes are accustomed to define reality by their own wishes. He dismisses Cornelia as "mad" and then, ignoring her attack on his perversion of public as well as private duty, simply inverts her religious terminology: he accuses her of being "uncharitable." Such emphatic and willful linguistic distortion is characteristic of the politician's expedient way with language: like Octavius and Volumnia, Bracciano seeks to impose on the value-charged concepts of traditional culture his own self-interested meanings. Far from having its intended effect on Bracciano, Cornelia's speech precipitates his decision—"Send Doctor Julio to me presently"—and evokes the kind of blame-shifting so admired by great men's apes. Refusing to defend his actions, Bracciano sweeps out on the declaration that Cornelia will be at fault for "all ensuing harm" (1.ii.307). Flamineo is left to argue morality with his mother and imitate his master if he can.

This mother-son encounter is brief but electrifying; it is the confrontation toward which the whole scene has been building. Gone are the various screens between us and the action's focal point, the comic di-

gressions and byplay. We are returned to the raw emotions and philosophical antitheses of 1.i, but this time the confrontation is real. Old
world meets new, and the spokesmen are unshakably committed, articulate, and diametrically opposed. The coda to the play's first movement, the debate allows Webster to establish Flamineo's centrality while
clarifying fundamental issues. As active manipulator, Flamineo sought
to control events physically as well as intellectually; yet he was also a
peripheral figure, hovering on the true action's sidelines. He now steps
forward, in his own voice revealing the rage as well as the bitter wit
which completes this scene's echo of 1.i. (Indeed, Flamineo's account of
his spendthrift father underlines the spiritual kinship with Lodovico.)
Defending himself, Flamineo openly enunciates the attitudes generating
this world's ceaseless struggle for personal advantage. He stands for all
the reduplicated intriguers, and, in himself, he displays some of their
principled egotism's natural consequences.

Despite a widespread belief that Flamineo effectively "answers" his
mother's traditional objections, his counter-accusations reveal more than
they convince.[13] He willfully misconstrues the "honour" Cornelia tries to
save: taking it in the worldly sense of the respect and privileges due to
rank, he accuses Cornelia of violating the "honour" due Bracciano as
duke. In *Bussy D'Ambois* Monsieur shocks Bussy, and us, by turning
back against him the satirist's rhetorical question: " 'Tis a great man's
part. / Shall I learn this there?" We discover that Monsieur, at least, has
no doubt that he and Bussy share the same corrupt goals and discourse.
Similarly, Flamineo pounces on Cornelia's rhetorical and, she thinks,
unanswerable question: "What? because we are poor, / Shall we be
vicious?" (1.ii.314–315). But as Monsieur cannot negate Bussy's criticism, only reinterpret the court's prizes with an ethic extolling the fruits
of Fortune's banquet, so Flamineo cannot "answer" Cornelia's question
except by redefining her terms. In effect, he too shifts the blame for his
behavior—to his parents and to the same corrupt system of "courtly
reward and punishment" that justified Lodovico's villainy. Flamineo
opposes Cornelia's traditional values with the conviction that the only
vice *is* poverty. One must do whatever society demands in order to
rectify that condition.

Flamineo's is a "reasonable" as well as a rationalizing argument. We
have heard it before, in the persuasive voice of the empiricist who
sensibly suits his behavior to the world as it appears to be, not as it is

defined by tradition or wishful fancy. Given Flamineo's aspirations, it is of course also self-interested. Like Lodovico, he defines a world in which unrestrained action may hope to satisfy ambition.[14] That he is only a would-be Lodovico, and more uneasy about his "court" ethics than he will admit, is fairly clear. His violent attack on Cornelia reflects a passionate need to overwhelm doubt with excess justification. He insists there is no honest service, yet admits that advancement rests on deeds whose nature requires the use of "lusty wine / 'Gainst shame and blushing" (i.ii.331–332). He had denigrated Vittoria, Camillo, and the lovers' passion in order to deny their value or individuality as human beings, let alone relations with special claim to his care; the same self-justifying compulsion drives him to grasp any argument that will convince Cornelia (and himself) that his chosen path is both right and necessary. When he cannot sway Cornelia, he denies her by wishing to have been born a courtesan's bastard. Like Tamyra's desperate self-exoneration, in which she amasses "reasons" for her personal inability to resist adulterous passion, Flamineo's compulsive justifications invoke necessity—in this case economic necessity. Such reasoning absolves his guilt for having succumbed to the court's temptations; it explains his failure to return a true satirist instead of "more lecherous by far, / But not a suit the richer" (i.ii.326–327).

Hints of a few lingering doubts aside, Flamineo has successfully outgrown his mother's milk. With gusto he has adopted a philosophy that encourages looking after oneself, values a truly protean adaptability, and erases any distinction between honorable and dishonorable action. Elevating the individual's solipsistic desires, it erodes traditional ties of family loyalty: Flamineo does not even offer his mother Tharsalio's rationale of familial as well as private ambition. He acknowledges no ties: he denies his mother and redefines his sister—here to Cornelia and later to Marcello—as merely "a path so open and so free / To my preferment" (i.ii.328–329; iii.ii.36–37). Flamineo styles himself a free individual, master of the "winding and indirect" policy he soon eulogizes and a man no one can shackle. At the same time he claims that the natural order bears responsibility for his way of life. Just as in soliloquy he soon asserts, "We are engag'd to mischief and *must* on" (i.ii.347, my italics), Vittoria was urged to accept Bracciano with promises of luxury and the assurance that "'tis fix'd, with nails of diamonds to inevitable necessity" (i.ii.159–160). Flamineo's parting thrust mocks

Cornelia's righteous security and the whole world of transcendent values he rejects. Wittily shifting his argument's grounds from questions of chastity and honor to the rational "ethics" of animal husbandry, Flamineo suggests that the Cardinal himself might approve of adultery as good breeding policy.

Flamineo has not won the moral argument; he and Cornelia achieve an ethical stalemate. Flamineo and Cornelia live in different worlds and inhabit different plays. Cornelia's is an old-fashioned didactic tragedy. She sees clear examples of virtue and vice and expects immorality to receive due punishment. Webster obligingly provides some evidence to support her generic expectations. There are virtuous good ones who resist the time's corruption, and the play even offers some traditional schematic oppositions: good brother balances bad, loving and self-sacrificing wives exist along with unfaithful and ambitious ones. Some villains return to the fold, like Monticelso after his elevation, and some children retain their innocence. Cornelia and Marcello may be qualified by their apparent willingness to profit from the corruption they condemn, but they remain staunch critics of the pervasive opportunism. Innocents may die and their own persuasions prove ineffectual, but they maintain their interpretation to the end. The murdered Marcello directs our attention not to the triumph of evil but to a larger, awesome, yet biblically appropriate justice: "There are some sins which heaven doth duly punish / In a whole family. This it is to rise / By all dishonest means" (v.ii.20–22). In the final bloodbath the stage seems purged of villains, and, in the traditional reassuring coda, the lonely young remnant of slaughtered virtue asserts the old moral order's victory.

Such interpretations remain in character; they do not adequately sum up the play's experience. These characters do not dominate, either as spokesmen for traditional virtues and responsibilities or as guides to our dramatic expectations. Their appearances are brief as well as ineffectual; in dialogue, their proportion of the conversation seldom exceeds Cornelia's in her interview with Flamineo. More importantly, they remain flat, uninteresting figures whose trite expressions and often smug certainty calls attention to their personal limitations.[15] What power they possess derives from their symbolic status, and from what is done by others to those symbols. As examples of the life lived according to traditional moral and perceptual categories they do not live at all, not in the explosive, intense, ever-changing environment the play provides them. They simply exist to be sacrificed by a world with which their inherited and unquestioned categories cannot deal.

Flamineo offers a different interpretation—one apparently much more attuned to the reality we have seen, not just in the seduction scene he engineered but in the ambitious and self-seeking courtly world beyond his active control. He seems, indeed, what J. R. Mulryne calls "the least deceived character in a world of false appearance."[16] In a world atomized into individual desiring egos, prizes go to the clever, not the good. Even though he lacks a prince's material power, the man "who knows policy and her true aspect" may hope to advance himself by molding circumstances and controlling those who blindly follow appetite's dictates (1.ii.353). Webster has shaped his first act not only to substantiate Flamineo's pragmatic assessment but also to encourage our adoption of his attitude over Cornelia's. If Flamineo exemplifies the witty, detached stance he extolls to his mother and admires in great men, that stance seems adequate to the first act's largely comic maneuvering. Although perhaps less immediately attractive than Freevill or Tharsalio, Flamineo's hard, nasty edge suits a world where aggression and desire lie closer to the surface than either city comedy or tragicomedy will openly admit. Despite Cornelia's objections and Lodovico's threats, it seems a world where life might safely be treated as a game: murder has only been mentioned, silly husbands cuckold themselves, and prostituted sisters willingly seek dishonor's advancement.

Action soon becomes more serious, but *The White Devil* does not immediately darken or adopt the high tragic tone. Certainly, the play's middle acts lack the firm sense of structure that so effectively controls the crowded incidents and varied groupings of act 1 and, to a large extent, act 5. Yet although new characters appear, side issues multiply, and the central action advances in the jerky, episodic leaps and bounds of disconnected "big scenes," some patterns seem clear. The confusing juxtapositions of melodrama and farce remain important structurally, at least on the local level of Webster's scenic development. Further, despite a strong and at least partially sympathetic introduction to the lovers and titular protagonists, as well as an apparent focus on Flamineo as vocal manipulator, Webster seems determined to block emotional involvement either with the romantic couple or with the play's witty interpreter.

In part, Webster keeps us distant from the lovers' passion by withholding scenes of intimate affection or self-revelation. Unlike Bussy and Tamyra, Bracciano and Vittoria are never alone together; nor when on stage do they transcend their accompanying entourage, as do Antony and Cleopatra. Indeed, Bracciano and Vittoria do not reappear as lovers until IV.ii, in the House of Convertites, and though that scene of jealous squabbling ends in romantic rededication, Flamineo's maneuverings make it a repetition of I.ii's distanced, ambiguous accord. Bracciano's, and perhaps Vittoria's, consuming passion is one of the play's givens, despite the presence throughout of Flamineo's mocking disbelief, but the nature of that passion is not allowed to become the play's main concern.

Interposed audiences and dislocations of perspective distance us from the lovers in I.ii and IV.ii; they also force our detachment from nearly all scenes of melodramatic excitement. Like Shakespeare's soldier by-standers, the roving ambassadors provide unbiased commentary at key points; they also remain on stage as active spectators during Vittoria's big moment, the arraignment. The rather awkward conclave scene intervenes between the flashing tempers in the House of Convertites and act 5's carefully managed suspense. It provides visual spectacle and "time" for Francisco to organize his revengers, but even though it ends with the dramatic shifts of the Pope Paul IV–Lodovico interview, we are largely diverted from our primary interests while tension dissipates in ecclesiastical minutiae. The ghosts, too, block rather than intensify involvement. Silent, stylized reminders of the stage's separation from "our" world, they attempt, rather frustratingly, to bridge the gap between Cornelia's world of ministering spirits and potent curses and the "modern" court's more detached response to psychological projections. They are treated by Francisco, and even the more nervous Flamineo, with familiarity and disrespect. Webster may be travestying the conventions of his genre or foreshadowing his later mocking tone toward the last reality in a tragic play, "the business of dying itself"; for whatever reason, he seems quite willing to blunt the edge of some of his most theatrically promising moments.[17]

Framing exciting and emotional scenes with comic "business" and tonal contrasts further enhances our uncertain, complex relation to the staged action. The double murders of II.ii, a notable opportunity for thrills and pathos, fade into "staged" unreality, formally presented by an anonymous conjurer as silent vision. They are also preceded by

Flamineo's gleeful eulogy of Doctor Julio's wit and cunning and by Camillo's "merry parting" from his uncle and Francisco. Eschewing the doctor's moral significance, Flamineo with fantastical inventiveness elaborates the stolid figure we see before us into the quintessence of a politic duplicity that "will fetch up lungs, lights, heart, and liver by scruples"; he then falls in love with his own comically grotesque caricature and offers to "embrace thee toad, and love thee O thou abhominable loathsome gargarism" (ii.i.309–311). The victims' individual sufferings then pale in dumbshow murder. Instead of the expected pathos, Webster builds on Flamineo's witty prologue: we witness Bracciano's cool performance as Flamineo's admired Machiavel.

The situation is less complex than i.ii, with its series of competing responses to what is already ambiguous action, but the murders are not deemphasized to encourage sympathy for the lovers.[18] Here we observe a most unambiguous performance, ordered, watched, and commented upon by Bracciano; inevitably, we compare our spectator's response with his. In this way the victims can be relatively unimportant, yet our revulsion at the show's "producer" is intensified by his callous reaction: "Excellent, then she's dead" (ii.ii.24). Watching Camillo's death, Bracciano acts out Flamineo's infatuation with politic contrivances: he wants to "taste" more fully each cunning circumstance of his servant's "quaint" device. The scene closes, too, on an unexpectedly humorous note: the conjurer shifts both Bracciano's and our attention from contemplated illusion to the stage audience's immediate need to "make out by some back postern" (ii.ii.52). The escape underlines the essentially comic predicament of Flamineo and his model, Bracciano. This reversal is the first hint that they will be *trompeurs trompés*. Despite Flamineo's boasts that his "politic strain" will make murder appear accidental, no one believes Camillo slipped on the rushes;[19] Bracciano himself is almost caught in the act of savoring his protégé's artistry.

The arraignment of Vittoria which follows is justly famous as a showcase for her "brave spirit" and, despite the ambassadors' comments and Bracciano's blustering intrusions, Vittoria and Monticelso by and large manage to dominate their audiences and appeal directly to our judgment or sympathy. Yet here, too, contrasting modes frame the arraignment's high drama. Before the trial begins Webster prepares our response, first in Monticelso's admission that its real purpose lies in making Vittoria "infamous / To all our neighbouring kingdoms" (iii.i.7–8), then in the comic duel of wits between Flamineo and a lawyer. The lawyer proves himself brother to Lear's lustful beadle, and Flamineo's baiting exposes a lubricious interest in Vittoria's behavior shared by his equally humorous latinate brother and purposefully titillated by Monticelso's detailed yet allusive "character of a whore." Flamineo's satiric "presentation" of the ambassadors further establishes a comic perspective that qualifies the trial's gravity or impartiality. His "feigned garb of mirth" may not gull suspicion, but his bawdy jibes hold all questions at wit's distance; they even contain Marcello's repetition of his mother's dour laments and moralistic advice.

The trial itself maintains the play's characteristic balancing of biased and partial viewpoints, though in this case self-proclaimed innocence and righteousness prove on both sides to be merely acted. Since not justice but the publication of a decision already reached by Monticelso and Francisco is the trial's goal, it becomes a rhetorical battlefield with each side assuming whatever role will most effectively sway the stage audience to which they both self-consciously play.[20] With a new aggressive vitality, Vittoria picks up her brother's tone and tactics in ridiculing the lawyer's pompous obscurity, then counters Monticelso's old-fashioned "character" with the same witty deflation.[21] By exposing a vindictive, petty individual hiding beneath the official cloak of moral purity, she attempts to turn him, too, into the comic butt of our laughter.

Like the rest of the play's debates, the arraignment "proves" nothing. It reveals no new damning facts about Vittoria beyond her ability to dissimulate with the best. The objects of this rhetorical display, the ambassadors, split their comments and, significantly, their allegiance: they reappear both at the Cardinal's elevation to the papacy and at Bracciano's wedding to Vittoria. In demonstrating the corruption of justice by powerful self-interest, however, the trial brilliantly displays the public world to which Flamineo and Vittoria aspire. The Vittoria who fled her mother's curse has learned to manipulate the new world's weapons—allusion and analogy as well as outright hypocrisy; they cannot cow her with Cornelia's language because for them such terms are only rhetorical ploys. She can effectively turn back her judge's charges— "As if a man should spit against the wind, / The filth returns in 's face" (III.ii.150–151)—because there is in fact little or "no difference between accusers and accused."[22] Strictly speaking, both dissimulators ravish justice. The difference is that Monticelso has the power to force justice to do his "pleasure." The trial's comic prologue turns out to have been a not wholly irrelevant introduction to this travesty of justice. The Cardinal's verdict was a foregone conclusion; when it comes, his pompous linguistic impersonation of justice is comically undercut by Flamineo's witty aside. Finding that Zanche, not he, has been publicly named as Vittoria's bawd, Flamineo sighs to find himself "a sound man again" (III.ii.265).

Varying rhetorical styles and conventional expectations, multiplying perspectives or framing major scenes with disquieting generic contrasts, Webster shows the same interest in controlling aesthetic distance, and with it our immediate response, that he dramatizes in the theatrically self-conscious Vittoria and Monticelso.[23] He prevents our accepting any one character or viewpoint by repeatedly asking us to see characters and issues in different and often mutually contradictory contexts. We are refused melodramatic involvement with any single perspective. That the radically opposed generic contexts represented by Cornelia and Flamineo also express the play's thematic concerns simply facilitates Webster's exploration of the ways individuals maintain personal equilibrium and seek to control their lives.

But Cornelia's and Flamineo's are not the only plays in progress. Webster uses his revenge action as more than the convenient generic peg on which to hang a theatrically exciting denouement. Through it he not only presents the world beyond the Corombona family's private concerns and valuations, he also validates Flamineo's satiric assessment while undermining Flamineo's stature. The arraignment scene forms part of this expansive movement, and the trial's revelations suggest that Flamineo is not wrong in seeing great men's motives as "ambition / Or idle spleen" (III.i.48–49). In this society, even on its best behavior, the appearance of virtue merely aids in manipulating public opinion. Ideal standards mask the pursuit of individual goals; private passions hedge public enactments of objective moral judgment. Monticelso desires to avenge his family honor, but his passion is hardly unique. The central scene of public justice is punctuated by Vittoria's cry for vengeance and Bracciano's proud threats of violent retaliation. It is followed by Flamineo's defense of his family honor, since he strikes Lodovico for calling Vittoria "whore" as well as for breaking their "housekeeping" agreement, and by Francisco's own determination to revenge his sister.

Webster has, of course, taken pains to establish his revengers early.

Explosive, retaliatory drives shape *The White Devil*'s world from the start. After the barely contained violence of I.i, Lodovico's reputed lust for Isabella and Flamineo's ill-judged provocation seem almost unnecessary further motivation. The lengthy scene of Isabella's interviews with husband and protectors characterizes the powerful princes as much as it displays Isabella's exploited and discarded virtue. The disputants are all men of rank, but they reveal the same obsession with personal honor and the power to enforce their will that governs lesser hearts. Although Monticelso and Francisco occasionally echo Octavius's criticism of Antony's public derelictions (II.i. 26–42, 84–87), neglected political responsibility is only a marginal topic. They do not pursue Cornelia's concern with the dial of princes' lives. Francisco and Monticelso are clearly angered more by Bracciano's implied insult to their family honor than by any harm done to Camillo or Isabella. Sister and nephew are important in only a limited sense. After Isabella disobeys her brother by cursing Vittoria and divorcing her husband, Francisco promptly joins Bracciano in laughing at her; Monticelso is only too eager to "stake a brother's life, / That being wrong'd durst not avenge himself" (II.i.393–394). They willingly bait Bracciano because they have the inclination and power to threaten him. In turn, Bracciano's former idealization of Vittoria becomes as irrelevant as their present denigration: she is Bracciano's possession now, as whore or goddess, and he defies their ability to "supplant her." Bracciano's threats here and at Vittoria's arraignment have the violent force and arbitrariness of Lodovico's in I.i. Though he can sound like a traditional moralist, Francisco lacks Cornelia's faith in divine decorum and himself appropriates godhead's prerogatives. He *says* that "lust carries her sharp whip / At her own girdle," but immediately claims he will personally ensure Bracciano's proper punishment: "Look to 't for our anger / Is making thunderbolts" (II.i.70–72). Instead of the real moral contest that closes act 1, the contrived staging of Francisco's and Monticelso's admonition recalls the moralistic hypocrisy of Gasparo and Antonelli.

The princes reflect Flamineo's assumptions; by word and act they foster not Cornelia's ideal but Flamineo's amoral battleground. They create a world that recognizes only the freedom of the self-centered will;[24] their lives, too, mirror the price of unrestrained solipsism. In act 1 Webster focuses on the dissolution of blood-ties. Flamineo's self-promotion and Vittoria's ambitious, not to say ambiguous passion rend the

Corombona family from within, and neither Cornelia nor Marcello can stand against a falling fabric. The family unit is atomized; what should be a vital organism instead feeds off itself. The brother and uncle, Francisco and Monticelso, extend Flamineo's personal detachment into other families as II.i emphasizes the disintegrating bonds of marriage and parenthood. Although not an especially attractive figure, Isabella is as virtuous as her source-original was dissolute; her nobly intended parody of Bracciano's divorce underlines the ease with which he shatters personal and religious commitments. Further echoing Cornelia's ideal world, Monticelso pictures the exemplary father Bracciano might be, the "pattern" of "a stock of virtue that may last" (II.i.105–106). In private, Bracciano curses not only Isabella and his marriage, but "even my issue" (II.i.191). To the men she becomes a comic shrew and object of laughter, yet the audience's privileged view includes Bracciano's cowardly opportunism and Francisco's self-important concern with his status as prince and mediator rather than with his sister's "killing griefs." More important, young Giovanni movingly embodies the worth of the family structure here destroyed. His naïve precocity and pathetic hopefulness highlight the surrounding scenes' hostility; his happy innocence more compellingly dramatizes the loving ties of blood and marriage than Cornelia's sententious concern with family honor.

Webster later uses both son and mother to remind us of family values and human emotions nowhere else acknowledged. Not simply further victims of callous aggression, like Camillo and Marcello, Giovanni and Cornelia illustrate the love they symbolize, and Webster allows each a powerful moment of undistanced pathos. The "amoral context" established by the arraignment's pervasive and witty hypocrisy is shattered by Giovanni's unfeigned grief for his dead mother. The moment is melodramatic, but within its context this glimpse of genuine emotion dissolves the sense of "game" underlying the trial's battle of wits and words. It condemns the surrounding impersonations of natural feeling: the Cardinal's "natural" revulsion at Vittoria's corrupted life; Bracciano's "natural" grief for his wife's death; Francisco's cooly contemplated and short-lived concern for his sister; Flamineo's "natural" madness "for the disgrace of my sister" which in fact aims only to "keep off idle questions" (III.ii.305–306).

Cornelia's sorrow in v.ii recalls Giovanni's eloquent grief. Again, the scene's structural significance lies less in its exploitation of pure pathos (although this is truer of the dirge scene inspired by *Hamlet*), than in the force of its juxtaposition with others' unnatural responses. Only the courtier Hortensio demonstrates real pity for Cornelia. Bracciano uses this "misfortune" to revenge himself for Flamineo's insubordination in the House of Convertites; Francisco and his henchmen remain intent on their own revenge and the piquant irony of its appropriateness to a murderer himself pardoning murder. Desperately attempting to salvage the remnants of her family, Cornelia strikingly answers their cold solipsism. Provoked, Marcello had disclaimed any fraternal bond; Cornelia insists that man's arbitrary will cannot abrogate such fundamental truths. She tells Flamineo he has killed half of himself. Strict justice would claim the other half, but Cornelia upholds the bond of love perverted, in some way, by each of her children. Refusing to break the kinship bond for personal revenge, she pointedly corrects her own impulse to punish and asks that "the God of heaven forgive thee" (v.ii.53). She lies to protect Flamineo from the law, hoping that his deed will find its proper end in repentance. This is true charity and opposes the murderous Capuchins' inversion. The repentance for which Cornelia prays also mocks the "contrition" that later urges Zanche to betray and rob Vittoria. In Flamineo's casual sword-thrust, arbitrary and ruthless egoism has reached a new, frenzied stage of self-assertion. Facing a world where selfish calculation no longer offers an opportunist's rationale, where Marcello dies even though "here's nobody shall get any thing by his death" (v.ii.28), Cornelia goes mad. The fully realized pathos of her confusion and madness challenges the play's prevailing ethic. At the same time, her naïve confusion illustrates her creed's inadequacy: Flamineo appears unchanged, and his murderer's spotless hands frustrate the beliefs by which she had tried to live.

Such scenes of undistanced, unmocked emotion are important in their contexts, but also in their rarity. Like the gnomic couplets, they burst upon us, unanticipated and startling; when they end the onlookers cooly reknit the plots in progress, for the most part unchanged by intimations of tragic suffering. Cornelia's scene (v.ii) is the longest and most powerful, for it must help shape the play's climax and rekindle, however briefly, her son's suppressed compassion. Giovanni's moving exchange with Francisco in iii.ii is briefer, and the stage is immediately regained by Flamineo and the bitter jests of his politic "mad humour." In each instance the moment of pure pathos, however melodramatic in content, explodes the fundamentally amoral context which both major factions impose on all experience. Giovanni's unexpected interruption is also the play's turning point. In itself it recalls a world of real suffering ignored by quaint devisers and ingenious rhetoricians; its information transforms the play's genre and provides new goals, new intriguers.

In disgrace and hampered by a sister whose verbal brilliance earned her imprisonment, Flamineo has yet succeeded in dominating the first three acts. Though not always on stage or central to every action, his mocking cynicism frames or "is made to play about almost every scene and incident; it sets at a distance the anarchy the play embodies and yet in some ways intensifies it."[25] Whatever their concerns, other characters seem merely to confirm his viewpoint and, hence, the intellectual mastery he claims. Revelations of pervasive egoism and its corrosion of social institutions and restraints may not justify Flamineo's actions, but such self-seeking opponents create a world in which Flamineo and Vittoria deserve whatever they can wrest. The established "good" characters offer occasional and important disruptive commentary, but they remain helpless, unable to cope, or dead.

Webster uses his revenge action to reexamine Flamineo and the detached, amused attitude he represents. Now redirected, the play loses its center (an admittedly amoral one) along with the generic cues supporting Flamineo's intended comedy. Partly, of course, Giovanni's poignant grief, and the fact that murders only hinted at in act 1 have been committed, however wittily, by act 3, discourage our acceptance of Flamineo at his own valuation. If the play is not to be city comedy, that genre's attitudes may become uncomfortably inadequate. Partly, with the revenge action begun, Flamineo's advancement intrigue slips out of his control; he becomes an unwitting and therefore potentially comic actor in a larger play directed by Francisco. Yet while he is the object of revenge, Flamineo is pitted not against his moral opposites, but his equals. If the play is not to show simply the amoral operation of a suddenly murderous farce, as many believe it does, Webster must prove the bankruptcy of Flamineo's witty detachment while suggesting Flamineo's ability to find an identity and attitude beyond his own initial definitions. Webster's plot lacks the central opposition that unifies heroic tragedy. Daringly, and confusingly, he offers not his protagonist's apparent antithesis, the politician who tempts a tragic hero to betray his ideals, but multiple images of the antiheroic intriguer himself, men who illustrate in full perfection Flamineo's own avowed principles.

Flamineo's likeness to the violent Lodovico, only hinted at in i.ii's witty allusions, becomes the subject of their "strange encounter" after Vittoria's trial. Flamineo's response to Giovanni's news affords the meeting's preliminary parallels. Adopting an antic disposition, he hypocritically laments his unrewarded service, the devilish cunning of politicians, the power of gold to corrupt everyone. In his angry disregard of the trial's "proofs" and scorn of the ambassadors' "comfortable words" he recalls the opening dialogue between Lodovico and the moralizing courtiers. Both malcontents are unrepentant; both rail against the inequities of a world where "noblemen are privileged from the rack"; both suggest that bolder perversions of justice sanction their own deeds. Flamineo's feigned "humour" parodies Lodovico's earlier display, though the mock-satiric attacks on corrupt religion, politicians, and mushrump gentility are remarkably close to his usual bitter wit.

We are not allowed to take seriously either the satiric pose or Flamineo's success in duping the foolish ambassadors. The scene of feigned melancholy-madness becomes a comic duet when Lodovico decides to "wind" Flamineo with his own parody of the malcontent stereotype. Marcello's direction to "mark this strange encounter" encourages our comic detachment and emphasizes the interlocutors' conscious self-dramatization.[26] i.i's parallels are developed: the two actors appear as mirror-images of each other. Each strikes his pose to discover the other's intentions, yet neither fully controls the scene. Pretending to reverse the courtly decorum of hypocritical flattery, they achieve instead a comically inverted variation.[27] The parodic use of stoic maxims in fact undercuts both men's stature as self-styled satirists or master politicians. Misfortune, far from teaching them "to scorn that world which life of means deprives" (iii.iii.97), spurs them on to additional disguises and hectic intrigue. The turn of Fortune's wheel unbalances their calculating self-control: Lodovico's pardon makes him scornfully overconfident, and he taunts Flamineo into a foolish, ill-timed defense of Vittoria's "honor." Antonelli and Gasparo close this scene as they had i.i, again mocking Lodovico's blustering pride.

Like Flamineo, Lodovico is both a comrade and an intriguer to great men; he shares Flamineo's delight in witty intrigue. Though he kills

Flamineo, the same delusive self-confidence invites his own death. Yet if Lodovico is Flamineo's apparent double, Francisco is his ideal. While the would-be Machiavels fall to threats and violence, Francisco has no trouble sustaining his chosen "parts." His impersonation of the good prince, piously rejecting Monticelso's incitements to revenge, suggests his future mastery. Distrusting his former cohort, Francisco adopts a Cornelian pose and defends his portrait of an ideal ruler: a prince who thinks first of his "poor subjects" and, shunning deceitful "undermining," cries instead, "Free me my innocence, from treacherous acts: / I know there's thunder yonder" (IV.i.22–23). He fools Monticelso and, momentarily, us. In soliloquy he reveals his true disregard for subjects or heaven: contemplating Monticelso's black book, he finds only a piquant irony in the fact that by such officious lists "poor rogues" are kept "knaves still," blackmailed by men like himself into becoming "agents for any villainy."

The play's form changes as Francisco usurps Flamineo's role in determining plots and (as intermediary commentator) attitudes. Francisco, too, shows himself a very literary, self-conscious playwright, well aware of his genre's requirements. Unlike Flamineo, uneasily struggling to shape unlikely material to his own comedy of advancement, Francisco does not need to persuade himself or others of his control. He does master events and gives careful attention to theatrical effects. He summons up the necessary ghost from his own dramatist's imagination, self-consciously plays with the possibility of questioning his own vision, then banishes her as "a melancholic thought" irrelevant to the cool plotting of one who must "meditate upon revenge." No longer does a ghost appear unbidden to demand revenge from a surprised and baffled relative. Determined already, Francisco allows Isabella no supernatural status—wisely perhaps, for as "real" ghost the Isabella who perjured herself to preserve Bracciano and his subejcts' weal would make an unlikely proponent of revenge. Far from acknowledging in private the "thunder yonder" he espoused to Monticelso, Francisco's self-conscious use of the traditional revenger's tag only underscores his complete lack of faith in, or appeal to, either human or divine justice. His *will* demands vengeance, and he vigorously excludes the possibility that a supernatural power exists either to judge him or to dictate his revenge. Isabella's brief and silent appearance is thus for Francisco merely part of the conventional machinery: it is "like an old wives' story," as aesthetically motivated as his moral "old tale" to Camillo in II.i. Having dismissed emotional burdens—the killing grief associated with those "tombs, or death-beds, funerals, or tears" that he decides economically to skip over—he sets about writing, directing, and starring in his own revenge tragedy. Given such detachment, it is not surprising that "this weighty business" turns farcical. A genre whose conventional values, stock characters, and typical situations best suit it to Cornelia's old-fashioned expectations must now, in the sophisticated present Francisco shares with his audience, "have some idle mirth in 't, / Else it will never pass" (IV.i.119–120). Francisco maintains a distanced, mocking attitude toward the revenge, its ghosts and properties, and the victims whose passion his "idle mirth" parodies.

Francisco's plotting soliloquy reveals a man in love with his own cunning, another favorer of quaint devices over brute strength. As Flamineo's control of viewpoint and events falters, Francisco's witty and inventive theatricality eases the play's transfer of trickster-commentator functions. Francisco's apparent mastery forces a new distance on Flamineo, and the aspirant politician recedes into a world of variously successful intriguers. Webster shows Flamineo constantly but unsuccessfully trying to make his world conform to his own image of it. He gulls Camillo and tries to control the lovers' meeting, yet Cornelia intervenes; he is arrested, though not held, immediately after his politic killing of Camillo; he ridicules lawyers and the processes of public justice, but it is Vittoria who effectively checkmates the Cardinal's rhetorical dexterity, and neither Flamineo nor Vittoria can prevent her imprisonment; he tries to gull Lodovico with a playlet of his own devising, only to discover Lodovico playing the same trick on him; he prides himself on his cool, amoral detachment, yet is moved at the most inopportune times to defend his and his sister's honor. Francisco, however, already possesses both the power and the politic brain to which Flamineo aspires; he is, as Gunnar Boklund says, "a projection of Flamineo . . . a Flamineo as the latter would like to be."[28] As model of everything Flamineo and the other intriguers admire, Francisco places them all in a new, often comic light.

The first scene of Francisco's revenge play is enacted in the House of Convertites, and his "juggling" love letter elicits precisely the desired response. In parodying the Petrarchan rhetoric with which Bracciano himself wooed Vittoria, Francisco also initiates Webster's bold combination of allusive parallels to earlier scenes. Flamineo's caustic remarks on the letter echo his earlier commentary in I.ii. Bracciano now plays the jealous "husband." Given Francisco's ultimate control, the enraged Bracciano appears almost as ridiculous as Camillo, reduced because manipulable. Seeking the pleasures of moral superiority, Bracciano tries to alter the scene's structure: he assumes Monticelso's trial rhetoric and shifts all blame to Vittoria. She is a "whore," a bewitching "devil in crystal" who led her passive victim "like an heathen sacrifice, / With music, and with fatal yokes of flowers" to his "eternal ruin" (IV.ii.88–91). Vittoria will not allow the claim of injured innocence to go unchallenged, and in an echo of the trial scene, she takes the offensive. Choosing Cornelia's voice as the most appropriate "answer," Vittoria insists on the responsibility he shuns—for Isabella's death (which "God revenge / On thee most godless duke"), for staining the Corombona honor, for her present shameful abode. He becomes the active ensnarer and she the helpless victim who will now turn her thoughts to heaven. When Flamineo takes his master's part Vittoria turns on him, too: in response to his attempt to evade a pander's guilt by asking, rhetorically, "Am I the author of your sin?" she answers "Yes" (IV.ii.137–138).

As it did in the trial scene, righteousness confronts righteousness, but the extreme, unexpected, and rapidly shifting rhetorical postures suggest rather the comedy of Antony's amusingly high-toned attacks on Cleopatra's malign influence. After such confusing role-reversals, the participants retreat to a repetition of the first wooing. Francisco's ploy not only inspires the flight he "instructed"; through it Webster also allows the lovers to undermine their own heroic claims. We are returned to I.ii, but with a new perspective. We can believe the strength of Bracciano's passion, but not his conscious elevation of it. We have witnessed his dissimulation and cowardly opportunism with Isabella, his cool delight in two artful murders, his hypocrisy and blame-shifting with Vittoria. Vittoria's angry attack matches the splendor of her trial defense; innocence lends her words force, and her accusations certainly strike home truths. Yet she is not completely disingenuous here either, and she seems ready to accept a duchess's title rather than "go / Weeping to heaven on crutches" (IV.ii.122–123). More importantly, Flamineo's smutty devaluation and self-interested coaching dominate the final accord, as they did not in I.ii.

Behind the whole recapitulation of I.ii stands Francisco. Present through constant reference to the letter, his god-like perspective frames and distances all the reversals and maneuverings. Characters whose previous actions had meaning for them (or Cornelia) as free moral choices now suffer a reduced stature: though not comic stereotypes like Camillo, they do demonstrate a diminished capacity to perceive truly or to act independently. Flamineo and Vittoria may reject Bracciano's reduction of them to patient scapegoats for his sins or to "dogs" too servile to disobey his wishes, but in Francisco's diabolic plan they are all actors meekly responding on cue. Within this perspective, their reasserted self-confidence is comically demeaning. Neither Flamineo nor Bracciano penetrates the depth of Francisco's craft, and his project, "whether in love or gullery," appears good to them. Flamineo indeed deceives himself about Bracciano as well as Francisco. The same unpolitic temper that roused him to strike Lodovico for insulting Vittoria has led him to brave his master and even exchange insults. He has revealed that he "knows" Bracciano and his own precarious position "methodically": "You're a great duke; I your poor secretary. / I do now look for a Spanish fig, or an Italian sallet daily" (IV.ii.57–60). Bracciano's wrath had demonstrated the "lamented doctrine" of Flamineo's smug warning to Marcello—"Alas the poorest of their forc'd dislikes / At a limb proffers, but at heart it strikes" (III.i.53–54)—but Flamineo ignores his own "knowledge." He still maintains that "knaves do grow great by being great men's apes" and insists that he controls the present action by his "varying of shapes" (IV.ii.246–247). We see him, as well as his master, in the ironic posture of the guller gulled.

That Francisco's control it total is made clear in his awkward, self-congratulatory aside during the papal election. As we watch him shape the various stages of his plot, his presence forces us to share his detached and amused perspective. Revenge itself is not enough for Francisco, nor is the godlike presence-in-absence of the House of Convertites scene. As revenger, Francisco is a farceur, his wild justice a series of practical jokes. He wants to play with his victims directly, to elaborate endlessly what Lodovico admires as "the art, / The modest form of greatness" (IV.iii.143–144). In adopting Lodovico as his tool he insists on his part in both the danger and the glory; later, their argument reveals a shared concern with a plot so "ingenious" it will be "hereafter recorded for example" (v.i.75–76). Yet though he calls Lodovico "noble friend" and offers the respect and equality Flamineo coveted with Bracciano, Francisco in fact trusts no one but himself. Rightly suspecting both Monticelso's and Lodovico's constancy of purpose, he makes assurance double sure by sending Lodovico gold in the new pope's name.[29] The cynical trick works and reestablishes Francisco's superiority over his clever tool. Francisco's duping of Lodovico is followed by the equally successful but far more satisfyingly elaborate gulling of Flamineo and Bracciano in the victim's own palace. Indeed, the last act's structure, with its many brief scenes of gloating conspirators, continually reminds us of Francisco's ultimate control in the midst of his victims' apparent success.

Flamineo's opening self-congratulation establishes the ironic tone which generates act 5's pervasive, often grotesque humor. Finally, Flamineo has reached his goal: "In all the weary minutes of my life, / Day ne'er broke up till now"; Vittoria's marriage "confirms" his happiness (v.i.1–3). He could not be more mistaken. Though Flamineo demonstrates a strong admixture of the malcontent villain who admires the Machiavel's ruthless cunning, he is also adolescent, exuberant, and playful in a way neither Bracciano nor Francisco is. For him, the challenge of a cuckolding offers the same excitement as a politic murder. Recently and bitterly shaken out of what he considers the childish innocence of Marcello, he plays the preferment game according to rules established not by his mother but by the great men who seem life's best players. The "necessary" murder of Camillo does not change his view that the game is one of wit, that in good city-comedy fashion the clever can parlay native ingenuity and family attractions into wealth and freedom from the servitude of poverty. Every effort to gull others is directed toward one bourgeois goal—economic and social advancement. Flamineo labors under some severe misapprehensions, of course: he consistently ignores the possible consequences of even witty murder, of politicians' true ruthlessness, and of his own susceptibility to manipulation. In his eyes, he is the hero in a drama where intellectual superiority in the intriguer is the prerequisite for success, and marriage to wealth and power the goal. Flamineo's play should end here, with the successful marketing of his sister Vittoria.

Flamineo is instead already an unwitting actor in Francisco's play, the comic butt of a laughter he no longer controls. Immediately, Hortensio mentions "the Moor that's come to Court," and Flamineo, puffed with his "knowledge" and success, offers his report of the visitors' character and history. Fooled by the very malcontent pose he had self-consciously acted with Lodovico in III.iii, Flamineo admires the stoic commonplaces uttered by his nemesis. The favorite moralistic tag he so approvingly repeats—"Glories, like glow-worms, afar off shine bright / But look'd to near, have neither heat nor light" (v.i.41–42)—has ironic bearing not only on his own "confirmed" happiness but on the Moor he praises with such surprising sincerity.[30] Flamineo condescends to give Mulinassar "politic instruction"; later he sagely agrees with the Moor that Bracciano's death was "very likely" Florence's handiwork and proceeds to eulogize "the rare tricks of a Machivillian" to Francisco himself. On no other subject—not women, family, or even strictly monetary gain—does Flamineo wax so passionately eloquent. The irony of Flamineo's praising "quaint knaves" to his disguised rival underlines the fact that Flamineo is indeed in love, physically and morally, with his own destruction. We remember his grotesque affection for the subtle Doctor Julio.

Francisco supplants Flamineo in more than symbolic ways. The gusto with which he becomes Mulinassar reminds us of Flamineo's love of "mad humours" and cunning devices, and when Francisco playfully taunts his victims with gnomic wisdom we are reminded of how Flamineo had mocked Camillo with *doubles entendres* and amatory lore. Zanche's advances are comically swift and pursued through a hilariously smutty parody of her mistress's courtship-by-dream. The irony of Zanche's transferred affection lies not simply in its mimicry of her betters' easy betrayals, but in her having discovered in Mulinassar a black, and better, Flamineo. As doubles of Flamineo, both Francisco and Lodovico reveal that dark side of the Middletonian trickster-intriguer we have seen explored in ironic tragicomedy. They create a world that takes his cynical assumptions with deadly seriousness. As guller gulled, Flamineo shares a Follywit's blind confidence in his own ingenuity, but he is not so endearing a rogue. He lacks the "justification" of a Witgood, out to win back what was originally cozened from him, or the soothing moral rationales with which Freevill and Tharsalio palliate their witty but more nakedly egoistic intrigues. Yet the presence of reduplicated intriguers also enforces Flamineo's uniqueness: he differs both from the man who shares his destiny, his social double Lodovico, and from the ideal princely Machiavel who dupes them both.

The final confrontation is between brother and sister and the revengers, with Francisco's spirit lurking in the shadows and speaking through Lodovico. *The White Devil* concentrates on distinguishing among them, and not on opposing murderous egoism with transcendent romantic passion. Webster's play is simply not an awkward imitation of *Antony and Cleopatra*.[31] Despite the many linguistic and structural parallels with Shakespeare's play, Bracciano is dismissed as of less interest than his secretary or his mistress. Bracciano lacks the intellectual vitality and aspirations shared by Flamineo, Vittoria, Lodovico, and Francisco; no witty Machiavel, he depends on crude threats and the power of rank. He suffers a conventional villain's death and thus offers a lone example of the condign punishment so satisfying to Cornelia and her avatars. Bracciano pardons murder while the poison is sprinkled for his own death; the executioners' methods—the barriers, poison, strangulation with a "true-love knot"—wittily recall Bracciano's motives as well as his crimes. He dies amidst a parody of true church ritual and Christian charity, just as his divorce had parodied authoritative religious decree. A binding covenant between him and the world rules his life as it did Flamineo's and Vittoria's, but it makes Bracciano deeply afraid of death. He gestures toward the heroic love in which "infinite worlds" were "too little" for Vittoria (v.iii.17–18), but such hints of love's transforming power remain undeveloped.[32] Bracciano ends the helpless victim of a dramatized delirium, and the conventional mixture of small amounts of sense with large swatches of comic babble drains his last moments of dignity or pathos. His death is carefully framed and distanced, then forgotten. Given his behavior with Isabella and at the arraignment, then in the House of Convertites and in his own palace, it is evident that Bracciano's early ambiguity and potential complexity are, like Francisco's, progressively simplified.

For all his very real viciousness, Flamineo possesses a moral sensitivity and complexity lacking in the revengers as well as in Bracciano. Although there is no doubt that Webster gains sympathy for Flamineo and Vittoria by purposefully blackening Francisco and Lodovico, villainizing the revengers is not just a theatrical trick to lend the victims a spurious innocence. That they are not innocent Webster makes clear in the final scene. Yet they are their own victims more than Francisco's, self-deluded and finally lost in a world whose complexities make Cornelia's clear-cut moral distinctions—or Francisco's easy, amoral dismissal—impossible for them and for us. They have suffered Webster's mocking scrutiny along with the world whose prizes they sought. In the end, sexual passion offers no alternative to the world's claims; whether love or infatuation, it has revealed none of the ennobling glories that promised Antony hope in the midst of self-betrayal and loss. To restore Flamineo's and Vittoria's stature and our interest in them, Webster requires other means to convince us of a potential, however limited, for self-transcendence.

While other characters become simplified or lose themselves wholly in the conventional attitudes of their "parts," Flamineo and Vittoria remain aware of the moral imperatives that condemn them. As a differentiating technique, such reminders are abstract; they lack the sympathetic force or encouraged emotional involvement of a mutual romantic passion. They are also appropriate to the isolated, self-obsessed souls who until the very moment of death maintain such distance between themselves and any inhibiting emotions or beliefs. Webster insinuates relatedness as well as alienation by alluding to a common history of suppression. In order to forge their own strong hearts' covenant with the world, they have had to deny part of themselves, a heritage symbolized by the persistent voice of Cornelia and reflected in Flamineo's compulsive self-rationalization as well as Vittoria's intermittent attacks of guilt. Despite the rationale of cosmic as well as economic determinism, both brother and sister are haunted by a suspicion that the moral life is not just an empty social form. They fear they have condemned themselves by making choices they were in fact free to refuse.

Offered diametrically opposed interpretations—ultimately, Cornelia's and Francisco's—they are forced to choose between them. Each side claims certainty and refuses contradiction; though incompatible, each interpretation of the natural order demands total allegiance. Francisco sees only the physical world and his power to shape it to his will: will is sufficient to make his actions "justified," and the "glorious" murder's fame, not its justice, "shall crown the enterprize and quit the shame" (v.iii.270). In Cornelia, Isabella, and Marcello, clear moral significance inspires its appropriate response and banishes doubt.

Though Francisco directs the denouement's revenge, *The White Devil* is of course not his but Webster's play. And Webster dramatizes the ambiguities and contradictions that both sets of limited characters willfully ignore. Confusingly, there seems no middle. The only characters capable of perceiving the metaphysical problems of existence instead eagerly suppress their knowledge to achieve the same untroubled assurance in which others so easily act. In this drama of delusion and self-denial, Flamineo is the focal point. Progressively stripped of his imagined happiness, unable to justify his deeds by success, he must finally recognize the full inclusiveness of those pragmatic observations with which he berated Marcello and rationalized his own dishonesty. He had asked, "How shall we find reward?" (iii.i.49). The answer remains ambiguous, not only in his intended economic sense but in its older, spiritual meaning as well. Villainous service under Bracciano earns Flamineo no more than Marcello's honest soldiering; at his master's death Flamineo is appalled to find that at the "end of all my harvest, he has given me nothing" (v.iii.187).

Under pressure, Flamineo becomes increasingly cynical, demanding, and violently resentful, first with Giovanni and then with Vittoria. The sterile egoism demonstrated in Marcello's murder, the cynical repudiation of love either for Zanche or Bracciano, and his disbelief in the sincerity of Vittoria's grief or prayers all depict a nature capable of sinking to Francisco's state of cold depersonalization. Yet the confident self-control, repression of feeling, and critical detachment from his own choices and acts as well as others' also prove illusory. Flamineo insists on viewing the "superstitious howling" of his mother's grief, but instead of amusement at religion's hollow consolations he finds "a strange thing . . . compassion" rising from the conscience he thought safely dead. The callousness of Flamineo's recent jests, the shocking insensitivity with which he projects his own ambition to "ride in the saddle" onto the mourning young Giovanni, allow Webster powerful effects of contrast: Flamineo's apparently unemotional response to his mother's grief—"I would I were from hence" (v.iv.91)—carries the enormous emotional force of simple understatement.

The gulf between Flamineo's "merry" villainy and inner doubts is now made explicit; "riotously ill" living and a face wreathed in smiles have disguised the "maze of conscience," not resolved it. As Flamineo had earlier hoped, the ghost of Bracciano appears, bearing emblematic messages. The ghost may be as much a psychological projection of Flamineo's melancholy as Isabella's was of Francisco's, but Flamineo lacks Francisco's amused self-control or the power to banish his silent visitor. Flamineo actually wants this ghost to be "real" so that it can tell him the final reward—"yon starry gallery" or "the curs'd dungeon"—

for practicing a Machiavel's worldly knowledge. Information that would solve the maze of conscience is withheld. Indeed, Bracciano seems as sadistic in death as he was in life. The ghost's gestures inspire courage, but only of a despair that dares fate's worst, and Flamineo retreats from the self-knowledge that introspection might bring. He suppresses all hint of responsibility for his predicament's "horrors" and turns to Vittoria as his last hope of earthly "good." She is to be his justification.

The final scene brings the unmasking Flamineo and Vittoria so assiduously tried to avoid. Webster's primary interest in man's most fundamental bonds is clear: pitted against each other are the brother and sister whose unbridled egoism helped destroy two families and dissolve the fragile legal and religious covenants that bind individual wills to communal purposes. The family unit is indeed consuming itself. In formally sundering his relationship with Flamineo and redefining them as "the two slaught'red sons of Œdipus" (v.i.205), Marcello had returned in kind Flamineo's contempt for family affection. Now brother and sister face each other as enemies, strangers fighting for the same earthly throne. If Cornelia is right about Marcello and Flamineo, to turn against each other is to destroy part of themselves; yet Flamineo and Vittoria now willingly sacrifice each other in a bitter struggle for self-definition as well as self-preservation. Flamineo still justifies himself by others' baseness. He assumes Vittoria's devotions are hypocritical: her prayers can be easily dropped for "worldly business," and he claims "reward, for my long service" (v.vi.8). Vittoria's answer recalls her denunciation of Bracciano at the House of Convertites. Sounding like an uncharitable Cornelia, Vittoria reasserts the personal context both brother and sister attempted to deny. She deliberately twists "reward" and promises Flamineo only Cain's fate for "having slain his brother" (v.vi.14).

Each refuses the other's definition, and Vittoria's words remind us of the bond they do not feel, the self they have denied. Each seeks a controlling part, one that would win this final game of wits. In the role of good servant and moralist, Flamineo urges her devotion and his promise that neither would survive their lord Bracciano. He taunts Vittoria by parodying her own brave words to Monticelso: "I would not live at any man's entreaty / Nor die at any's bidding" (v.vi.48–49). Vittoria counters with an equally hollow attempt at religious dissuasion; when words and cries for help fail, she accepts the noble lover's role her brother suggested, but her words mock Bracciano as well as

Flamineo. The rhetoric of passionate abandon—the "flaming altar of my heart" and willingness now to "sacrifice heart and all"—only emphasizes how little she intends to die for either love or nobility. Together with Zanche they travesty the sort of exchange through which Antony and Cleopatra prompt each other to increasingly exalted declarations and, finally, actions. We know Vittoria's and Zanche's intentions from their asides, and neither intends self-sacrifice. Self-interest hedges with irony the noble rhetoric and repetitions of "love."

Vittoria's trick is contained by Flamineo's, for the whole series of burlesqued "tragic" responses to death is Flamineo's last practical joke. He plays it out to the end with witty theatricality, and we are delighted when he pops back to life. Flamineo's play has, in good comic fashion, exploded Vittoria's moral pretensions—her religious devotions, the condemnation of her "villain" brother, the noble rhetoric with which she welcomed honorable death. In naked fear and hatred Vittoria and Zanche trample on Flamineo; neither brother nor lover, he is no more to them than a "fire" that threatens their "ruin." Unwittingly, they imitate the gleeful sadism of Gasparo and Lodovico; they echo the earlier parodic last rites, and they curse Flamineo to hell with all his sins upon him. Yet though the resurrected Flamineo laughs at his dupes, he is neither physical nor moral master of the situation. He, too, acts in a larger play, and his sense of control is as illusory as Volpone's or, in *Michaelmas Term*, Quomodo's. In the immediate situation he has "try'd your love," but in that precious quality all have been found wanting. Calculated hypocrisy has merely debased and distanced both sides; neither Vittoria nor Flamineo could be farther from our sympathy. The comic butt of the other's trick, each has proved to be totally self-concerned, hardened in sensibility and sufficiently ruthless actually to delight in killing a sibling. In each other, brother and sister face themselves.

Flamineo's farcical playlet, where nothing is real and the defeated spring back, proves to be only a rehearsal. The conventional revengers' masque offers Flamineo and Vittoria a second chance; they may yet turn savage farce to tragic knowledge. Instead, they begin to reenact their roles. Flamineo hates Vittoria, would willingly kill her for "ingratitude," and blames the external necessity of that spaniel Fate for his present plight. Vittoria repeats her earlier placating response; desiring life, she will pay any price—a share of her goods to Flamineo, herself to the revengers. Like Bussy D'Ambois, Flamineo slides through a series of tragic postures as he tries to find a satisfying public stance. The ludicrously bloodthirsty revengers, eager to repeat the pleasure of torturing a fearful Bracciano, deserve the humor with which Flamineo defeats their expectations and trivializes both them and the life they take. It is classic gallows humor, the basis of Freud's definition: the ego triumphantly denies the external world. Concentrating on defying his executioners, Flamineo also avoids facing himself; he will think of "nothing" because a man's own thoughts provide "infinite vexation." The self-hatred in which they turned on each other, still grasping for the world's rewards, now turns outward and fuels defiance.

Only when death is certain, when prostitution of the self and others can gain no possible advantage, do they break their covenant with the world. Only when forced to give up the world can they find each other. Yet their final recognitions are the more powerful for this last, dying acknowledgment of the natural bond their egotism had renounced. Vittoria joins her brother; with the same wit she scorns to play the parts assigned by Francisco and Lodovico. Flamineo discovers, to his surprise, "I love thee now" (v.vi.242). His stature, and to a lesser extent Vittoria's, rests not merely on a final heroic pose, proudly defying both man and death; after all, the bloodthirsty Lodovico, Flamineo's double in active villainy, can also defy Giovanni's soldiers. Rather, they raise a united voice against the world that sundered them and then turn inward to face the maze of conscience Lodovico had felt only briefly, when admonished by the newly elected Pope Paul IV.[33] Acknowledging a justice in her death, Vittoria recalls Marcello's moralization of his own fate; as "a ship in a black storm," however, she lacks his complete certainty of moral meanings and ultimate destinations.

Flamineo and Vittoria have the capacity to suffer tragically. They have indeed often been understood as tragic heroes, though usually (like Bussy D'Ambois) of the courageously defiant stamp. By lowering their rank and claim to grandeur, by confining their small-souled ambitions to the pursuit of economic and social advantage, Webster denies them the fullest potential for tragic knowledge. Endlessly vocal, Flamineo is not a strong character; he more resembles Tharsalio and Freevill than tragedy's traditional protagonist. His wit and pragmatic intelligence have been expended in the world's service, in arranging satisfactory accommodation, and not in defining its inadequacy. In the mock suicide both Flamineo and Vittoria show natures almost subdued to the solipsistic intensity of the world they worked in. Yet after such savage distancing, our final involvement depends upon more than admirable and theatrically exciting defiance, or a few aphorisms appropriate to death's final simplification. They try, however briefly and inconclusively, to find a larger meaning in their fate. We applauded the courageous, amoral wit with which they challenged their masters and refused all judgment; by suggesting their continued duality in an increasingly stylized world, Webster encourages sympathy and interest as well as critical detachment. We sense that as intelligent and complex beings, they alone—and especially Flamineo—represent the possibility of a sane balance, our hope to discover through experience those humane values lacking in both self-absorbed Machiavels and self-cloistered moralists. Unlike Bussy or Vindice, they deliberately chose the world's wisdom, yet they can never completely forget the knowledge of another wisdom by which they stand condemned.

What moral understanding they do attain is limited by their own natures, unprepared for this single, final attempt to transcend what they have made of themselves. Confused, they struggle to fit the knowledge of bitter experience to the rigid formulations of proverbial truth. Vittoria retreats to Cornelia's phraseology, moralizing her death (blood's payment for sin) and its lesson: "O happy they that never saw the court, / Nor ever knew great man but by report" (v.vi.261–262). Vittoria's final knowledge may indeed be to discover by experience the truth of such maxims, yet the trite, simplistic formula inadequately expresses our own response to her life or her death.[34] This dissatisfaction is intentional. Vittoria's echo of Cornelia and Marcello reminds us of their inability to explain fully the events they moralized. The hinted pastoral ideal emphasizes that such an "answer"—physical flight from temptation and ambivalence—is not an option the play offers. Unable to retreat or, really, to cope, goodness's moral naïveté subjects it to the taints and compromises, as well as the triteness, we find in Marcello, Cornelia, and Isabella.

Flamineo faces more firmly the intellectual dilemma his argument from economic necessity had tried to simplify. Realizing that the path to freedom leads only to death, Flamineo's own conventional responses hint, in their imagery, an awareness of the personal cost of his "service." Not being Fortune, he has been its knave; as Bracciano's creature, he knows what it is to "belong to great men," to spend a life aping others. Though resolved to be his own man at the last, Flamineo derives from experience neither regret nor moral assurance. He can face the "maze" that has plagued his life and admit that "while we look up to heaven we confound / Knowledge with knowledge" (v.vi.259–260). Yet since no one, least of all Bracciano, will return from death either to confirm or deny the "knowledge" of faith, he can only see all life's action as wearingly futile: death alone brings rest from the "busy trade of life . . . where all seek pain by pain" (v.vi.273–274).

Flamineo's weary despair is not, or should not be, our own. Webster has placed Flamineo's and Vittoria's deaths with some care. The comic antimasque of mock suicide offers two possible "deaths": one a hero's, crowned with noble speeches; one an egotist's, buying life by trampling one's kin. In the actual event, their deaths are both less than one and more than the other. Most striking after such theatricality is the final inwardness, the intellectual compulsion to find in their own lives a universal meaning. The moral awareness distinguishing Vittoria and, especially, Flamineo, even while it divides them against themselves, also stands in stark contrast to the revengers' submission of self to role. Lodovico has been Flamineo's "fate" in more than the obvious sense, but Webster at the end reminds us of the gulf separating these apparent alter egos. The deliberately stylized Lodovico gives a conventional villain-revenger's speech that rivals Vindice's in its narrow self-absorption; he glories in the violence by which he has lived and finds his satisfying "rest" in the fact that his last "night-piece . . . was my best" (v.vi.297). In death he offers no hint of change, self-doubt, repentance, or any tragic awareness of conflicting demands; neither he nor Francisco, whose primary concern his words echo and recall, cares about justice in any sense wider than personal vengeance.

Against their moral callousness is set Giovanni's naïve confidence that the revengers' fate illustrates a natural moral order which he upholds. Behind such assertions we may hear the echo of Francisco's delighted laughter, for, as has often been pointed out, he remains untouched by the justice he scorned. We are, moreover, pointedly reminded that Francisco is yoked by blood and political authority to the righteous young prince: Lodovico defends the "massacre" by informing Giovanni that "thy uncle, / Which is a part of thee, enjoin'd us to 't" (v.vi.285–286). We may or may not suppose that Giovanni will mature in this pattern, that power corrupts, or that, as Flamineo bitterly observed, "he hath his uncle's villainous look already, / In *decimo-sexto*" (v.iv.30–31). Rather, the conclusion's force lies in the very distance separating Francisco from Giovanni and both from Vittoria and Flamineo. The cast of characters may have changed, but we are faced with the same two confident and contradictory interpretations of experience on which the play's dynamic has been constructed. In Giovanni we see again Cornelia faced with her own kin's denial of her beliefs. The murder of Vittoria and Flamineo provides plausible but incompatible meanings to each interpreter—Lodovico (and Francisco) see "glory" and Giovanni takes it for a moral *exemplum*—but neither view is satisfactory to us. Generically, their responses define two different plays, but neither is the dramatic experience Webster has given us. Flamineo and, to some extent, Vittoria prevent *The White Devil* from falling into either of the melodramatic genres it employs. We alone see their tragedy.

Such frail vessels allow Webster not merely to explore the personal effects of their narrow, exclusive devotion to themselves, but also to portray the dark, claustrophobic world such attitudes create. Ruthlessly pursuing willful desire, they deny each other and help undermine fundamental bonds of consanguinity and marriage. Their petty, temporally bound lives form one instance of the pattern suggested by references to Cain and Abel and the slaughtered sons of Œdipus: the recurrent rending of human bonds by pride and self-assertion. The play is composed of a series of betrayals of intimate relationships, and dramatic structure further illustrates man's capacity to fall, self-deluded, over and over again. The temptation and fall of i.ii is repudiated, then reenacted, in iv.ii. In v.iii it is echoed in parodic form by Francisco, Zanche, and Lodovico. The recurrent parallels do distinguish among characters, for Zanche debases Vittoria's behavior, but the variations themselves suggest a pattern, one which belongs to and helps define the dramatized experience's wider meaning. The cry for personal vengeance runs through the play, and the ego's delight in punishing and humiliating others is everywhere apparent, from the laughter of Julio's murderous assistants to Vittoria's and Zanche's imitation of Gasparo and Lodovico as they gleefully trample Flamineo. Human beings seem unable to profit from the meaning of either their own or the race's experience. The times are corrupt and certainly have contributed to Vittoria's and Flamineo's degeneration, yet the horrors we see are not bound to or distanced by a

melodramatically Machiavellian Italy. The "old tales," the frequent repetitions and parodies of earlier actions by different characters, the mythic
allusions, all suggest a pattern more permanent than Jacobean.[35]

Flamineo and Vittoria illustrate both the perennial temptation to unleashed self-interest and the personal cost of accepting the meaningless universe such amorality postulates. Their life was indeed a "black
charnel," for they hardened their own hearts, applied their intelligence
to deluding themselves as well as others, and created by their choices
the "inevitable" conditions of their death. They destroy themselves, not
in the way that all the variety of devils, by working "together" in
pursuit of selfish goals, can be said to depict evil consuming itself, but in
a more tragically significant, though equally pointless way. They oblit-
erate themselves as individuals, consciously lose their unique identity by
adopting a less fully complex and human ideal.

Flamineo had hoped, like a trickster-hero, to attain more personal
freedom than constraining social definitions would allow; by standing
outside society and its various roles, he thought to find self-expression
as well as social promotion. Flamineo, like Freevill, Tharsalio, and Lucio-
Vincentio, defined a world in which he could act and (what is just as
important) from which he could protect himself. All are private, self-
isolated men who stand outside the communal group, with no sense
that they owe others truth or good faith. Unlike them—or Lodovico—
Flamineo discovers that assuming universal competitive and aggressive
motives has limited his self-expression, shaped another identity, and left
him without the self he might have been. Flamineo comes in his last
moments to the edge of the tragedy he had avoided; he recognizes, as
the tricksters refuse to do, that erecting subjective will into moral standard and refusing to treat life as more than private game has simply left
him empty. Confused by a sense of infinite, if indefinable, loss he wants
only to pack in a losing game. Since he *is* aware, his moment of despair
is deeply moving in a way that Lodovico's equal "loss" can never be,
for Lodovico offers no hints that his life and death are not completely to
his satisfaction.

In casting their lot with the worldly Machiavels, Vittoria and Flamineo "aspire" to a rigid, obsessed, and ultimately comic "greatness"
whose envied freedom is only apparent, not real. Witty, intelligent,

poised in the beginning, they become the snarling animals of v.vi, puppets of the blind instinct for self-preservation they had exalted as nature's only imperative. That they fail to reach their goal is no adequate condemnation of their attempt. Francisco, operating on the same values, acts successfully. We are in no more doubt about his ability to arrange his victims' destruction than about Monsieur's or Octavius's or (once Coriolanus changes sides) Aufidius's. Unlike Giovanni, we cannot look to external guarantees. The tragedian must make us believe the "realists" are wrong about the nature and value of man, just as Flamineo himself learns the inadequacy of the knowledge he shared with them. The flattening of Francisco's and Lodovico's characters suggests the worldly ideal's limitations, just as the moralists' blinkered somnambulism undermines their certainties. The revengers adopt the conventional limitations of their role; while striking a theatrical pose, equally conventional in its own way, their victims have momentarily dropped all roles and looked at each other and at themselves to find the complex and lonely humanity they had denied.

The White Devil is not a tract, not a simple denunciation of corruption or an exaltation of courageous defiance. Nor does it answer the questions it so pointedly raises about how to cope with the gap between traditional moral imperatives and the demands the world makes and, apparently, rewards. It offers no moral exemplars, but we may be wrong to require of all tragedy melodrama's predictable affirmations.[36] The careers of Vittoria and Flamineo reveal most forcefully self-absorption's corrosive power. Yet Flamineo, especially, suggests—and hence in a sense affirms—the human capacity not only to perceive another's hypocrisy but also to transcend self-delusion. Although realization is partial and comes only at the moment of extinction, almost against his will, he does acknowledge both the moral ambivalence of the world he claimed to know and the desolate harvest of his own solution to the problem of competing imperatives.

Flamineo's compulsive honesty, his discovery of an ineradicable moral sensitivity, suggest the possibility of coming to terms with the divided self and hint that, in a world which refuses to offer it, meaning might yet be created. Although Flamineo and Vittoria fail to transform themselves at the last, in their failure Webster intimates the possibility of another response to experience, a choice which they refused but for which they alone reveal the capacity. There is as little consolation in their lives and deaths as in Bussy's or Coriolanus's, and as little comfort in the unchanged world they leave behind. We mourn their loss because they were more richly human than the voices that condemned them; beyond this, the tragic experience that remained unavailable to the stage audience has shown us something of lasting and disturbing value about ourselves.

CHAPTER IV

"The Duchess of Malfi"

ELF-KNOWLEDGE in *The White Devil* is limited, despite Webster's care in distinguishing Vittoria's and Flamineo's dying moments from Bracciano's and Lodovico's. Both brother and sister transcend mere defiance of their murderers, yet the brief confrontation with herself before death leaves Vittoria tritely moralistic, unable to conceive any remedy beyond flight. Flamineo dies still confused by the failure of his world to fulfill its golden promises. They are very nearly heroes in a totally ironic tragedy of ignorance and self-delusion, one where "the protagonist, far from returning to his former, or better, self, instead bears out even to the edge of doom his new world-encumbered self."[1] It is Lodovico, however, who remains the deed's creature, bound even in death to a worldly idea of glory. Flamineo does recognize, finally, the quality of his life. He can see that the values he rejected "confound" those he adopted, though the contradiction defies resolution.

In the *Duchess of Malfi* Webster reconsiders such partial recognition of failure and self-delusion as he explores contiguous moral terrain. In some ways each play is romantic tragedy, and both plots revolve around women who pursue private goals through what prove to be disastrous marriages. Both plays portray court corruption stemming explicitly from the political and social rulers, yet such evil remains stylized, its representatives flat and in themselves uninteresting. Webster's focus lies rather in corruption's effects on the private lives and personal relationships of those who seek fulfillment in a world where they can exercise little control.

The Duchess of Malfi, of course, transforms both its heroine and the nature of the central romantic alliance. Vittoria Corombona is her brother's twin both in ambition and, at the final confrontation, in ruthless egotism; the Duchess enjoys at the outset the social position Vittoria and Flamineo coveted, yet finds it without real value and attempts to escape in a most unadvantageous marriage. Both women seek the freedom to be what they wish and to gratify their personal desires, but the two marriages are as different as the two ideas of what constitutes contentment. In their search both move beyond their society's prescribed limits, but the means employed differ as much as the ends sought. Vittoria and her brother pursue advancement—which only the society they despise can confer—through murder as well as cleverness and deceit; the Duchess seeks an intimate and enduring family relationship—which her society cannot provide—in a secret marriage that requires deceit and violates both custom and her brothers' wishes. Each attains her goal, however briefly. Faced with society's punishment, however, Vittoria repudiates her desire as well as her corrupted life; the Duchess upholds her choice even as she admits personal frailty.

Superficial similarities between the women's positions emphasize basic antitheses, but likenesses between the plays' cynical commentators are more fundamental. In motivation and response, Bosola offers a variation and development of Flamineo rather than a contrast. Drawn to court service partly by economic necessity, both men also feel the court's perverse attraction and envy the amoral freedom as well as the luxury they satirize. Although both hold themselves critically distant from the great men they serve, the apparently successful manipulation of people and events lures them into adopting their masters' psychology. Accurately perceiving—or so they think—the world's daily operation and rewards, the realists go on to assume they understand that world's metaphysical foundations. Both servants are deluded: seeking preferment and self-realization, each finds instead frustration and constraint. Flamineo thinks that mastery of the court's ways will bring freedom and power, yet discovers that no matter how far he seems to advance, someone more cunning and powerful still stands between him and his goal. The trial scene's forced injustice, the insistent theatrical images, the "playwright" Francisco's successful redirection of Flamineo's drama, Giovanni's ban on Flamineo's presence, all indicate Vittoria's and Flamineo's restricted control. Their freedom, even of movement, is progressively limited and circumscribed even as they feel they are approaching their plans' fruition.

As the Arragonian brothers' tool, Bosola is more passive than Flamineo. He is also more clearly self-divided than *The White Devil*'s vociferous schemer, who so wholeheartedly preached the duplicated intriguers' Machiavellian philosophy. Although Flamineo pleads economic necessity and "inevitable fate," he sees himself as both master manipulator and vitally self-creating, self-sustaining artifact. Despite Webster's allusion to a shared pedigree as disappointed university men, Bosola seems older, wearier, more disillusioned. Knowing his service may again be rewarded by the galleys, Bosola is no misplaced city-comedy farceur. He lacks Flamineo's adolescent exuberance and smug self-confidence. Bosola hopes only to wrest a living from his world, not dominate it; in him, skeptical detachment's primary function lies in self-protection and self-definition.[2]

Bosola also lacks Flamineo's fantasied independence from his superiors. If Ferdinand's need for a master/servant relationship is obvious, both in his anger at the laughing courtiers and his refusal to explain why he opposes his sister's remarriage, Bosola shares his master's dependence. Despite his contempt for Ferdinand's self-puffery, Bosola lacks the courage of his own aphorisms, and he seeks external moral authority to direct him. Ferdinand's "curs'd gifts" allow Bosola to reassign moral blame to his patron: he can deplore the fact that "bounty, / Which makes men truly noble, e'er should *make* / Me a villain" and enjoy the irony of a situation in which, "to avoid ingratitude," he "*must* do / All the ill man can invent" (1.i.271–275, my italics). The earlier ethical juggling—"It seems you would *create* me / One of your familiars"—is made clear. As Robert Ornstein says, Bosola is the "feudal liege man brought up to Jacobean date."[3] By transforming payment into the "bounty" which binds recipients to loyal service, he creates a context to justify his "service." In such a hypothetical feudal relationship, refusal is simply inconceivable. Bosola turns his bitter wit against himself as well as others, but psychological needs outweigh self-disgust; he willingly becomes Ferdinand's creature.

Reliance on moral sophistry and intrigue proves ill-advised for Bosola, as for Flamineo; yet Bosola's earlier awakening requires that he act upon his new knowledge. Just as the Duchess has at her play's beginning found Vittoria's goals inadequate, so in act 4 Bosola discovers, through suffering but not death, the insubstantial fabric of his "sweet and golden dream." Bosola is, in effect, given a second chance. Both he and the Duchess become disillusioned with the court before death instructs them; in different ways they struggle for that self-realization and enriched humanity from which Vittoria and Flamineo were barred by their own willfully limited perception and necessarily diminished moral sensibility. In Vittoria and Flamineo *The White Devil* sketched a fragile potential for discovering alternatives to the Machiavels' and moralists' narrow and contradictory interpretations of experience. *The Duchess of Malfi* explores one alternative and its consequences.

Transforming the central protagonists and their relationship entails major modifications in Webster's dramatic technique. On the broadest level he adopts, with only partial success, the dangerously disrupted, broken-backed structure of Shakespeare's *Antony and Cleopatra*. The Duchess's death in act 4 provides the romantic tragedy's climactic moment; it also marks the larger play's generic turning point. With characteristic perversity, in neither *The White Devil* nor *The Duchess of Malfi* does Webster fulfill normal expectations raised by the potentially heroic and romantic couple's apparent centrality. Bracciano's lover and secretary carry on, little changed by his demise. Antonio plays no Antony to the Duchess's Cleopatra, and he wanders helplessly through act 5 to an ignominious death. The Duchess gains a new and different admirer, and the play's form and focus shift: murderer rededicates himself as Petrarchan lover, and historical romance dissolves into a travesty of revenge melodrama.

In providing his cynical reductionist with a real challenge, not just the trite advocates of traditional codes who pop up briefly and ineffectually in *The White Devil*, Webster also complicates the neat antitheses of his earlier play. Traditional ideals operate more centrally in *The Duchess of Malfi* and are variously represented in Antonio, Delio, Pescara, and even Bosola, while the opposing politicians remain distinct instead of collapsing into the doubles, Lodovico and Francisco. Even though she also shares Vittoria's vacillation between conventional submission and defiance, the Duchess provides a third, ambiguous, but clearly different perspective. Moreover, since the Duchess's marriage is both secret and, in its naïve impracticality, beyond Bosola's ken, the central romantic alignment is neither the commentator's prime target nor a prominent confirmation of his philosophy's adequacy. Bosola's cynical wit is largely diverted outward, to the court, and his role as passive witness rather than intriguing participant enforces his resemblance to the traditional satirist: as the "only court-gall" and framer of traditional set pieces in the *contemptus mundi* tradition, Bosola often sounds more like Malevole than Flamineo.[4] Neither disguised prince nor, despite his murderous past, a very actively intriguing villain, Bosola becomes more clearly a mediating figure. Physically, he moves between the first scene's antithetical groups; he later represents the Arragonian brethren in the Duchess's court and, finally, brings Malfi to Milan.[5]

More concerned with a broad spectrum than with neatly balanced characters, *The Duchess of Malfi* varies its use of conflicting, rather than unifying, dramatic techniques. Beneath opposed rhetorical surfaces, characters in *The White Devil* initially all sound alike: each knows what he wants and grasps the nearest way to procure satisfaction. Until Cornelia's entrance late in act 1, no one resists the assumed amorality in which self-seeking cynics maneuver for individual goals; when she appears, the contrast is total. Although in his second play Webster still favors developing plot and character through contrasted perspectives and shifting patterns of opposition, the tight concentration of Machiavellian realists who stand opposed to conventional moralists relaxes into the varied components of the first act's leisurely groupings. Sharp juxtapositions and violent rhetorical contrasts melt into simultaneous action and almost indistinguishable voices. Instead of Gasparo's and Antonelli's urbane and taunting unconcern, we find a polished court whose good manners and judicious moral assessments contain disruptive threats. Instead of Lodovico's aggressive egotism, Antonio's eulogy of the French court seems to provide a social and political model by which subsequent action may safely be judged.[6] The static opening is succeeded by casually scattered conversational units more concerned with observing and wittily describing each other than with present action or violent foreboding. Far from being thrust into the plot's action, we can discern no plot at all; we are lulled by a panoramic overview of normality, a sense of both social and moral security.[7] Commentators abound and, though elsewhere opposed, both Antonio and Bosola here ground their satiric "characters" in the same traditional values. That calm surface will of course explode, and we may hesitate over the murderous Bosola's quest for service or the violence of Ferdinand's admonitions to the Duchess. More important, Webster himself soon mines the intellectual distance and firm moral schema offered by Antonio's and Bosola's evaluative commentary.

The French court provides the model for a healthy commonweal we never see. Its political formulae immediately prove inadequate to Malfi's realities, yet when Antonio insists that morality and statecraft are interdependent, Webster approaches his play's true focus: the moral status of the world in which his characters must act. If "blessed government" requires moral clarity in the "common fountain" and conscientious royal counselors "who dare freely / Inform [their prince of] the corruption of the times," then this ideal uncovers existing faults before the Duchess even appears. Recipes that reduce states to the "fix'd order" so beloved of political theorists fail of their goal without the prescribed ingredients. Quite happy to tell prince or pauper of the time's corruption, Bosola is yet introduced as one whose "railing / Is not for simple love of piety" but for envy and a host of equally dangerous emotions (I.i.23–28). A man who thinks it a "miserable age" when virtue is its own reward bears little resemblance to the needed provident counselor. Although, paradoxically, he is almost alone in sharing Antonio's vital concern with moral depravity, the ambiguity of Bosola's position as corrupt castigator of corruption only underlines Malfi's vulnerability and the naïveté of Antonio's formulae for good governance.

Purity in the royal fountainhead seems equally hard to come by. The Cardinal and Duke Ferdinand are immediately described by Bosola (and later, in a variation, by Antonio) as "standing pools" who support, use, and introduce into others' courts the very people a good statesman should eliminate (I.i.49–52, 161–163). Antonio has impugned Bosola's credit as impartial judge, but Bosola can here claim first-hand knowledge. The Cardinal urges honesty on Bosola, yet if princes determine their land's health, little guidance can be expected from a divine able to "possess the greatest devil, and make him worse" (I.i.46–47). Although Ferdinand lacks his brother's opportunity to bribe his way into the papacy, he is in quality the Cardinal's twin, and his "perverse" nature bends the law's public justice into a "foul black cobweb . . . to entangle those shall feed him" (I.i.178–180). The truth behind the brothers' "characters" is immediately demonstrated in their colloquy about Bosola's employment, in their objection to Antonio's honesty, and in Ferdinand's interview with Bosola. This world's fountains of morality have reversed the proper order; instead of preserving the commonwealth, they feed off, or poison, those they govern.

Although structure here favors simultaneous groupings rather than the receding observer-commentators of *The White Devil*, Webster works to enforce the same aesthetic distance, the same sense of interpretive stalemate. No one is allowed the role of unchallenged judge. The politic Bosola acquiesces in the present state of things; as one of the brothers' "flattering panders" he would happily use their corruption to his own profit and "hang on their ears like a horse-leech till I were full, and then drop off" (1.i.53–54). Familiar with courtly corruption, he understands the throat-cutting service implied by Ferdinand's gift of gold. Yet Ferdinand's answer also undercuts Bosola's satiric righteousness, for he tells his cynical servant that "your inclination to shed blood rides post / Before my occasion to use you" (1.i.250–251). If Bosola seems over-eager for iniquitous employment, he yet refuses Antonio and Delio the privileged moral position assumed in their stance as commentators and presenters. He pointedly reminds them of their own involvement, for the hierarchy of worldly reward is continuous: no man has the right to "scorn" another when, in the court as in the hospital, "this man's head lies at that man's foot, and so lower, and lower" (1.i.66–69).

Antonio indeed demonstrates his naïve understanding of both the cynic's attitude and the "cure" for a malcontent's "foul melancholy." In Antonio's view, Bosola's problems stem from neglect, the "inward rust unto the soul" caused by inaction and excessive contemplation. Yet the problem is more complicated than simply "want of action" for, given his past patronage, service to the Cardinal is hardly likely to preserve or encourage whatever of "goodness" Antonio sees in Bosola. Moreover, Webster immediately shows us Ferdinand, bored and seeking to "fall to action indeed" (1.i.92). While the action that engulfs him may take the "inward rust" from his soul, it also drives him mad. Antonio's description of the French court holds out a hope that moral degeneration is not the norm in this play's world (as it seemed to be in *The White Devil*), but as a moral standard it only accentuates the corrupt and limiting context in which they must all act. Antonio and Delio fail to understand the subtlety of the vices they condemn; indeed, Delio later competes with the Cardinal for Julia's favors. What they do perceive, neither they nor the Duchess have the power to correct. Even before the Duchess rashly accepts Bosola as her servant and marries her steward we are clearly shown the inadequacy, as a practical guide to conduct, of Antonio's version of Cornelia's dial-of-princes' lives.

Antonio's conventional standards, like Cornelia's, ill suit him to deal with tragic complexity in character or situation. Webster undercuts Antonio's naïve political ideal by juxtaposing it with a "real" court, and this technique is echoed in the way he plays Antonio's idealized portrait of the Duchess against the earthy, willful woman we see. As the "wire-drawer with her commendations" Antonio praises the Duchess as a romance heroine, diametrically opposed in "temper" to her princely brothers. The later interview reveals likeness rather than difference. The purity of "so divine a continence / As cuts off all lascivious, and vain hope," whose sleeps must be "more in heaven than other ladies' shrifts" (1.i. 199–200, 203), manages nevertheless to bandy bawdry with her brothers about diamonds and jewelers and then to lie unequivocally about her intention never to remarry.[8]

For three hundred lines Webster has withheld his heroine. She moves forward at last, simultaneously to complete the first act's panoramic view and to plunge us into the play's action. Webster's dramatic skill is evident not only in her suggested complexity,[9] but in the wooing scene's structural effectiveness. More strongly than with *The White Devil*'s adulterous relationship, Webster introduces a potentially comic dilemma: young lovers frustrated by tyrannic family opposition.[10] He encourages our sympathetic rejection of the brothers' peremptory and gratuitously nasty demands. Equally clearly, however, her solioquy reveals that the Duchess shares her brothers' indifference to the claims of either "simple honesty" or public duty. Ferdinand's demeaning image of the self-confident "irregular crab" who thinks its own way "right" is not inaccurate. Her sudden resolve to make her "royal kindred" into "low footsteps" to her will suggests she shares their stubborn egotism and even accepts their rebuke as a challenge to her sovereign freedom. The battle imagery in which she couches her decision hints a recognition of danger but also recalls the Arragonian family penchant for self-aggrandizement. The Duchess may reject future critics as "old wives," but Cariola's ambivalence encourages our own: free of Ferdinand's personal animus, Cariola sees her mistress's action in ominous domestic terms, as dangerous poison. She is not at all sure whether the proclaimed heroic endeavor is urged by "the spirit of greatness" or merely a private woman's foolish will (1.i.504–506).

Certainly in the wooing itself the Duchess demonstrates both sides of her character. She seeks the domestic satisfactions of love and marriage, but in her reckless willfulness seems possessed by a quality as perilous as what Antonio calls the "great man's madness," ambition. Surrounded by fawning suitors and flatterers, ambition becomes dangerously convinced of its power (made "lunatic, beyond all cure"); to obtain its desires it feels justified in leaving "the path / Of simple virtue, which was never made / To seem the thing it is not" (1.i.446–448). She dismisses as insignificant Antonio's realistic fears about her brothers' reaction; she refuses to be bothered by nebulous consequences and shrugs off a tempest that "time will easily / Scatter" (1.i.471–472). Paradoxically, in trying to set aside her nobility she exercises the very dignity, courage, and stubborn willfulness natural to her royal position. Yet the Duchess is foolish as well as charming, and an ominous undertone in the courtship's imagery combines with Cariola's assessment to make us uneasy about the choice itself as well as its prospects for worldly happiness.[11] The wooing both initiates the plot's action and prepares us for its course. However variously our uncertain response to this marriage may be explained away by critical appeals to contemporary opinion, Webster himself creates the internal contradictions that ensure ambivalence.[12]

Structurally, the wooing brilliantly focuses the first act's seemingly aimless social maneuvering while it also balances Antonio's opening speech. In playing off Antonio's recipe against a leisurely exploration of princes' courts, Webster has suggested Malfi's urgent need for attention to public matters. In this context, the audience's own feelings about second marriages violating degree are irrelevant: unconcerned with her duchy's political health, the Duchess seeks private happiness at the expense of public stability. As a ruler, she can no more be lauded for the example she sets than her brothers. Each sibling pursues an essentially private will, and Clifford Leech rightly notes that she "only refers to her people when she is concerned with how her reputation fares at their hands."[13] Yet everything in the wooing scene militates against the terms set up by Antonio's prologue, and the initial public context comes to seem less and less relevant or helpful in explaining our response. Webster supports the Duchess's verbal attempts at divestiture by briefly eradicating all but that personal "circumference" she seeks to establish. Dubious but sympathetic, even Cariola is relegated to the scene's borders; no interposed commentators degrade the lovers' vows or, for the moment, interrupt our sympathetic involvement in domestic romance.

Webster allows us to experience the Duchess's goal, a haven beyond the aggressive, treacherous world of political maneuvering, and we come to value her for precisely the nonpolitical desires she here represents.[14] She may be a "bad" ruler, certainly a poor example of Antonio's ideal; yet any political consequences of her decision are to her accidental. She should not be—and does not strive to be—a ruler at all. The Duchess

does not so much misuse or evade public responsibility as seem unaware of its claims. The political world that reappears throughout the
play—in satiric "court" scenes, in the Cardinal's military investiture, in
conversations about war and horsemanship and impatience with inaction—is in her eyes "irrelevant." The Duchess continually closes out
the great world to which she inextricably belongs and instead attempts
to establish a private sphere, a world of intimate relationships and
family concerns to which she can devote herself as private individual.
Royally cavalier about deception, about her general responsibilities,
about her marriage's social or political ramifications, the Duchess denies the world act 1 portrays; yet that rejection paradoxically takes the
form of an affirmation we can only applaud. Her private, domestic, and
comic drama is one of courtship and marriage. By creating two of the
most powerfully affecting scenes of domestic happiness in theater history, Webster lets us, too, withdraw momentarily from the public arena
where time is history and individual happiness irrelevant.

In this play the two worlds, like the scenes that represent them, are in
opposition. We do not see the Duchess, or Antonio, try to bridge this
gap; indeed, their attempt to divorce public and private, day and night,
ensures their helpless vulnerability in a world inimical to romantic comedy's assumptions or goals. By endowing these lovers with the sympathetic wit, charm, and harmonious accord appropriate to their purpose
(and denied Bracciano and Vittoria), Webster can use his generic contrasts to dramatize the desirability of the Duchess's choice as well as the
impossibility of its attainment, both her culpability in political and
social terms and the unimportance of any terms that inhibit reestablishing fundamentally valuable human relationships.

In sexual and maternal love the Duchess alone is fruitful; society is
preserved in her, though its order may be questioned. Paradoxically, the
political world seems to support, even necessitate, the cynical watchful-
ness of Bosola's self-protective "realism." The Duchess's chamber, the
lovers' new world, is circumscribed, penetrated, and destroyed by the
great world it cannot exclude. Yet enclosing comedy within tragedy
allows Webster more than the sentimental poignance of blasted happiness. Through the Duchess's choice, and her refusal to repudiate comedy's goals when called to tragedy's accounting, Webster suggests what
is perhaps a blind, but certainly ineradicable human drive toward relatedness, union, and love's self-effacement. Although Bosola and An-

tonio are in many ways elaborately paralleled throughout *The Duchess of Malfi,* in generic terms it is Bosola and the Duchess who prove to be the play's real antagonists, the poles of its dialectic.

In acts 2 and 3 Webster pulls us back from the wooing scene's narrow and sympathetic concentration on the lovers; we see their intimate harmony only once more, in the hair-brushing scene whose domestic security and easy banter collapse when Ferdinand usurps both Antonio's place and the first husband's right to vengeance. Although he does not provide the devastatingly juxtaposed commentary of *The White Devil,* Webster yet holds us back from the lovers and unsettles his romantic focus. The lovers' discovery and flight is crosscut with scenes of satiric comedy, abrupt shifts from Malfi to Rome, and in general a return to the panoramic view that places all characters at the critical distance enforced by Bosola's reductionist observations. Seen from outside their affection's "circumference," the lovers themselves shrink to the surrounding court's common humanity. Preoccupied with ugly physical details, Bosola's jaundiced eye sees an unattractively pregnant woman: the Duchess "is sick o' days, she pukes . . . she wanes i' th' cheek, and waxes fat i' th' flank" (II.i.64–66). Bosola's coarse devaluation is answered by no Petrarchan hyperbole; irritable, short-winded, greedily hungry, the Duchess herself contributes to his reductive picture. Bosola's conclusion—that such "tetchiness" and "vulturous eating" are "apparent signs of breeding"—is accurate in point of fact, and the Duchess's behavior corroborates his bold assertion that the "souls of princes" are not "brought forth by some more weighty cause than those of meaner persons," since the "like passions sway them" (II.i.101–104).

As secret lovers, Antonio and the Duchess often seem comically inept, and their plight is distanced by comic interludes as well as by demeaning commentary. Dramatic tension encouraged by the Duchess's dangerously sudden labor dissipates in comic repartee with the Old Lady and uproarious laughter over the Switzer's lethal codpiece. So too later, the dramatic confrontation in Ancona is deferred for a reprise of I.i, with its pithy "characters" and "irrelevant" witty banter about Malatesta's Parolles-like soldiery and the coming war. The potentially melodramatic banishment is distanced by dumb-show and superseded by the Cardinal's spectacular investiture and the pilgrims' judiciously "objective" commentary.

Under pressure, Antonio is "lost in amazement" and bumbling. The "politic safe conveyance" for the midwife proves ineffectual; he rashly insults Bosola, then drops the nativity figure at the intelligencer's feet. Despite Ferdinand's presence in Malfi and her people's rumored censure, the Duchess eagerly believes that asserting her submission ("When I choose / A husband, I will marry for your honour") and hypocritically appealing to Ferdinand's trust and "fix'd love" have "purg'd" all "deadly air" (III.i. 42–43, 52, 56). Naïvely self-confident, she insists on having her man and her position too; even after Ferdinand's nighttime visitation she seems to think preserving her "weak safety" depends on only one more "enginous" ruse, the *magnanima menzogna* that will "shield our honours" (III.ii.176–181). During Antonio's "trial," as J. R. Brown notes, both lovers delight in playing publicly the game of ambiguous meanings.[15] Like comedy's self-deluding fools, the Duchess follows Bosola's advice because he tells her what she wants to hear.

That the lovers should lack Bosola's finesse in courtly intrigue is neither surprising nor blameworthy, but lack of skill in deception does not guarantee the deceivers' innocence. Antonio's self-accusation carries weight: "The great are like the base—nay, they are the same— / When they seek shameful ways, to avoid shame" (II.iii.51–52). In pursuing all her desires the Duchess is like her brothers: she wants both Antonio and her duchy, while the Cardinal maintains his public position and secretly enjoys Julia on the side. In wanting the game's prizes, the Duchess has accepted its rules; the easy lies, the "shifts" and paltering, demean the lovers even while naïve ineptitude makes them comic dupes of Bosola's more skillful maneuvering.

Yet though the lovers suffer personal as well as social exposure in acts 2 and 3, they do not, like Bussy or Antony, claim a superhuman stature in the face of demeaning reality. Indeed, the lovers see themselves in no more heroic terms than Bosola's. Antonio remarks to Delio that his wife is "an excellent / Feeder of pedigrees" (III.i.5–6); content with being a nighttime lord of misrule, Antonio's first concern, both before the marriage and after its discovery, is for safety.[16] The Duchess asserts to Ferdinand her ability to live or die like a prince, yet hers is no heroic passion. Her true context is the private and domestic sphere of wifely devotion. Bosola's scathing analysis of court loyalty and hyperbolic praise of her steward give the Duchess her chance to acknowledge Antonio with honor, and she cannot resist a display of connubial pride: "This good one that you speak of, is my husband" (III.ii.275). In proving her claim to Antonio's virtues she reveals the true locus of her concern; the boast to "have had three children by him" suggests the standards by which she defines her own value. She naïvely expects Bosola to honor the trust she asks for; she allows her new friend's "direction" to lead her "by the hand" (III.ii.313).

Bosola's sarcastic descant on the idea of marriage as a suitable reward for service makes the proud wife before him rather ridiculous, in her role as duchess. Yet Bosola's ridicule also demonstrates how much her acts exceed his understanding, how inadequate the context in which he places them. Her gullibility, too, sets her apart. She did not marry Antonio to reward his long service to virtue; that is merely one of the wooing scene's private jokes. Rather, his virtues helped win her love, and love is outside the world of service and payment which Bosola's speech portrays. In this sense, it is Bosola who does not understand. To him the central meaning of her life, which she has just revealed in wifely pride, is marketable information for which he is "certain to be rais'd" (III.ii.330).

Both here and after the banishment Bosola speaks for as well as serves the antagonistic outer world that denies the Duchess not only her life but the values by which she has lived. A world of covert, variously illicit amours—from Castruccio and the Old Lady to Julia's several relations with the Cardinal, Delio, and Bosola—it can never rise above the level of brief, embittered, and commercialized sexual encounters. Sexually as well as politically, from the Arragonian brethren to the petty courtiers whose youthful sins are "the very patrimony of the physician," self-seeking egoists exploit each other's needs. The inconstancy attributed to women is shared by their lovers: when the Cardinal swears to "love . . . wisely" he means "jealously," self-protectively; Julia has become his "ling'ring consumption" before she seeks sexual excitement elsewhere (II.iv.24–25; V.ii.228). Bosola's complete detachment is only an extreme version of the cynical defensiveness that distinguishes other relationships: if we are essentially coterminous with our animal bodies, we can seek momentary physical pleasures or, like Bosola in his "meditation," strip human beings of their material masks to discover nothing "in this outward form . . . to be belov'd" (II.i.45–46).

The only extreme, "heroic" passion is Ferdinand's, but it is merely the distorted complement of his brother's cool rationalism. In both brothers, self-interest dominates their personalities' narrow concentration: they seem the unintegrated halves of one solipsistic being. The Cardinal exhibits in perverse, Machiavellian form his sister's intelligence—the wit and judgment with which she prizes Antonio's virtue and directs the wooing scene, the calm self-acceptance with which she faces adversity. While the Cardinal remains cool and noncommittal until scene 5 of the fifth act, Ferdinand shares and debases his sister's passionate physicality and tenacious emotional commitments; impetuous, unreflective egoism loves and fears the blood they share. Identifying himself with his sister as well as with the husband's role he cannot quite usurp, Ferdinand can in her punish himself, and by fixing her in "a general eclipse," quench his own "wild-fire."[17]

Ferdinand's prurient sexual fantasies have as little to do with the Duchess's private world—those tender but prosaic scenes of companionable raillery between husband, wife, and friend—as the Cardinal's cold generalities about women and marriage or Bosola's certainty that ugly (albeit "natural") sexuality drives her to employ her steward as pander. The Duchess's self-appointed judges neither pity nor understand her. They cannot conceive of a love which also prompts rational choice, an affection embracing but also exceeding sexual desire. Her particular violations of their code lie beyond their categories. Explaining Malfi's response to Delio, Antonio finds the same misinterpretations there: the common people think her a strumpet while "graver heads" believe Antonio an unscrupulous opportunist, but "for other obligation / Of love, or marriage . . . they never dream of" (III.i.35–37).

The demeaning acts, the foolish choices that deny the lovers' heroic stature and demonstrate their practical naïveté, also set them apart from the world they inhabit. The hair-brushing scene gains power from its precariousness, suspended as it is on the thread of Ferdinand's anticipated entrance, but also from its apparent impossibility when so many deny even the emotions that created it. Challenged by her brother, the Duchess cannot explain, let alone persuade. She places her case in a generalized human context, urging the marriage's naturalness. Disingenuously, she suppresses the obvious fact that, for a woman in her position, this particular marriage has indeed "gone about" to create new "custom"; she equivocates about her reputation's safety. Yet Ferdinand's hysterical revulsion overshadows her evasiveness. Like Bosola and the Cardinal, Ferdinand sees only one meaning in "love" and "marriage": his passion focuses on a sexual union which must be punished.

As Ferdinand's fable makes clear, his notion of love has nothing to do with the court; love exists, if at all, only in a make-believe pastoral world ("'mongst unambitious shepherds, / Where dowries were not talk'd of") or between impoverished, equally unambitious cousins "that had nothing left / By their dead parents" (III.ii.127–130). Ferdinand cannot see her truth, for the Duchess has found love in the courts of princes. Yet in pursuing desire beyond society's prescribed bounds she has ignored his truth, for Ferdinand's instances suggest the only genres in which such love may be safe.[18]

Ferdinand flees, refusing to meet again his sister's eyes; the Cardinal directs from Rome the revenge to which he vowed to sacrifice his sister's wedding ring. Bosola is their perfect agent and representative. Personally bound to Ferdinand yet sharing the Cardinal's cool detachment, Antonio's social equal and philosophical opposite, Bosola usurps brothers' and husband's place alike. That he does not share Ferdinand's punitive obsession, the goal of despair or madness, is clear, though he paradoxically carries out his master's orders with both gusto and reluctance. In his perverse way, Bosola woos the Duchess while tormenting her. She alone challenges the carefully constructed philosophy by which Bosola has accommodated his bothersome conscience to the world's demands. As a man who has intentionally, though not wholly successfully, chosen to "look no higher than I can reach" (II.i.89), Bosola's bitter humor attempts to reduce all others to his own level of self-disgust. He pushes, prods, taunts the Duchess, trying to force the acquiescence that would justify his life. Yet the compulsive honesty evident in Bosola's earlier self-laceration forces him to accept whatever she can, under pressure, become. Having seen through the trappings of metaphoric as well as real cosmetics and found nothing worthy of love, he grasps an opportunity to search the inward man. Unlike Ferdinand, Bosola is not impelled to destroy whatever resists his definitions; he carries on Ferdinand's "persecution" in the impersonal, detached mode of his earlier meditation.

From the Duchess's arrest in act 3 until her death at Bosola's hands, Webster focuses his play on their confrontation. Bosola's discussions with Ferdinand, the waxwork display, and the dance of the madmen serve not as misguided fragmentation but rather as punctuation to that central dialogue toward which Webster has moved us. The Duchess's "play" is over. Her romantic comedy is shattered by the violent egotism that, unleashed, issues both in Ferdinand's insane aspiration to godhead (for he wishes not merely to usurp divine punishment but to create in the limited world of her prison his fantasy's mad sister and dead family) and, ultimately, in the madmen's complete solipsistic alienation.[19] Stripped not only of her title but also of her drama and its sustaining props, she is forced to discover how the values she lived by may sustain her in another drama, defined by Ferdinand's "properties," in which she must "play a part . . . 'gainst my will" (IV.i.85). To Antonio she admits both guilt and doubt, but she does not fully join his retreat to conventional, aphoristic acceptance of the world's injustice as God's inscrutable wisdom. Although Bosola presses her admission of pragmatic folly, she cannot be forced to admit worthlessness in Antonio or error in marrying him; she refuses Bosola's or her brothers' right to judge or punish her.[20]

The Duchess does not simply defy Bosola. She challenges the assumptions on which he bases his taunts, forces on him the dilemma of knowledge confounding knowledge. To Bosola's certainty she returns a question: "I prithee, who is greatest? can you tell?" (III.v.123). As her parable of the dogfish and salmon points out, our humanity binds us to frailty, yet man's imperfection implies for her no cynic's assurance. Nor does she maintain that Antonio's merit raised him in any worldly, social sense, only that "man is most happy when 's own actions / Be arguments and examples of his virtue" (III.v.120–121). In the pragmatic terms by which Bosola has lived, a "barren, beggarly virtue" is meaningless, but he is to learn that there is fulfillment in "so good a quarrel," even if the price of that satisfaction is death.

Majestic in adversity, the Duchess demonstrates that disdain of the world which Bosola affects; by incarnating one side of his personality, she offers him a different model from Ferdinand and the greatness he represents. To some extent, she has shared Bosola's ambivalent attitude toward the world's prizes: she wanted her duchy, yet also denied its claim to define or constrict her identity. Waxwork tortures and the threat of death bring her to see that the two positions she valued— duchess and wife—are incompatible and that to only one of them is she ultimately, mortally, committed. The pilgrims acknowledged the injustice of her persecution, yet accepted it as the way of the world. The Duchess will not, cannot accept; her greatest achievement lies in discovering the strength to find life unworthy of such a price. With her husband and children "dead," life has no significance, and she begs death's mercy. Bosola cannot yet either understand or believe such a discovery, for he has made life itself, at any price, his highest value. Torn between pity and mockery, he suggests that Ferdinand has appeased his wrath: in Bosola's eyes her mourning is "vain sorrow," and she should be happy if her family's deaths can purchase her own life.

As confident of his own understanding of the game and its rewards as Flamineo was when toying with Vittoria and urging the suicide pact, Bosola provides the mocking antiphonal response to the Duchess's cosmic imprecations. If "the stars shine still" upon human misery as well as happiness, then the curses' invocation of heavenly absolutes is a comical and futile self-delusion. Yet Bosola's mocking ironies fail to protect him. The woman he cannot understand begins to mine the bases of his self-definition; she moves him to inexplicable pity. The man he thought he understood moves beyond explicable motivation's reasonable bounds; Ferdinand refuses "comfort" because he demands despair as well as death. Bosola's world as well as the Duchess's is shaken. Perhaps for Bosola, too, the madmen's "noise and folly" represent the real, while silence or logical discussion would be false rationalization, ultimately so out of touch with mad reality as to induce true insanity.

Like his master unable to bear the Duchess's direct gaze, Bosola doffs "mine own shape" for the old man's disguise.[21] The only "comfort" he can now bring is the persuasiveness of his own contempt for humanity. As the choric voice of the *contemptus mundi* tradition, Bosola extends the satiric reductionism of his earlier "meditation": the body's grossness now hedges and infects the soul, and a heaven that reflects merely the "small compass of our prison" renders meaningless both earthly acts and religious certainty. The pressure of such nihilism forces the Duchess beyond resignation to necessity's "sad misery"; against its terms she must define herself and her life. Bosola insists on her common humanity as well as her mortality; he has never granted rank any automatic moral stature. The Duchess's famous reaffirmation of her social identity—"I am Duchess of Malfi still"—is met with the impassivity of the death Bosola represents. He reiterates her title's significance: examined closely, such worldly glory signifies broken sleeps and offers "neither heat, nor light" (IV.ii.145).[22] What was an ironic truism in *The White Devil,* a linguistic expression of the worldly Francisco's disguise as stoic Moor, here takes on a more complex meaning. In Bosola's role as bellman the maxim is straightforward moral counsel; in his ambivalent position as follower and servant of greatness, even while he criticizes it, the advice calls attention to his own self-delusions as well as those of the Duchess. Ironically, by violating her title to assume that maternal identity so strongly emphasized throughout the play, the Duchess has created life, both "heat" and "light." Her self-discovery holds a proleptic significance for Bosola; it will shatter the compromises by which he now straddles two roles.

The Duchess's acceptance of Bosola's new "comfort" is swift, complete, and far greater than Bosola himself can grasp. Adjusting to the waxwork "dead" had already loosened her hold on life; incarceration and torture both challenged and clarified the significance of her worldly identity as duchess. Bosola's "plainness" shows her the emptiness of titles when men no longer choose to recognize them, or when confronted with death. With extraordinary poise she jokes with Bosola about the time's fashion in tombmaking, even about the manner of her own death. Instead of Vittoria's and Flamineo's sarcastic defiance, we are returned to the light banter of earlier domestic scenes.

The Duchess both accepts Bosola into her "last presence-chamber" and marks the gulf that separates them. Bosola has prostituted himself to a world that disdains the ideals by which he judges both it and himself. His death remains "a hideous storm of terror," just as his life was "a general mist of error." To his surprise, the Duchess not only receives death "now I am well awake, / Best gift is they can give, or I can take" (IV.ii.224–225), but seems even eager for it. She holds to a reality beyond man's arbitrary redefinition, one in which significance does not lie at the mercy of the powerful. At times her defense is couched in terms of traditional absolutes, as when she reminds Ferdinand that he and (by implication) the Cardinal violate sacraments they cannot in fact abrogate. Yet the Duchess lacks Cornelia's unshakable faith: at least momentarily unsure of posthumous union or the "eternal Church," she, like Flamineo, wishes for "some two days' conference with the dead" to settle all doubts about this world's conduct (IV.ii.21–23). Mystery does not confound the Duchess, however. She chose to believe and act in a "knowledge" Flamineo rejected for lack of guarantees; her assertions are the more powerful for her only intermittent participation in Cornelia's certainties. Though without either "path" or "friendly clew," she has entered that uncharted land of the values men make for themselves, and the unknown world of love has given her life a meaning sufficient to withstand her torturers' jerry-built reign of terror. Having known that good, she can brush aside the fear of death which "should," according to Bosola, afflict her. Hers has not been the weeping from birth or mist of error of his dirge. She draws strength from what her persecutors cannot understand; in her final composure she transforms former curses into forgiveness of her executioners, her wish for general chaos into concern for Cariola and for her children.[23] In the face of death she transcends self-absorption and despair.

Regal poise gives way to impatience with their amazed procrastination: "any way, for heaven-sake, / So I were out of your whispering" (IV.ii.222–223). She remains Duchess of Malfi "still"; while suffering and loss have brought some clarification of her world, her relation to it, and a sense of her own hierarchy of values, she remains that curious and confusing mixture of womanliness and nobility, self-sacrificing dedication and willfulness. Webster seems self-consciously to play his Duchess's death against Cleopatra's. The loves for which they die differ markedly, but the Duchess's purely domestic and maternal concern is quite clearly, however unusually, its own value and not merely a watered-down, misunderstood version of Cleopatra's heroic aspiration. Still, with perhaps Shakespearean inspiration, Webster has managed in terms of his own play's values to fuse in one final paradoxical heroism the "spirit of greatness" with the apparently incompatible, willful, and earthbound "spirit of woman." In the end, the very behavior that had in earlier acts diminished the heroine's stature both fuels and lends additional power to her final self-transcendence. The Duchess commands her own executioners, even summons "violent death" as if it should do her bidding; yet she assumes in the same moment a posture of true humility that denies the arrogance of "princes' palaces." As she goes toward heaven upon her knees she has yet a moment to spare for one last unholy message to her brothers.

Webster has taken some care to avoid the univocal pathos of martyred innocence. While the spectacular trappings of this ritualized murder encourage a stereotypical response, the Duchess herself prevents such simplification. She retains her complex, earthy individuality to the end, and the comedy of Cariola's futile evasions returns us promptly to the world of scrambling vitality to which the Duchess too belonged. The play does not turn elegiac, nor does it affect domestic tragedy's pat conversions or the saintly exaltation of *Sophonisba* or *The Second Maiden's Tragedy*.

Ferdinand may be struck by guilt, but Bosola quickly drops his appeal to "pity" when he sees his master falling into "ingratitude." An element of bizarre comedy hedges the dispute waged over the dead woman's body, as master and servant try futilely to transfer their own responsibility and self-hatred. At base, it is a serious struggle to establish the terms in which Bosola's "service" should be interpreted, a test of the Duchess's effect on the worldly ethic she finally transcended. Although Ferdinand turns moralist, condemning Bosola's failure to be the "honest man" who, "bold in a good cause," would oppose his sword "between her innocence and my revenge" (IV.ii.274–278), the high moral tone is both hypocritical and laughably inappropriate. The two of them have helped create a world in which this ideal cannot exist, or exists only to be spurned in the way Ferdinand and the Cardinal rejected Antonio as "too honest for such business" as theirs (I.i.230). Bosola maintains that the issue is not one of right or wrong, by which both men stand condemned, but of payment for services loyally rendered. The wheel has come full circle, and Bosola is again asking reward for murder; but he now seeks more than physical self-preservation. Bosola's and Ferdinand's opposed voices spring from the same desperate solipsism. Seeking moral justification, each refuses to be defined as this deed's creature; each uses his general argument to dissociate himself from the body they both deny.

The "play" has broken down again. The "villain's part" with which Bosola protected himself explodes when Ferdinand repudiates his "service" and identifies actor and man. For this end to his "sweet and golden dream" Bosola is even less prepared than was Flamineo when Vittoria willed him Cain's reward instead of the successful pander-servant's due payment. Instead of the playwright's delight, the intriguer's pride in his ingenious "night-piece," Ferdinand's "revenge" dissolves in guilt and madness. Webster's generic juggling, even fragmentation, reflects not loss of control but increased mastery of his drama's components; the more flexible use of revenge conventions aptly serves this play's development. In *The Duchess of Malfi* the repeated collapse of individual dramas seems to suggest the futility of human hopes and plans more emphatically than *The White Devil*'s untroubled villains and wholly successful revenge play. Yet in the *Duchess* failure depends only partly on chance, though that demigod presides over a good deal of the fifth act's comedy of errors. While the clash of powerful wills threatens any individual's external ordering, the intriguer's plans now founder equally on his own unacknowledged complexity. Even those who reject, ignore, or exploit conventional religious sanctions exhibit an innate moral sense that conflicts with, even undermines, their proclaimed self-sufficiency.

The Duchess's death forces upon her tormentors what her living, misunderstood presence could never accomplish. Each finally confronts his own nature's contradictory impulses. Ferdinand escapes his deeds in madness, but even insanity cannot free him from his suppressed conscience, the self who was his sister's twin and his "dearest friend"; he tries in comic earnest to kill the shadow-self that dazzled him in the dead woman's eyes. The Cardinal is briefly troubled by his pond's reflection, a "thing arm'd with a rake" that mirrors his inner wasteland, yet in his nearly complete emotional ennui he can lay by as "tedious" his conscience's awkward promptings. It is in Bosola, where strong contradictions have run close to the surface throughout, that the Duchess's murder creates as well as destroys. Yet even here her effect is not immediate; it comes only after Ferdinand has demolished the bases for Bosola's service to him and bondage to the world. The would-be Machiavel's credo—that by seeing into society's dark heart he can use its evil for his own worldly gain—is finally exposed as the foolish obverse of idealism, for he has naïvely believed that if goodness is scorned then loyal service to evil will be rewarded. Arguments from both personal loyalty and economic necessity have earned him nothing. Clearly distraught at losing his devious and delicate adjustment to what he had thought were life's realities, Bosola faces an appalling freedom. Without a justifying patron, Bosola is left with Ferdinand's demand that he accept the very moral responsibility he has carefully argued he does not possess.

Violent disillusionment cannot itself take even the conscience-ridden Bosola much farther than Flamineo's despair, and the ex post facto resolution that "were this to do again" he would not sell his "peace of conscience" cannot solve his present predicament. The Duchess's momentary return exacerbates his sense of spiritual as well as physical loss, but also offers him a way to redefine his empty life. Needing both moral support and personal commitment, Bosola fastens upon the re-

viving Duchess as his key to atonement and salvation. In shockingly
Petrarchan terms he woos the woman he murdered. Belatedly, he grasps
her significance and seeks his own "heaven" in love and dedication. He
tries to transfer the "love" he bore Ferdinand to one who might help
him realize his "better nature." His own *magnanima menzogna,* assur-
ing her that Antonio is not only alive but reconciled to her brothers,
seems part unconscious tribute to the love that absorbs even her last
flicker of life, part pity and the "comfort" Ferdinand had refused, and
part a selfish desire to revive her as his new guide by giving her reasons
to live. In *The White Devil,* Flamineo's self-absorption isolated him; he
denied human relatedness and found others useful only as properties in
a private drama of advancement. Bosola explicitly admits that he needs
a Beatrice to "take me up to mercy" (IV.ii.349), and this admission also
frees him to acknowledge the naturalness of humane feelings, the "penitent fountains" that bind people. The Duchess dies, but Bosola has
found in her a significance around which his despair of advancement,
frustrated good intentions, pity, and guilty conscience can organize the
ambiguous "somewhat" worthy his "dejection."

As many commentators have noted, act 5 pursues the consequences of
the Duchess's murder. It could also with some justice be called Bosola's
Revenge, for this murderer has assumed the part usually reserved for
relative or lover. Yet the act is hardly distinguished by tight construction, and it lacks the unity and suspense gained by the constant presence
and ironic control of *The White Devil*'s revengers. *The Duchess of
Malfi* has largely eschewed the earlier play's abrupt juxtapositions and,
except in the distancing shifts between Rome, Malfi, and Ancona, has
determined its focus with smoothly flowing scenes and internal commentary. In act 5, however, we are returned to an "objective," panoramic view, crowded with characters pursuing separate goals. Webster
only gradually directs his characters, and our attention, towards the
denouement's final "presence-chamber" in the Cardinal's palace. The
irony now lies not in the revengers' ultimate control but in Webster's,
and in the cool detachment with which he reveals their inability to
command even their wills, much less events. The characters, like the
scenes, seem to move aimlessly, paradoxically determined to shape
what safety they can yet also hesitating, waiting for others' direction
or chance's resolution.

Charges of poor dramatic construction, of anticlimactic thinness, fall wide of the mark if based solely on the Duchess's "premature" death. Webster's theatrical sense may have faltered; certainly the act lacks a focus, a hero. Yet this choice is purposeful, not inherent in the material. Webster denies Bosola and Antonio the prominence or development by which either might dominate act 5 as a male Cleopatra or determined revenger. Moreover, although the Duchess in some sense stands behind the events of the act and the assemblage of corpses with which it closes, hers is not the revenging spirit of Shakespeare's Julius Caesar, omnipotent even in death. Act 5 demonstrates all too clearly how little she has affected the quality of life in this play's world, for the lesson of her wilderness voyage was a private one, and her final affirmation was quite literally incarcerated in act 4. Those who presided at her death were fundamentally affected, yet one finds refuge in madness and the other is more confused than transformed by what he has learned. The rest of their world was insulted against the impact of her imprisonment. The Duchess dies, as she had tried to live, in private.

Both the dramatic tension and the sense of significance generated by the fourth act's confrontations and violent murders dissipate in the play's concluding movement. Yet Webster does not simply demonstrate "how restricted is the power of virtue and how problematic the transformation of evil."[24] Though he has recourse to conventional stereotypes of good and evil, Webster is interested rather in discovering those pragmatic values that make life meaningful; he is interested, that is, in his Duchess, not in Cornelia or Isabella. He is less concerned with evil as a satanic moral force, struggling against good in some cosmic plan, than as the human consequence of self-limiting choices. In *The White Devil,* Lodovico's and Francisco's "development" into stereotypical villains suggests the ultimate fruition of their worldly solipsism, and this retreat from full humanity is emphasized by Flamineo's perplexed admission that the self-centered ego has not satisfactorily determined all value. Through both character and structure, act 5 of *The Duchess of Malfi* explores more subtly, and in more variety, the effect of belief on action and of action on the perceived quality of life.

Part of the fifth act's impression of unfocused triviality comes, of course, from its juxtaposition with the unmediated complexity and power of the Duchess's death and Bosola's personal crisis. Comic, even farcical intrusions further block our sympathies;[25] they also help characterize the individuals who remain. Into a world ignorant of the Duchess's

murder comes mad Ferdinand, himself now one of the obsessed caricatures of humanity with which he tortured his sister. Ferdinand's confused babble and the comic exchange with the buffoon doctor which
breaks down in fisticuffs form an interlude of low comedy. Our response is double: from our distanced, privileged position Ferdinand's
ravings are also powerful, grotesque reminders of what he has done. We
know the deed he cannot name and refuses to confess; we see the grisly
connections between a dead man's leg and the Duchess's final message
that her brothers might now "feed in quiet"; we feel the utter inap-
propriateness of using salamander skin to cure the "cruel sore eyes"
that dazzled at the sight of a murdered sister.

Our knowledge keeps us critically distant from the stage maneuverings, and Webster continues to enforce this rapid oscillation between
comic and grotesque. Ferdinand's humorous violence with the pompous
doctor is succeeded briefly by the Cardinal's evasions and his order for
Antonio's murder, then by Julia's misguided travesty of romantic comedy. It is, of course, her unconscious imitation of the Duchess's wooing,
and Webster can use its superficial resemblances to define more firmly
the Duchess's real singularity. More important, the comic associations
of love-at-first-sight, coupled with a woman's bold and witty wooing,
become shockingly misplaced both in the context of death and madness and when the principals are not young lovers but murderers and
adulterers. Light banter plays effectively against the situation's realities and lends power to the "romance's" concluding triple betrayal.

Julia here functions as more than the Duchess's foil. Like the comic
doctor, she represents a self-deluded, pleasure-seeking world that knows
nothing of the Duchess's life or death and remains unconcerned with
the nature of the power which provides its sustenance. Frivolously pursuing their own immediate goals, these people are insulated against the
horror that surrounds and directs them. Misfortune may be accepted
"philosophically," as it was by the pilgrims at Loretto, but most escape
knowledge of their world's real inhumanity or learn it only when they
suddenly become caught in the struggle, like the Duchess, Julia, and the
nameless servant dispatched by Bosola. Julia dies a pawn in a game she
did not even know existed; she is both pathetically innocent and also
part of the commonplace world that seeks, in public and private realms,
its own petty desires. Dying, she finds her life meaningless, yet like her
betters she cannot escape the void within. Unable to face what "should

have been done" in her life—" 'Tis weakness"—she dies an intellectually and morally coarsened version of Vittoria Corombona; she goes she knows not whither (v.ii.287–289). Like Vittoria, Julia retreats to the traditional moralist's pat explanations, but here such assertions ring particularly hollow; for betraying a murderer's confidence her own death hardly seems the "equal piece of justice" she claims.

In this lethal but trivial world the Cardinal plays a chief role. His cool, unemotional detachment is more terrifying than Ferdinand's impassioned raving. Almost inhuman, he requires neither the emotional satisfactions of affection nor the intellectual consolation of rationalizing his deeds. If Ferdinand claims too many motives, the Cardinal offers nothing beyond his agreement that the Duchess taints their noble Arragonian blood. Yet the shedding of his "blood" seems not to touch him. The murder lacks personal importance or the power to astonish him. Although he seems to occupy in *The Duchess of Malfi* Francisco's position of master politician, Webster's structure denies him Francisco's stature or control. The Cardinal shares with Francisco an existence predicated on intellectual mastery of a world whose total corruption he assumes; lacking Francisco's vitality and gleeful manipulation, the Cardinal seems rather an automaton than a trickster villain. Indeed, the narrow self-absorption marking his lost humanity now also ensures his comic downfall. Unable to see beyond the prison of his own nature, he becomes the inflexible victim of his own craft. Himself indifferent to the Duchess's murder, he assumes he can still employ the usual politic lies, the usual rearrangement of others to further his own dark ends. Offering the same old methods and expecting the same results, he promises Bosola that for one more "thing" in service he will "make you what you would be" (v.ii.115–117). When Bosola discovers him to be a "fellow murderer," the Cardinal still expects proffered fortune and honors to ensure his tool's loyalty. The smug certainty of psychological penetration and control no longer adequately corresponds to reality. Others now resist their place in the Cardinal's drama. Bosola has learned the practical lesson that suing to fortune is "the fool's pilgrimage." He can withstand the fearless image of the man who "bears up in blood" both because he guesses the Cardinal's real intentions—to hide his murderer's identity "i' th' graves / Of those were actors in 't" (v.ii.300–301)— and because the Duchess's very different image still haunts him.

The Cardinal's misprison is given comic scope: the arch-Machiavel churchman becomes the ridiculous and ineffectual plotter of farce, hoist with his own petard. The carefully, even comically elaborated instructions to his courtiers set up a practical joke on the world which kills him; we watch as his almost compulsive plotting weaves the web of destruction intended for others ever more closely about his own person. If earlier commentary portrayed him as a center of evil and corruption, act 5 defines him as a fool. In this new perspective we see him deceived by his own cynical reductionism, confident that his "tedious" conscience is his only worry since men will always act according to a few basic, manipulable emotions. Though the Cardinal begs for life, he dies under the merciless doctrine by which he ruled. The courtiers' mocking comments, highlighted by the good Pescara's single dissenting voice, only emphasize how completely the Cardinal's ethics guide his court.

In *The White Devil* Francisco's dominance, his final looming presence behind even the ending's hopeful coda, provides its own disturbing commentary. Although Webster's stylization sets the price of such detached control, the play's world by and large still answers to Francisco's assumptions; only in death do some characters come to doubt the values by which they all lived. In *The Duchess of Malfi* the villains are not merely unsuccessful in practical terms, they are dismissed by Webster's dramatic treatment. As powerful princes they can wield destruction, but in act 5 Webster's comic reduction undercuts their initial dark persuasiveness. In other ways, too, the later play suggests that the Machiavels' worldly ethic inadequately encompasses their world. Although the courtiers who laugh at the Cardinal's pleas remind us of the false friends who spurned Antonio's "decay'd fortunes," they do not fully represent either Malfi or Milan. Malatesta and other courtiers whom one can look quite through are balanced by Delio and Pescara. In *The Duchess of Malfi* goodness is neither relegated to peripheral commentators nor qualified by its own trite and formulaic generalities. Fallible worldlings perhaps, though for that reason the more persuasive, good men exist at all social levels and even, like Pescara, function successfully in positions of power. Though Bosola may betray the Duchess's trust, Delio and Cariola remain faithful, and (departing from his source) Webster has some of the Duchess's servants follow her in adversity. If loyal service without reward is known to this world, so is unfeigned friendship. Delio offers Antonio support in all danger, for friends' lives "keep rank" together. Pescara refuses to bestow upon his friend "so main a piece of wrong" as Antonio's "ravish'd" lands; he chides Delio to ask only "noble things of me, and you shall find / I'll be a noble giver" (v.i.44—54). Some courtiers, or a Julia, seek to "fortify themselves" with others' ruin, but Pescara displays an innate sense of justice that the play suggests men may either ignore or follow.

Such departures from the prevailing opportunism, together with a surprising persistence of conscience in even the most hardened Machiavels, should produce a world of comparative sweetness and light, one in which exterminating this particular nest of vipers might indeed leave man free to pursue his "better nature." Optimism is not, however, the play's dominant impression, and over Delio's last hopeful words hangs the shadow of the fifth act's uncertain, self-perpetuating world. Although man's moral freedom in smaller matters is given more emphasis in Webster's second play, individuals seem less able to command their lives or claim authoritatively to understand their world. The earlier play's oppositions dissolve into more widespread confusion. One of the fifth act's most striking features is the very lack of inevitability in its deaths. Moreover, while some characters accept their fates as just retribution for sin, others can find no meaning beyond chance in the final events of their lives. It is just this bumbling quality of purposes mistook and accidental judgments that keeps us aloof from assertions of supernatural direction, whether benevolent or malign.

Here, where either Bosola or Antonio might offer to penetrate the play's mist, Webster enhances rather than resolves perplexity. The Duchess found—created—self-giving love, trust, and even humility in a world where nothing, even language, is what it seems and all absorb themselves in self-assertion and preferment. Yet the two men she most vitally and creatively affected can draw no positive significance from her life or death. Both are as burdened by their past actions and habits of mind as they are liberated from their attempts to satisfy the world's demands. Far from being the just revenger Bosola contemplates joining, Antonio desires only an end to indecision and his nebulous, fugitive state. If, as Delio says, the Echo can be shaped to the speaker's wishes, Antonio makes it reflect his own desire for release.[26] Once a virtuous follower of stronger wills, he now presumes on "necessity" to compel him toward some resolution; in seeking a "fate" he cannot fly, he refuses the good counsel of Delio and the Duchess-echo. Though he says he wants reconciliation with the Cardinal, we watch an unarmed man walk meekly to his death.

Disillusionment saps Antonio's life even before he offers it to the Cardinal's "worst of malice"; more concerned with maintaining his own slippery footing, Bosola can find no positive direction for his devotion, only uncertain gropings toward an ethic of revenge. Individually they move in and out of the last act's loosely structured scenes, contributing their own uncertainty to the final grisly comedy. Bosola, man of action and professional murderer, rashly kills Antonio instead of the Cardinal and thus ironically fulfills the Cardinal's orders to the letter, though Antonio is the man he would most have spared. This last "direful misprision" caps a life spent misprizing value, and Bosola's habitual inclination to deny responsibility for failure finds immediate rationalization: "We are merely the stars' tennis-balls, struck and banded / Which way please them" (v.iv.54–55). The virtuous Antonio, others' passive instrument throughout, even more strongly feels himself the victim of a malevolent universe. Two such apparently different lives have brought these courtiers to the same blank despair.[27] For Antonio, too, "in all our quest of greatness . . . we follow after bubbles, blown in th' air" (v.iv.64–66). Despite his share in the domestic felicity from which the Duchess drew such strength, Antonio finds in that relationship neither positive countervalues nor even an intuition of real possibilities for meaning. Knowledge of her death for him merely confirms life's essentially penitential nature; its pleasures seem only the "good hours / Of an ague" that humanity is well out of (v.iv.67–69).

Each character dies bound to the life he has lived. The Cardinal prevaricates to the courtiers with his last breath; then, perhaps with a glance toward that family honor he has at least nominally been protecting, he asks to "be laid by, and never thought of" (v.v.90). Bosola, too, is the deeds' creature. His intuition of another philosophy, another way of life, has altered but also confused him, and the Cardinal perceptively notes that his murderer's "great determination" is "mix'd with some fear" (v.v.9–10). Though he can "glory" at the Cardinal's cowardice and in killing Ferdinand claim his "revenge is perfect," Bosola remains self-concerned and discontented. He dies rationalizing his own part ("much 'gainst mine own good nature"), complaining still of having been "neglected" (v.v.86–87).²⁸ Reckless fear and hatred of the Cardinal cause him to murder Antonio, but that death is unintelligible to him— "in a mist: I know not how" (v.v.94). New and old knowledges shape an impossible conclusion: the world's "deep pit of darkness" daunts fearful men, who are "only like dead walls, or vaulted graves, / That ruin'd, yields no echo"; yet men should also live moral lives, not fearing to "suffer death, or shame for what is just" (v.v.97–104). He knows, really, only that he has failed to respond to such a complex challenge, that the "good quarrel" has come too late and that his "is another voyage" (v.v.105).

Bosola's double vision of both depravity and possibilities for hope, the tempering of his earlier fatalism with a final affirmation of free and responsible choice, confirms our own ambiguous response to act 5 and its reflection back upon the play. The whole of the final act, and especially the echo scene, attests to the fact that men are not merely "dead walls." The echo of the Duchess affects all the principal characters, though only of Bosola might it be said that the effect was beneficial and illuminating.

Yet even here Webster clearly demonstrates a tragic sense both of man's personal limitations and of his world's distortion of individual attempts to coerce it into humanly satisfying shape. The larger world's resistance qualifies both Bosola's exhortation to virtue and Delio's sanguine expectations for "this young, hopeful gentleman." Delio's concluding assertions are as wide of the play's mark as Antonio's opening disquisition on the ideal commonwealth. In both public and private spheres, the just or humane life proves elusive. Bosola must be denied any prospect of worldly advancement or reward and forced, like Vittoria and Flamineo, to abandon his strong covenant with the world before he will face himself and his life's meaning. Then, bitter and needing a new source of moral direction, he identifies himself with the avenging sword of justice—with the spirit, that is, of the Duchess's curses. But the Duchess's last word was "mercy," and the Cardinal echoes her just before Bosola stabs him. The Cardinal, of course, is selfishly begging for the life he has so thoroughly forfeited, but his cry reminds us of those larger questions of value which the play has raised. Is there a place for mercy or love in this world? Delio introduces Antonio's son and heir in the hope that there is, yet both Ferdinand's fable of Reputation and Antonio's dying injunction that his "son fly the courts of princes" must give us pause. The "young, hopeful gentleman" may inherit only sorrow.

Our perplexed response to both the young ruler and Delio's final speech, our suspicion that perhaps nature seldom if ever fashions men "lords of truth," is heightened by our inability to comprehend the workings of the nature that presides over the play's world. Each character lives according to his own understanding of the natural and cosmic order and, taken together, they interpret their experiences in as contradictory ways as the play's critics. Webster's ironic structure, especially in the last act, only increases our uncertainty. If a cosmic order exists, allowing us to seek our lives' direction in the stars, then men have not found the proper means of communication: the son and heir whose horoscope predicted most horrible and early death is one of the few characters to remain alive at the play's end. If there is justice above— and *The Duchess of Malfi* offers this claim more support than the earlier play—then it operates as enigmatically and inefficiently as Albany's heavenly "justicers" in *King Lear*. In this world, too, "one thief hangs another" and the widow who violated social codes, the innocent servant, and their murderers all receive the same sentence. Yet set against such suggestions of chance or, worse yet, an indefinable "mist," we feel Bosola's assumption of the revenger's role to be significant. His execution of punishment, however distorted, not only illustrates his belief in an order of justice but also, by realizing that belief in action, in a sense demonstrates its existence.

The play itself seems to indicate neither an optimistic nor a totally pessimistic author, only one acutely aware both of life's possibilities, given man's potential for exaltation as well as self-delusion, and its ultimate mystery. Webster seems finally no more certain of the heavenly absolutes to which the Duchess kneels in act 4 than he was of the just moral order invoked by Cornelia, Marcello, and Giovanni in *The White Devil*. He is sure only of what men do to themselves, of the psychological effects of their own deeds. Each play demonstrates man's freedom to interpret his world according to his own predilections and limitations; his deeds in turn shape not only his own character but the world in which he acts. The relative optimism of *The Duchess of Malfi* depends less on the absence of a Machiavel lurking behind Delio's hopeful words than on the positive example, however qualified, offered by the Duchess's life: one character enacts a different "interpretation" or possible meaning only hinted in the earlier play. Bound neither by the moralists' rigid traditional codes nor the cynics' denial of all but self-interest, the Duchess ventures beyond that point, on the brink of self-realization, at which Vittoria and Flamineo die.[29]

If man does, partly, fashion his world, then the Duchess is more important for the new, unprecedented world she sought to create than for her proud refusal to recant when threatened with death. Looking for romantic comedy she finds instead a tragic world, one in which discovering possibilities for true creation arouses the opposition that will destroy it. Her stubborn courage both creates and jeopardizes her unorthodox relationship; the venture's success is affected by her personal human frailties and also undermined by external limitations of social position and her more powerful brothers' opposition. For the latter barriers she bears no responsibility, but over them she has little control; her attempt merely to deny them is both naïve and dangerous. Romantic naïveté characterizes tragic heroes as well as comic lovers, of course, and she continues to haunt us, and her survivors, because she eludes the meanings imposed upon her. She is not simply Ferdinand's lustful widow; she belongs neither to Bosola's revenge play nor to Delio's tidy melodrama.

The Duchess exemplifies the limits and triumphs of the tragic hero's paradoxical freedom; she also marks Webster's final alteration of heroic tragedy. As the titular, if not the only, protagonist, she is an unambitious woman, defined by basically bourgeois goals and committed to pettily hypocritical, irresponsible as well as foolish, means. Despite her soliloquy's proud defiance, she does not initially have a hero's stature. The aristocratic pride that leads her to assert that she can live or die like a prince is finally substantiated in her death; yet royal strength and willfulness coexist with the common physicality and domestic yearnings that lead her to choose her steward as husband and become "an excellent / Feeder of pedigrees." The world does not offer her an Antony or a Bussy, but neither does she seek heroic passion. Without the suffering that exposes illusions and ends in death she would have remained the reckless, happily self-indulgent woman who defied public responsibilities as well as her brothers' commands. Nobility appears only under pressure; then, unexpectedly, from her only partially realized and always threatened domestic idèal she draws the strength to withstand grisly and bizarre attempts to force submission or madness.

However unheroic her stature or the private and individual alternative she tries to forge, she shares with other tragic heroes the ability to discover value for which her world—and her own life—offers neither precedent nor example. Like them she seems initially other, and less worthy, than she finally proves herself to be. In the intimate domesticity of her longings she sounds the note not of Cleopatra but of newly wise Lear, discovering sufficiency in a walled prison with Cordelia, or the prematurely aged Macbeth who laments his destruction of the friendship and trust that make life meaningful. Yet neither her briefly glimpsed life nor her death in themselves suggest the scope or deep significance of Lear or Macbeth. The values for which the Duchess so nobly dies are not hard-won discoveries. She chooses them instinctively, and though desiring her rank and social position, she easily turns her back on the delusive attractions of power. Indeed, despite the effective immediacy of her three major scenes, the Duchess is kept as remote and distanced as Shakespeare's later tragic heroes. Her "story" gains full significance only in Webster's context, in conjunction with that opposite and "lover" who both qualifies and extends her private meanings.

In discarding Antonio in favor of Bosola, indeed fashioning him out of even skimpier source material than went into Flamineo's christening, Webster shows as much daring as in the portrayal of his resolutely unambitious heroine. He throws away Antony to accept an Enobarbus substitute and so redirects the possible triumph of romantic passion into a less exalted but also less exclusive sphere. Bosola's mocking voice bars our fully sympathetic involvement with the Duchess. As interposed commentator his cynical observations undermine her stature; as trickster-intriguer he finds her comically easy prey. Even more than Flamineo, Bosola in mid-play stands between us and the action. To a large extent Webster allows this "presenter's" stance to control our response, and he thus builds our identification with this surrogate audience. Witty, cynically realistic, detached, Bosola exhibits some of Enobarbus's charm and a good deal of his commonsensical persuasiveness in a world given to hyperbolic exaggeration. Like Enobarbus and Flamineo, Bosola brings himself close to us, for he represents the rationalizing spirit of accommodation in us all. He offers us the distance he tries to establish in his own life, that protective gap between the coolly observing self and the dangers of belief or commitment. He gains prominence as Ferdinand and Antonio fall away; he becomes the play's second protagonist and through him we participate in the Duchess's death. In his revaluation and transferred allegiance Bosola carries us with him and alters our sympathetic delight in the two lovers' witty poise and warmth. His gritty resistance to the Duchess's charms, his stubborn reluctance to admit her effect or renegotiate his life, set off but also blunt the melo-dramatic thrill of stoic majesty in adversity. Bosola survives, and his plight ensures our concentration not on the Duchess's brave death but on the meaning of the life that gave her such strength, on precisely what significance it can bear for us beyond its obvious private and individual value. Her courage becomes important less in its own right than in its effect on Bosola, for in refusing to accept or justify his materialist challenges she undermines his assumptions about man's nature and value. In both subjective and practical senses, Bosola's apparent mastery breaks down.

Through Bosola we discover in the Duchess a term, a humanity, between the play's melodramatic villainy and its foolish heroine's infuriating refusal to pursue heroic stature. As observer and actor Bosola both distances us and yet draws us into the play, even involves us in her torture and death. He discovers and in part exemplifies her larger significance, yet he also marks its limits. Finding no action worthy his dejection, Bosola moves away from us into his own mist. Indeed, to the extent that we have shared Bosola's viewpoint, we are relieved when Webster severs our dramatic intimacy. Yet as Bosola recedes into the shifting groups of act 5, Webster's structure forces us to share his sense of disorientation and emptiness: though separate from him now, we are in a strange and impersonal way more discomfitingly identified. Webster has locked us within the particular "game" into which Bosola had sought to turn his life, the practical struggle for subsistence drained of all moral meaning. The last act's farcical treatment of tragic motifs is grotesquely compelling, unsatisfying, and beyond easy dismissal. Webster has thrown away the glorious intensity of act 4, as well as a possible romantic double climax, to gain other ends.

The fifth act's mixed modes and extreme distancing bring it close to *The White Devil,* and through his last act especially, Webster qualifies the simplified, potentially sentimental exaltation of a young woman's martyrdom. Setting *The Duchess of Malfi*'s affirmations against farce's closed world of ultimately meaningless aggression, Webster enforces tragedy's characteristically double response. We assent to Antonio's and Bosola's final despairing vision: their own thwarted good, rather than her brothers' unregenerate hostility, most powerfully argues the fragility of the Duchess's triumph. Yet we also deny the adequacy of their self-limited, self-concerned conclusions. If the Duchess's dismissal of death establishes anything, it is that worldly success proves an insufficient measure of value, that the individual ego's pursuit of life and security (that suburb of hell) cannot in itself answer the heart's desires.

CHAPTER V

"The Devil's Law-Case"

ESPITE flashes of greatness, *The Devil's Law-Case* is not a felicitous successor to Webster's tragedies. Its disappointments are in some ways surprising, for in temperament and style Webster would seem well suited to write the kind of pithy, intellectually substantial and disconcerting tragicomedy that had earlier molded his own dramatic technique. Certainly, some of the play's characters and thematic oppositions do continue the tragedies' preoccupations while also recalling the most interesting tragicomedies of a decade before—most obviously *Measure for Measure,* but also *The Dutch Courtesan* and *The Widow's Tears.*[1] Yet Webster's last unaided play neither re-creates earlier triumphs nor forms a satisfactory valediction to his tragic *oeuvre.* Our sense of dissipated intensity, even confused purposes, may be attributable to waning interest in his own dramatic career, or to tragicomedy's generic resistance to Webster's always insecure command of overall dramatic structure, however brilliant the smaller scope of individual scenes and sequences. Perhaps his earlier, less than satisfying reception at the Red Bull did not inspire Webster to full creative exertion. Still, explanations probably lie as much in the age as in Webster. The increasing prevalence of Fletcherian tragicomedy in the seventeenth century's second decade may account for some of Webster's difficulties. Interestingly, Middleton, too, though another promising candidate in this field (as well as Webster's admirer and later collaborator), in these years wrote tragicomic plays that fall far short of his accomplishments and innovations in either traditional genre.[2]

Our disappointment need not breed contempt, nor should Webster's turning from tragedy's particular ambiguities lead to ruthless simplification. *The Devil's Law-Case* is not, as some of its defenders would have us believe, simply the frustrated moralist's retreat to a pat Christian *exemplum.*[3] Webster's characteristic perspectivism, his penchant for opposing generic as well as thematic structures, precludes any such homogeneous effect. Webster again stretches his action between the poles of pragmatic materialism and romantic idealism; he seems as interested as before in keeping us aloof from his characters' private certainties. Traditional moralists and cynical realists describe events by their own lights, but Webster again undermines the claim of either extreme to interpret his dramatic action authoritatively.

Given his ultimately comic designs, the play's opening is disappointingly thin; it lacks the witty snap of earlier Websterian dialogues. Yet though this fifty-line prologue goes somewhat clumsily about its expository function, it sketches not only Romelio's character but the play's moral oppositions. We enter the money-dominated, urban world of city comedy Webster had helped define over a decade before, where all action, even love, seems conducted with one eye toward economic advantage. Romelio represents this world and gives it voice. He perceives himself as enviably successful and preternaturally beyond fortune's sway; his smug confidence is also supported by a community that admires his "world of wealth" and dubs him the "Fortunate Young Man." A self-satisfied and phenomenally rich merchant, Romelio resembles and occasionally echoes Marlowe's Barabas, even before he self-consciously mimics the habit and rhetoric of his spiritual forebear.[4] He also recalls Tharsalio, self-dedicated to Confidence and his own pleasure (yet also concerned to advance his house), as well as Flamineo.

Romelio shares the tricksters' vitality, their witty cynicism, their narcissistic complacency; intellectual superiority and a "true" grasp of the world's ways confer the right to manipulate others and dismiss appeals to love or nobility as "superstitious relic[s]" (1.i.39). And like Flamineo, Romelio suffers from a central and comic delusion. Complacent egotism blinds him both to feelings beyond his simple reductionist philosophy and to the possibility of stronger, craftier wills than his own. What he cannot command, he ignores. Like Flamineo, Romelio becomes the politic Machiavel, the role he thinks most appropriate and powerful in a corrupt world. Above idealistic illusion himself, he will control others by penetrating their unexamined roles. Each character discovers that through his own *folie de grandeur* he has lost control of events and become another plotter's comic butt. Finally, fortune's darling is shown his limits, by the seas he thought to master and by the mother and sister whose tame obedience he assumed.

Romelio's proud security initially seems well-founded, his world safely knowable within his categories. Attractive suitors pursue his sister and believe his lies; Leonora satisfyingly confirms Romelio's mockery of his sister's romantic protests against his choice of husbands. Although reluctant, Jolenta can be led to accept the most advantageous match and, later, be driven to the despair in which she agrees to pretend pregnancy and legitimize his bastard. In addition, Webster sketches a world that shares Romelio's values and, like him, will employ any means to ensure private satisfactions. It is largely an opportunists' paradise, where physicians are amenable to murder and blackmail, and lawyers' fees, rather than the case's merits, ensure eloquence. Less threateningly, it also includes expected city-comedy type-figures (humorous and none-too-scrupulous servants and lawyers, the wisecracking young wastrel Julio) and alludes to other common butts (from lazy court ladies to commodity-hustling usurers). Hypocrisy, deception, defamation all figure prominently in the trial scene, but scattered references—such as to the Duchess of Nottingham's betrayal of Queen Elizabeth and Essex or the fact that best friends "oft" prove the husband's cuckolder (III.iii.295–300; IV.ii.199–201)—suggest a universal condition. This is a world inimical to love, where betrayal is certain and trust is folly. Even blood ties—a brother's care, a mother's love or curse—serve largely as manipulative handles on otherwise reluctant actors. Thus in a city-comedy fashion not unknown to Webster's tragedies, sex and money dominate the action and characters doggedly pursue their own wills, either through martial combat or more typically Websterian intrigue. Such pervasive egotism supports Romelio's casual cynicism and promotes detached manipulation.

Dissenting voices are present, to be sure. The good-hearted Prospero opens the play, and his avatars or echoes reappear at intervals to remind us of the traditional values elsewhere flouted. By and large, such conventional spokesmen no more effectively challenge the prevailing self-interest than they did in the tragedies. As either victims or observers, Prospero, the Capuchin, Angiolella, all stand outside the lively, fast-paced world on which they tritely comment. In Jolenta and Ariosto we come closer to real and viable alternatives, witty and flexible idealists capable of living with some gusto in an imperfect world. Yet Ariosto's limited effect is saved for the trial and final sentencing and, for all her occasional wit and boldness, Jolenta becomes her brother's dupe and fades from view. We are encouraged to sympathize with her romantic idealism, through both her own speeches and Winifrid's earthy support of youthful passion over calculating familial concerns. Yet we glimpse Jolenta's feelings only briefly, and her romantic declarations are framed by others' cynical disbelief. In plot importance Leonora overshadows and soon replaces her daughter, and Webster's confusing use of the suitors further blunts the effect of Jolenta's opposition to Romelio's philosophy as well as his plans.

Indeed, the gentlemen lovers constitute one of the play's stumbling blocks long before they so easily and shockingly acquiesce in the denouement's assigned pairings. Generally high-minded, Ercole undergoes an apparently genuine conversion; about Contarino we remain unsure throughout. Although in 1.i Prospero defends Contarino on the solid, traditional grounds of accomplishments, birth, and worthy love, we are never wholly certain that Contarino does not share Romelio's equation of "true worth" with "riches," ancient or modern. His devious courtship, his insistent use of mercantile imagery in describing Jolenta (not only to her brother, who views marriage as part of the "business‐ of life," but to her other courtly lover, Ercole), and the eulogy of Leonora that most praises her taste in diamonds all suggest that this dissolute gambler keeps his eye on the main chance. Though Contarino may return Jolenta's love, he also partly substantiates Romelio's cynical observation that his sister's "portion," not her deserts, has brought her noble suitors. Contarino apparently shares Romelio's low opinion of female constancy or judgment: worried by Jolenta's letter, which leaves him wondering if she has "chang'd," he fears she shares her sex's inability to distinguish flowers from weeds (1.i.224–226). Romelio, of course, believes others are as selfishly devoted to monetary and social gain as he, but his mother, too, assumes Contarino's love may be purchased. The play's final alliances offer romantic idealists small comfort.

Contarino and Ercole—and their function in the play's structure—suffer not from complex but from inconsistent characterization. At times they reinforce Jolenta's idealism and support the possibility of unfeigned love as well as friendship. Ercole's Petrarchan compliments and stiff formality contrast sharply and favorably with Romelio's and Leonora's bawdy witticisms at the reluctant Jolenta's expense. Ercole wants Jolenta's heart, freely given. Understanding only sexual or monetary goals, both mother and brother disbelieve her protests and unite in sacrificing Jolenta's happiness to their private ends. Contarino offers Romelio a brother-in-law's friendship as well as a family alliance, and the two courtly lovers themselves at times imitate Damon and Pythias. Yet, at least before Ercole's "death" and redemption, Webster also undercuts his gentlemen's stature as either lovers or friends; they often suggest rather a sophisticated hypocrisy like Gasparo's and Antonelli's in *The White Devil* than any substantial alternative to self-obsession. They sink back into a world in which only their courtly rhetoric distinguishes them from Romelio and the foolish braggart Julio. In the second act's challenge scene Ercole and Contarino slide rapidly from haughty claims of individual "rights" in Jolenta to protestations of a friendship that would divide this jewel if it could, and, finally, to suspecting each other's honor as duelists. Both challenge and fight become ridiculous, and the distance between high-flown words and either love or honor is emphasized by the setting—Ariosto's and Romelio's baiting of Julio, and the young wastrel's own bawdy commentary on lovers' wounds.

Comic types and comic expectations repeatedly qualify our sympathetic involvement and deflect us from serious ethical concerns. Leonora and Romelio snicker at a lover's modesty they do not understand. They rely on wit, not conventional morality, and their busy maneuvering makes comic melodrama out of Jolenta's preference for death before dishonor (1.ii.245–247). Sympathetic Winifrid belongs to their world, not Jolenta's, and she shares with Romelio a taste for bawdy jokes and worldly knowledge. Her banter with Romelio interrupts Jolenta's interviews with the high-minded lovers, and together Romelio and Winifrid suggest an exaggerated, madly lascivious world worthy of the Jonsonian comedy from which some of their lines are cribbed.[5] Winifrid has the earthy charm of Juliet's nurse and, very clearly, the true comic accommodator's spirit. A robust and frankly sensual accomplice of young love, she will also spy for Romelio and support whatever lies her mistress chooses· to perpetrate on the court. She is a great comic creation, and we delight in her as we do in Cocledemoy and Pompey Bum. With her, too, shameless high spirits simply dissolve the conventional moral structures aimed at containing them.

With Winifrid the light-hearted side of city comedy penetrates the chambers of lovers and plotters alike, and other characters and scenes support the kind of response she encourages. Act 2 opens on the stock situation (and hilariously idiosyncratic development) of a disguised parent spying on his spendthrift son. Not unexpectedly, Crispiano finds

Julio more concerned with his inheritance than with the loss of his father. More important, Crispiano, like Winifrid, embodies comedy's positive values—that zest for life which floats free of the moralist's ideal of virtuous self-abnegation. A lawyerly Romelio or Volpone, Crispiano revels in his own ingenuity, and his "soul's felicity" lies in practicing his trade superbly. Reversing the expected argument about work as opposed to pleasure, he wishes only that his son enjoy spending the family fortune as much as he delights in earning it. Even moralistic Ariosto is swept into the scene's exuberance, and he joins Romelio in taunting the cocky and unrepentant Julio.

As the plots thicken and issues darken, Webster strives to maintain this carefree comic surface. In act 2, challenge and duel are followed by their parodic counterpart in the witty sparring of Ariosto and Romelio and by "stoic" Ariosto's predictable yet still humorous loss of patience. We are more than once reminded of the specifically comic irony inherent in honest women determinedly counterfeiting dishonesty. Even in iv.i, Ariosto's conventional horror at Leonora's proposed suit is framed by Sanitonella's and Contilupo's eagerness to do or say anything for money. Here the generic security implied by stock characters and situations plays against the scene's potentially shocking content, and Webster repeats this witty balance in the trial itself (iv.ii). He later plays off the trial by combat and the Capuchin's earnest moralizing against Romelio's jests and Julio's irrepressible insouciance. The two venal surgeons are frequently pressed into similar comic service, and their movement toward blackmail provides a humorous contrast to Romelio's deepened Machiavellianism.

Indeed, although Romelio's intentions turn murderous and he irritatingly declares his villainy (an infelicitous lapse in Webster's dramatic self-confidence), he betrays no remorse or self-doubt. Rather, as the merchant becomes more dangerous he also approximates more closely the witty trickster-intriguer. Bankruptcy stimulates both his imagination and his sense of humor. Contemplating his disguise's possibilities, he defines his new actor-director identity by self-consciously parodying Marlowe's Barabas. Delighted with his "shadow," Romelio does, as he fears, "lose" himself in his Machiavellian part and in the intriguer's concern with witty style and surface manipulation. To use Eliot's words, the "savage farce" to which Romelio thinks to turn events indeed comes about, but on a scale that includes him as one of its comic butts.

Excepting the extraneous III.i, in which Ariosto and Crispiano deliver some ill-motivated remarks on the dangerous power and "mad tricks" of contemporary ladies, Webster seems on surer dramatic ground in acts 3 and 4. Ercole and Contarino, even the more appropriately moralistic Capuchin, drop from sight. The pace regains II.i's sprightliness, and plot development springs from the principal intriguers' competitive struggle to effect their wills. Other characters join Romelio's turn to' action and share his self-conscious concentration on intrigue's mechanics—the setting, supporting actors, and physical properties of their private dramas. At least superficially, the play dissolves into farce's duel of wits and its matching of plot with counterplot; Webster is most effective when his satiric exposure remains largely implicit and dramatic irony illuminates his moral concerns.

As Romelio's plans darken, Webster's play moves rapidly toward the comic reversal completed in III.iii. The gap widens between dramatized reality and Romelio's assumption of both his control and a steady progress toward the "advancement of our house." Self-gratulatory and puffed with success in convincing Jolenta to feign pregnancy, he never understands the significance of his mother's response to Contarino's wounds. He fails to notice that his sister's reason for believing Lenora's unnatural love points to a truth behind his bold fabrication: Jolenta remembers that since Contarino's wound her mother "has been very passionately inquiring / After his health" (III.iii.118–120). Romelio's very real naïveté is evident. While violating traditional morality himself, he still unconsciously holds some tenets sacred. He believes the lovers will be bound by conventional restraints which he can use to his advantage; above all, he assumes the sanctity of family ties in others— a willing sister, a predictable and respectable mother. Private folly provides comic capital as he brags to Leonora of dispatching Contarino and assumes the cause of her distress to be not her own love for Jolenta's suitor but her daughter's shameful pregnancy. Romelio laughs at his private joke, thinking he has duped both mother and sister, but the audience also laughs at his credulity. No longer dominant, Romelio slips into the larger pattern of self-defeating intriguers. By III.iii he has become another "mad," obsessed fool, and in the trial Ariosto's comic commentary on the son's false righteousness makes us laugh at Romelio's shock.

The Devil's Law-Case fairly overflows with plots, and each falls ludicrously short of the plotter's intentions. Romelio's plan for his sister's marriage is frustrated by the suitors' "deaths"; his murder of Contarino by an unexpected cure; his plan to "breed" advancement from that death by his own admissions and his mother's counterplot. Leonora circumvents Contarino's marriage to Jolenta only to lose her love to Ercole's sword; Crispiano's presence at the trial exposes her counterfeit dishonesty. Contarino's plan to win Leonora's approval of his marriage to Jolenta backfires because he misunderstands the mother's passion. The surgeons intend to blackmail Romelio; instead Contarino lives, Romelio is bankrupt, and Leonora declares her son a bastard. Although the Capuchin withholds the information that Contarino is alive in order to bring Romelio to remorse, he is fooled by a feigned penance and locked in the tower room.

The point is not that Webster solves problems of dramatic structure and meaning with the "nearly perfect order" of his plotting,[6] or that increasingly complex intrigues demonstrate a providential design by which God subverts mankind's base maneuvers and transforms them into a campaign to reclaim proud sinners.[7] Webster's interlocked plots tragicomically avert disaster and at the same time explore one of his most persistent moral concerns: that violation of basic human relationships which both causes and reflects the more general social corruption. Each of Webster's plays presents the effects of lust, greed, and ambition in a variety of relationships—parent/child, husband/wife, lover/mistress, brother/sister. Further, willful destruction of the family unit corrodes the bonds of love and duty that constitute society's moral foundation. While the particular disruptive passion may vary, all are rooted in the individual's solipsistic isolation. Cut off from the emotional support but also the restraints conferred by acknowledged human relations, individual desire and self-regarding will threaten anarchy. Wholly committed to his private drama, each ignores the common endeavor in which all human beings are perforce engaged.

The tragicomedy's principal characters are bound to each other by ties of love and responsibility which they refuse to recognize. Here, as in *The Widow's Tears*, the most important and complex violations occur within the central family. Romelio will buy the "advancement of our house" first with his sister's unhappiness and later with murder and the shameful ruse which would produce a spurious heir for Ercole's fortune; finally, though he scoffs at religion, he hopes a convent may prevent Jolenta's ever marrying. Dividing the family against itself, he defames his mother and purposely sets about "to nourish craftily this fiend / 'Tween the mother and the daughter" (III.iii.211–212). Leonora threatens to curse her daughter if a marriage with Contarino frustrates her own lust; she later schemes publicly to shame her son and disinherit him. More pawn than selfish manipulator, Jolenta is sufficiently inspired by her brother's behavior to feign pregnancy and further tarnish the family's reputation: she is called "strumpet" and denied her dowry at the trial.[8] Plots frustrate counterplots, and Romelio's family, like Tharsalio's, disintegrates as he pursues its advancement.

In the surface comedy of crossed purposes we enjoy observing self-important fools outwit themselves. Our dissatisfaction with the equally superficial concluding discoveries and realignment of characters springs in part from the depths Webster has suggested about human relationships, the disturbing ramifications of that farcical violence which also delights. *The Devil's Law-Case* not only threatens danger and then avoids death; in the manner of earlier ironic tragicomedy it also suggests, behind the lively manipulation of events, a less "comic" self-absorption whose graver consequences may not always be so wittily averted. In the social sphere, the most serious result of abrogating natural bonds occurs at the trial. The egotist's willingness to publish outrageous and malicious lies defeats the institutions intended to safeguard veracity and fairness among citizens. In the welter of ridiculous accusations and false testimony, truth is not merely lost, it is actively discredited. Possibilities for certainty or trust crumble. As Winifrid explains to the surgeon, Ariosto will not credit her new sincerity because "he has heard me tell / So many lies i' th' court, he'll ne'er believe me" (v.iii.20–21). When the false charge of bastardy is fortuitously disproved, the accusation of murder is suspected as another preposterous fabrication. This "lie" is substantiated by Ercole's certain "knowledge," though in fact chance has made Romelio the physician instead of the murderer. The willful subversion of truth beneath this comic confusion implies serious consequences which the tragicomic unraveling cannot wholly disperse.

When the ideal of truth between individuals and the sanctity of bonds disintegrate, civilized society becomes impossible. At the trial Crispiano notes the radical threat posed by Leonora's unnaturalness. Condemning her efforts to undo her son, he voices clearly and authoritatively Webster's fundamental moral assumption—that principle of "Compassion-ate Nature" recognized by Flamineo after his mother's dirge and hypo-critically used by Ferdinand to comfort the imprisoned Duchess. It is the "obedience of creatures" to this natural law that is "the stay of the whole world" (iv.ii.264–268). The restricted decrees of civil law are only possible because guaranteed by a common belief in and adherence to the unwritten behests of this more inclusive and inherent principle. In *The Devil's Law-Case* we only glimpse the effects when "that law is broke," but this glimpse must qualify any manipulated happy end-ing. However felicitously events transpire, the bonds of "Compassion-ate Nature" have been so mutilated that "natural" beliefs are shaken. Jolenta accepts Romelio's accusation against Leonora and Contarino. Ercole and Contarino readily misconstrue Jolenta's explanation of her pregnancy: after the trial's revelation of perverse affection, there is no reason to think a "natural" horror of incest would restrain anyone.

If natural laws within seem dead, it is not surprising that their ex-ternal social agents—the civil law and the church—should be ignored or flouted. Ariosto's honesty is repeatedly admired as a rarity, and both lawyers and litigants evince little confidence in or respect for the law. The friar's simple faith ill equips him to maneuver actively for virtue's sake. He cannot see into Leonora's twisted heart, and Romelio's false conversion thoroughly beguiles him. Romelio openly scorns the church's rites, while his mother quietly employs religion as a stalking horse for private goals. She thinks nothing of using the Capuchin to bind Wini-frid's compliance with her plot, and when her lies are discovered she casually declares her intention of entering a nunnery. Indeed, as a reli-gious ideal the monastic life is abused by Romelio, Jolenta, and An-giolella as well as by Leonora.

While the social consequences of pursuing individual desire are also important in the tragedies, in both genres Webster cares chiefly about the effect of this pursuit upon the family and its members. If self-absorption makes one willing to use any means for private ends, deeds also operate reflexively upon desire to produce a gradual, self-protective hardening of the heart. Although he more fully explores it in the trage-dies, Webster sketchily suggests in Romelio and Leonora this ironic self-limitation in the witty pursuit of greater freedom. Romelio's social and economic goals initially require no more than forcing his sister to an advantageous marriage. Some violation of her wishes and his responsibility for her happiness is involved, but, with Leonora's help, Romelio can ignore such compunctious promptings. Economic disaster soon challenges him to recoup by craft what he lost in security. Both a cure for his financial straits and the intellectual stimulation of devising appropriate stratagems are important to him, but urgency provokes a new and ruthless approach with Contarino. The slandering of his mother and disregard for his sister's honesty or reputation complete Webster's sketch of his merchant's increasingly restricted moral perception. Rather than doubt his means or ends, Romelio loses himself in the Machiavellian role promising the greatest monetary rewards. In the "meditation" in II.iii he self-consciously jests at religious burial, and the heartfelt contrition of v.iv becomes merely another part, a cynical act to put off the tiresome Capuchin. The Capuchin *is* tiresome, and Romelio's barbs (abetted by Julio's unrepentant frivolity) emphasize this trite moralist's inability to direct matters of life or death effectively. Yet Romelio's superficial wit also brushes aside any consideration of his own past deeds or present fallacious defense of his "innocence" in battle. Only the immediate possibility of death in a bad cause brings him to question, momentarily and unpersuasively, this willed callousness and to echo Vittoria's doubt about "whither I am going" (v.vi.9).

Leonora, too, moves from comic obtuseness toward extreme, even grotesque moral insensitivity. Initially a supporting actor in Romelio's plan, she encourages him for her own ends and threatens to curse her daughter if the marriage with Contarino is consummated. Romelio's boasts of having killed Contarino inflame and further distort her passion. Unmoved by her daughter's plight, Leonora cares only for revenge on her son: the ritualized denial of relationship, even their common humanity, dramatically emphasizes the self-consciousness with which she divests herself of human commitments. Dead to everything but her own obsession, she declares Romelio a bastard and brings public shame upon herself and her family. She is later indifferent to her son's life or death and wishes to halt the combat only to preserve her beloved: "O, the saving Contarino's! / His [Romelio's life] is worth nothing" (v.v.9–10).

Restless pursuit of solely private ends gradually erodes the individual's humanity. Webster here averts those murders which in the tragedies are so casually executed, but the intent and its inner poison is present. It extends to a willingness to sacrifice one's family, and the family is an integral part of the self. This essential integrity of the family unit—the basis of any wider recognition of all men as compassionate nature's brothers—and the idea that destruction here annihilates the self receive, to be sure, less emphatic treatment in *The Devil's Law-Case* than in either tragedy. Yet Cornelia's admonition to Flamineo is echoed in Contarino's promise to Jolenta not to hate her brother's interference, since "he's part of yourself" (I.ii.296). Where Bosola learned belatedly that rationalizing murder involves first killing one's own better nature, Romelio self-consciously fears to "lose" himself in his Barabas disguise. More generally, Webster insists in all three plays that one's humanity is bound up with recognizing human relatedness and that within the most basic social unit all individuals are in some essential way members of each other. Cutting oneself out of the family destroys the possibility of civil society. Corruption in society's values may constitute the apparent source of this familial dissolution, yet until these primary bonds are recognized there can be no regeneration in the external social order.

Although Malfi's Duchess represents a major exception, many of Webster's tragic characters recognize at their deaths what earlier they had denied. Deeds against others may in fact define one more fully than a cherished self-image, and one must accept those deeds' consequences in order to restore the internal as well as the external moral order. In *The Devil's Law-Case* that crucial recognition is either lacking or only partially realized, though such final self-knowledge would be particularly appropriate at a comic denouement. Instead, the final disposition of persons seems superficial and inadequate. After such passionate if misguided intensity, Webster smoothly and disturbingly relieves his characters of any suffering. The casual ease with which Romelio's marriage to his pregnant nun is enforced, and accepted, completes the emotional disjunction of deed and finale.

The Capuchin believes Heaven has redirected man's disastrous private dramas into one harmonious and encompassing comedy, but his happy certainty hardly quiets our suspicion that for Webster fundamental questions remain unanswered. Such conventional ascriptions have already been mocked by Romelio and the Second Surgeon as a "superstitious" attempt to explain fortune's blows as God's benevolent intervention (II.iii.69–74; III.ii.167–168). However suspect the speakers, their disbelief deliberately balances confident references to the "hand of heaven" at work everywhere. Moreover, though Contarino thinks God umpires his duel with Ercole, the apparently mortal wounds suffered by both combatants suggest a heavenly reluctance to interfere in matters of earthly justice. The trial by combat in the fifth act, where Ariosto explicitly asks heaven to "determine the right," is never completed. Angiolella's explanation of her fall as a cautionary *exemplum* accords with the Capuchin's view of life as a morality play, but Webster's own tragicomedy offers little support for the pat assumption of happy endings created by divine fiat. We expect, vainly, an achieved inner peace to redeem the individual characters' emotional avarice and to guarantee the externally imposed social order. If we accept the Capuchin as a spokesman for the playwright, we must blame Webster's withered talent or a special ineptitude in tragicomedy. Yet no more than Cornelia does the Capuchin have the last word. Webster's own dramatic choices have created our dissatisfaction and encouraged us to judge, not merely to accept with laughter, both his characters and their final alignment.

We have concentrated primarily on the maintenance of Webster's comic surface, right up to the flippant request with which Julio almost closes the play. Supporting the more disturbing undertones, a number of frequently moralistic local techniques help to counteract the central action's farce tempo and carefree maneuvering. We enjoy the comedy, but Webster ensures our final discomfort. Although sometimes awkward and intrusive, contrasting perspectives repeatedly mark off the proper response to unnatural behavior by offering shocked reactions, such as Ercole's to Leonora's curse (I.ii.108–109) or Contarino's condemnation of the way Romelio has betrayed their friendship (I.ii. 273–276).[9] More subtly, the dehumanization implicit in Romelio's narrow monetary standard—earlier masked by witty cynicism about honor, nobility, and love—is emphasized by the trial's stark commercial language. As a disowned son Romelio is a "base coin" whom Contilupo "will sell . . . to any man / For an hundred chickeens, and he that buys him of me / Shall lose by th' hand, too" (IV.ii.144–146). Indeed, Romelio himself implies the standards by which he should be judged. In v.iv his pose as penitent sinner, meditating over his own coffin, concludes with forgiveness of others as the "way / To be forgiven yonder" and a belief in the vanity of man's ambitious "glory" (v.iv.148–152). Although the "miracle" of his "melted . . . heart of adament" turns out to be a joke on the Capuchin, the "part" provides more than comic preparation. Its enactment, however later denied, heightens our sense of

Romelio's—and others'—need for just such a miraculous change of heart.[10]

Implicit judgments thus reenforce both the Capuchin's traditional Christian maxims and Crispiano's and Ariosto's more generalized moral condemnation. In Ercole, Webster seems to suggest by example an alternative response to frustrated desire. Urged by the punctilious honor that Julio and Romelio ridicule, Ercole eagerly opposes Contarino in a violent, "fatal" duel. Restored to life, however, Ercole discovers a less self-centered love: penitent, he will live as the chronicle of his dead friend's nobility. He will marry the girl for whom they fought even though she apparently carries Contarino's child because, to his changed heart, "There never was a way more honorable / To exercise my virtue. . . . I never liv'd to do good act but this" (III.iii. 344–345, 361). He has learned the nature of true friendship: when Contarino finally throws off his disguise the delighted Ercole cries, "You were but now my second; now I make you / Myself forever" (V.vi.23–24). Ercole's brief appearances break the pattern of increasing self-absorption and aggression which leads to desperate, frenzied action in others. The contrast becomes explicit at the trial. Answering Ariosto's wonder that the animosity which provoked a duel should turn to defense of Contarino's honor, Ercole admits " 'Tis true; but I begun to love him / When I had most cause to hate him" (IV.ii.604–605). The morality on which society and compassionate nature depend is founded on that divinely disjunctive "but."

Ercole does not offer a strong contrast to the self-seeking world of *The Devil's Law-Case*. His appearances are infrequent and often awkwardly intrusive; he is also sketchily characterized and too cursorily differentiated from his friend and rival. Rather, the change of heart prompting him to virtuous action contributes to a suggestion, fully embodied in no one character, of the attitudes necessary to transform a world of social intriguers. Although less successfully than Marston in his handling of Crispinella and Tysefew or Chapman in his treatment of Lycus, Webster, too, offers some viable and attractive alternatives to his play's most extreme spokesman. Perhaps too allusively, he strives to suggest a moral center equidistant from the egoists' pragmatic vitality and the conventional moralists' prim disapproval.

The urban setting and generic cues of *The Devil's Law-Case*, as of earlier ironic tragicomedies, support an active, sometimes farcically frenetic world. Neither religious sequestration nor flight seem a possible or even desirable solution to social corruption. However falsely directed, activity and the full exercise of one's wit and ingenuity are at the center of the play's meaning as well as its source of entertaining suspense. Despite the Capuchin's emphasis on death and damnation, *The Devil's Law-Case*, like *The White Devil*, revels in worldly activity amid the temptations of wealth, power, and rank. Early in the play, Romelio affirms that the "soul was never put into the body . . . to stand still," and he defends to Contarino an active "honor," to be won individually through the virtuous exercise of one's own profession (whether soldier, scholar, or merchant) rather than inherited by noble birth (I.i.69–76). Romelio's argument fits the play's spirit and, like him, *The Devil's Law-Case* "labor[s] for life, for life!" (v.iv.63). *Contemptus mundi* is not the play's motto or goal. Rather, the threat of death or the possibility of love should awaken its protagonists to the self's real needs and proper aims.

Throughout the play, Webster shows energy perversely expended while simultaneously hinting an opposite, ideal activity. Romelio's obsessive accumulation of wealth distorts his eager enjoyment of the activity by which it is procured; finally, desire for possession and a desperate need to maintain his proud supremacy destroy any moral concern with the honorableness of the means employed. With Crispiano, Webster moves closer to an embodiment of virtuous individual action that in turn benefits society. Crispiano evinces no interest in the actual possession or conspicuous expenditure of his wealth; his "soul's felicity" lies "in the getting of it" (II.i.23–24). He shares with Romelio a trickster's delight in exercising his intelligence to outwit others, and the golden fees merely confirm his superiority in his profession. The echo of *Volpone* may not be wholly fortuitous, however;[11] while virtuous, Crispiano's activity is limited in scope and beneficial effect. His satisfaction is still bound to its tangible reward, and he remains unconcerned that his foolish profligate son wishes only to squander his patrimony in riotous living.

Wholly concerned with justice rather than his own successful legal practice, Ariosto stands as the only clear contrast both to Romelio's prostitution of his considerable intelligence and to the usual lawyers' and physicians' simple greed. Uninterested in monetary reward or the world's praise, Ariosto has found moral security beyond the quicksands of ambition, greed, and lust in which so many other characters are mired. Ariosto's moral effect is perhaps blunted by his clowning in scenes 1 and 3 of act 2 and as Romelio's unwanted "counsel" at the trial, yet he at least remains a fully realized, vital individual. In addition to his passionate concern with society's present health, he exhibits that liveliness and sense of humor so woefully lacking in the obtuse Capuchin and the wooden convert, Ercole.

Wealth and the false values it encourages are not, of course, the sole agents of this world's moral confusion. As Leonora tells her maid, she has for forty years indolently wasted herself "with talking nothing, and with doing less"; life has slipped away, "spent . . . in that which least concerns life, / Only in putting on our clothes" (III.iii.409–411). Dedication to courtly pleasure has produced good words "but no deeds." When frustrated passion at last drives Leonora to act, the exercise of her wit corrupts her maid, destroys her family, and introduces a public chaos that threatens to erase distinctions between truth and falsehood. Leonora shares her son's glee in "unimitable plot[s]" (III.iii.426), but activity in itself is no more a solution to personal fulfillment or social health than is monastic retreat. Action centered only on the self here produces a lighter version of that macabre comedy of errors which concludes *The Duchess of Malfi*. Although Francisco's demonic intelligence hovers over and directs *The White Devil*'s final bloodbath, in the later tragedy myopic personal vision and uncontrolled passion create a dance of death beyond individual, and perhaps providential, control. There, self-absorption is literally self-destruction, and even Bosola's good resolutions are twisted by the man his past actions have made him. In *The Devil's Law-Case* the fatal end toward which selfish action leads is (somewhat clumsily) averted, but the efficacy of even good intentions remains problematic. Ercole's defense of his "dead" friend produces the challenge to another bloody combat; Winifrid's confession is almost wasted; Romelio's unrepentant craft defeats the Capuchin's religious scruples about disclosing Contarino's recovery before the merchant's conversion.

The transformed heart and its attempt to enact new purposes, at first bumbling, are crucial to any real regeneration of Neapolitan society. Despite the play's disturbing undertones, sustained at the close in Contarino's and Jolenta's inexplicably altered affections as well as in Julio's and Romelio's failure to demonstrate signs of the generically appropriate reformation, Webster holds out some hope that the heart can change and human beings act on considerations beyond self-interest. In the comic wooing scene between the surgeon and his new love, Winifrid, Webster suggests the possible fruit of such alterations: beneficial social action and a reestablishment of humane values. The surgeon's joke about making Winifrid an "honest" woman wittily inverts the usual cynical meaning: honesty now has social and moral significance beyond the saving of reputation. Winifrid has perverted truth and civil law at the trial and earned her "filthy report"; to recapture her "good name" now she must "do some excellent piece of honesty" (v.iii.10−12). Good deeds, to match good words, must replace hypocrisy and the giddy changes of private passion. More persuasively than with Ercole, Webster suggests through the delightfully fallible Winifrid a comic norm (if no ideal) and reminds us of the human capacity for truth and "kindness" as well as for trickery and self-deception.

Webster refuses to gloze the difficulty of this apparently simple and unoriginal solution: external forces cannot change the human heart. Plots and counterplots have been the agency of both entanglement and final deliverance. That the self-interested intriguers should fail is comedy's form of justice, and Ariosto's final decrees complete the impression that some form of order has been restored. Yet this restoration is precarious and clearly provisional. Tragicomic finales often knit loose ends together rather hastily, and *The Devil's Law-Case* is surely no exception. Even more clearly than in earlier ironic tragicomedies, however, the final sentences here recognize both the urgent need for transformation and society's inability to legislate those radical inner changes necessary to personal and social harmony.

Romelio is forced to marry his pregnant nun, to make an honest woman of her in the most mechanical social sense. The other punishments are economic and hence fitting only in the sense that mercenary motives have been so prominent a cause for selfish action. Society's decrees may be satisfied without the change of heart necessary for regeneration and true stability. The law clerk Sanitonella as well as the carefree wastrel Julio remain unaffected by the play's events; Leonora's and Romelio's silence during the final sentencing leaves the extent of their self-knowledge and remorse in question. Ariosto knows his limits: the good judge can only hope that escape from egotism's "threaten'd ruin" has taught a new humanity, that the participants' "future life may make good use / Of these events" (v.vi.92–93). The "rotten ground" which promised personal loss and public chaos can be secured only by recognizing those inner natural laws which enforce relatedness and acceptance of responsibility, to others as well as to the self. If benevolent powers watch over and direct the human comedy, they ensure neither an earthly harmony nor individual salvation. At best, they offer conditions that permit individuals a second chance to find themselves.

Despite comedy's happy ending and nuptial prospects, the worldly condition of virtue, love, and truth remains frail. Renewal depends upon those private transformations which alone can guarantee society's health. Although in his tragedies the introspection forced by death brought an affirmation of that compassionate nature denied in life, Webster refused to bolster those hopeful realizations with the artificial comforts of full poetic justice. *The Devil's Law-Case* turns aside from death, yet its implications are not notably more optimistic. As in other ironic tragicomedies, tensions earlier sustained by dramatic means persist in the resolution. The ridiculous plots and delightful, Rabelaisian gusto with which characters pursue selfish ends are both funny and disturbing. The perspective is "comic," but it nevertheless reveals a progressive disintegration of natural bonds under the pressure of greed and lust. In several adamantine hearts substantive changes, rather than mere accommodation, remain problematic. Yet Webster insists that only through these weak, vacillating beings can individual relationships be restored and society renewed. As humanity's proper activity, the life of virtuous deeds can neither be imposed nor legislated. It must be discovered and affirmed by the wayward individual himself.

The World Within

E B S T E R himself invited comparison with his most famous contemporaries, and if I have not strictly followed the list that prefaces *The White Devil*, I hope this attempt to read Webster in his chosen context has helped clarify his involvement in some of the most exciting dramatic developments of his period. Old-fashioned neither in form nor content, both Webster's moral attitudes and his experimental dramaturgy grow out of the social, philosophic, and artistic concerns that dominated his best contemporaries' work. His apprenticeship, if not his maturity, was served in the explosive first decade of the seventeenth century, a period of intense, competitive interaction between public and private theaters as well as between individual dramatists; his later, unaided work draws on such generic experimentation and its products, plays that are iconoclastic and unsettling in both form and tone.

In seeking formal expression of his own vision, then, Webster reflects and extends in dramatic terms one aspect of his period's intellectual and artistic ferment. Historical studies of Mannerist style note its distinctive fluctuating tone, its use of intrusively shocking content and displays of self-conscious technical virtuosity to encourage both engagement and detachment; more psychologically oriented investigations treat disjunctive form as an expression of spiritual crisis. Stylistic innovation constitutes one reply to the failure of inherited artistic structures fully to satisfy contemporary needs. New forms both explore and are themselves responses to more general cultural and historical turbulence. A wide spectrum of Jacobean plays, even those as intellectually unsatisfying as Beaumont and Fletcher's, reflect this subjective turmoil in their technical and generic mixtures. In the dramatists' preoccupation with detachment's aesthetic as well as moral effects, philosophic interests merge with more purely literary fashions. Dramatic technique strains to alter the audience's response to traditional materials and conventional structures. Manipulation of aesthetic distance becomes a major structural and investigative tool, and formal experiments in distancing complement thematic ones.

On both public and private stages, new blends of comedy and tragedy explore those problems of distance which seem central to the period's philosophic restlessness. Seeking a stance capable of dealing with ambiguities of character and situation, these generically innovative plays propose variously successful intriguers whose mingled common sense and calculation continued to fascinate us and whose disturbing implications Webster further explored. They reexamine, and reject, the solution Altofront-Malevole had seemed to offer: a disguised prince objective enough to understand and intelligent enough to manipulate and even convert his enemies. Master of any style, his final success reestablishes both the style and values that the new dispensation had apparently overthrown; witty and adaptable, he conquers the Machiavel's weapons and places them in the service of traditional morality. However attractive the "white" Machiavel's solution, tensions implicit in his methods find immediate development in less hopeful tragicomedies. The cool disengagement that promised both psychological safety and external control, witty vitality and worldly success, comes under scrutiny as the new age investigates its own ideal.

Seeing through hypocrisy, pedantry, and the delusions of fools, society's critics now retreat and adopt a realistic philosophy denying the possibility of either nobility or self-transcendence. Society now provides no acceptable comic norm. Less than ideal, it becomes an active antagonist demanding conversion or acquiescence. Its smug mediocrity at best, and hypocritically filmed-over corruption at worst, provoke the protagonist's revolt and deepen our sense of the split between self and others, private needs and public satisfactions. Disillusioned with his world and unable to shape it to his will, the intelligent intriguer turns aggressively self-protective. Although society tries to enforce the union of appearance and reality, denounces playing with language and appearance as wrong, the unillusioned man enjoys the vigorous and elaborate play of self and roles. Through wit and self-conscious theatricality he tries to evade the moral and social categories he sees as inadequate. The cynic turns self-reflexive and with witty indifference resists serious endeavor and society's traditional moral imperatives and judgments. The self-referential farceur joins hands with the political Machiavel. Recognizing in man or nature no inherent morality, each accepts this world and its rewards as the only certain value; each finds in self-preservation and self-promotion humanity's chief "moral" obligation. He challenges society and tries to wrest from it, and from those depersonalized others of whom it is composed, some satisfaction of his private desires.

Tragicomedy's manipulators are happy with their engineered endings, although we are not. The playwright has shown us that the world they see is restricted and that what they exclude is of great value: the kind of loving commitment so attractively dramatized in Crispinella and Tysefew and suggested, though certainly not embodied, in Lysander and Cynthia. Instead, in order to interpret and control his world the intriguer disentangles himself from inhibiting commitments and injunctions; he adopts the coolly impersonal "knowledge" and amoral objectivity his urban, competitive life seems to reward. Accepting the world's perspective allows him to impose on it a form—*his* form, his plot; in defining the world he defines himself. Superficially, success is his. Material prizes are gained without loss of identity or vitality, and the individual apparently acts efficiently while eluding the lifeless categories into which society has forced others. Yet what seemed to offer a heady new freedom, to liberate the modern individual from outmoded codes of behavior and evaluation, proves unsatisfactory, in a new way even more constricting. Utter flexibility, the willingness to be whatever the immediate occasion demands, preserves no uniquely vital identity; indeed, it threatens dissolution. Trying to hold the self aloof while accommodating one's virtues to the time's demands proves impossible. Being a "man o' th' time" finally justifies the social order from which one had revolted and leaves the individual dedicated to the very trifles he had disprized. The loss or absence of a central self whose integrity lies safely beyond the pragmatists' quotidian accommodations—which we suspect in Freevill, Tharsalio, and perhaps Duke Vincentio—is starkly dramatized in Vittoria's and Flamineo's final despair. When the chameleon roles fall away, nothing is left.

Ironic tragicomdey shares with tragedy a devotion to exploring and renovating the terms by which the life we share may be considered moral and not just a community in the most mechanical and mercantile sense. Its failed resolutions signal the need for tragedy, for the kind of exploration and affirmation that we associate with Shakespeare's tragic masterpieces. The tragedian grants the "realistic" philosophy's pragmatic efficacy—in Monsieur, Octavius, and Aufidius as well as in Francisco—and allows its reasonable perspective to challenge his play's tragic issues and its protagonist's self-proclaimed stature. Something like the farceur's point of view repeatedly distances us from the tragic hero and suggests he is no great-souled visionary but merely comedy's self-deluded absolutist writ large. Yet the tragedian must also suggest that such wholly materialist assumptions wrongly, or inadequately, explain humanity's nature and value. In predicating universal competitive and aggressive motives, such a philosophy is like the spectacles Flamineo describes to his brother-in-law: they color all he sees with the same jaundiced tinge. Disengagement protects against suffering, but it also severs those commitments to external reality that make life meaningful. It values liveliness, intelligence, and vitality, and promises situational mastery, but in successfully accommodating us to a fallible, earthbound reality it also threatens the very values it aimed to ensure.

Heroic tragedy's protagonist admits no limits. Disdaining prudence and calculation alike, he seeks total self-realization and demands that reality fulfill the most ambitious of the heart's desires. The heroic image—an impossibly expansive ideal of self "past the size of dreaming"—reveals its limits when applied to the complex and fallible world of mortal men. Foolishly, the protagonists give to a metaphysical idea of freedom and self-fulfillment a local habitation and a name; they chase a tangible form which can only betray their dream. They are, moreover, victims of their own distorting ideals as well as of their imperfect environments. Their contradictory humanity stands between them and a self-proclaimed apotheosis; they are estranged from themselves as well as from others. Bussy D'Ambois, Antony, and Coriolanus display an acute consciousness of the requirements of the heroic image they have set themselves, and they act out this role to themselves as well as to their mocking antagonists. Final disaster confronts them with a physical failure they cannot argue away and so forces self-knowledge; up until this rude awakening they are deaf to others' criticisms and blind to any view of themselves that violates their mirror's image.

Partly, we find these protagonists so intensely alive and valuable because we respond to the quality of their illusion: we are awed by the visionary power of an ideal of nobility, or goodness, or unhampered freedom of the will that sets them apart from the soldiers, time-servers, citizens, and cautious relatives who surround them. They defy their critics' categories of virtue or vice, nobility or folly; they are not "of" their world, though they mistakenly try to find their happiness and identity within its institutions and available roles. Seeking public recognition, the validation of his private image in political power and social approbation, the heroic individual compromises and threatens those very qualities we prize. A corrupt society is no longer the guardian and judge of value, but to exceed its prescribed bounds shows a "fearful madness" compounded of weakness and strength. Fatal and at the same time salutary, it frees the protagonist from society's restricted perception and limitations on passionate commitment. In a world of shifting evaluations and pragmatic ethics, the protagonist must create the values by which he is to be judged: the heroic vision he cannot fulfill, the potential for a moral knowledge and acceptance of human bonds and responsibilities he refuses to pursue. Such men must be forcibly released from their strong hearts' bondage to this world before they can discover within themselves a source of meaning or finally declare themselves independent of public judgments. Our fascination derives as much from the way in which they fall short of their ideal as from their inability to transform their world by either rhetoric or force. Demanding a life worth living, they must find one worth dying for.

The heroic protagonist's failure of his own ideal as well as his society's demands is bound up with his private relationships to a remarkable degree. Indeed, sexual and familial affections dominate the world of Shakespeare's and Chapman's heroic tragedy. Strong women prove disastrous influences: they lure men from their epic mission and threaten soldierly supremacy; they tempt their men to turn politician and "flank policy with policy." Yet in exploding the hero's isolation and helping destroy his initial, martial identity they are also the means to whatever nobility beyond Herculean heroics he attains. They demonstrate the hero's confusing complexity: any single perception of him, whether his critics' reduction to comic stature or his own monolithic ideal, proves too narrow for his contradictory vitality. They also show us the hero's real singularity, for he is not simply nostalgia's spokesman for an impossibly outmoded warrior ideal. It is in the quality of his passionate involvement with others that the heroic protagonist stands, finally, opposed to the realist politicians who successfully destroy him.

These men fail—or feel they have failed—their life's challenge. As epic hero, each has tried to act as if a god alone while retaining his personal integrity. They exemplify the absolutist's inflexibility, but also his emotional grandeur in refusing to accept an expedient nobility. Finally, from the very traits they could not subdue to their chosen part's demands, they draw the moral strength to scorn their executioners. Paradoxically, in defeat they find a greater humanity, one capable of expressing, momentarily, an awesome harmony of all their complexly human and discordant elements. Unable to give substance to the epic hero's superhuman image, they also transcend its limiting contours. They die accepting a full and responsible humanity, their great souls worthily expended in conquering that self-division required of both successful heroes and politicians. In the end, there is no world elsewhere, only within. In discovering that world for us, if not for the play's survivors, these protagonists refuse to make the farceur's accommodation, to accept man "as is." Each fails to be his own hero but learns to be human, a much more difficult and unsatisfying identity.

In ironic tragicomedy we are haunted by the social consequences of forfeiting the ideal, of looking no higher than we can reach. In Shakespeare's and Chapman's heroic tragedies we see the individual cost of refusing the pragmatist's common sense, yet also see that the realist's world, expediency's reward, is indeed "common" and insufficient. Webster's witty intriguers stand in no danger of the tragic hero's spiritual obstinacy: resourcefulness and adaptability are their watchwords.[1] Their ambitions are more material; their goals of freedom and power are tied more explicitly to wealth and social position. (Even the Duchess's ideal of love finds expression not in trying to define the inexpressible through hyperbole, but in the solid facts of marriage—in a husband and children.) Webster's plays deal openly with the disturbing effect of wit's disengagement, its pliable and "realistic" outlook; his cynical antiheroes lack the vision of human possibility that sustains and illuminates the perplexing careers of Shakespeare's and Chapman's epic figures.

While the heroic vision may linger in the Jacobean period, social and political beings usually seek a more profitable control through manipulating the "natural," observable human laws of self-interest and survival of the wittiest. Like Octavius, Aufidius, or Monsieur, Flamineo and Bosola renounce any ideal of moral constancy or meaningful action. They adopt a conveniently limited role, one demanding less complex responses than those of which they finally prove themselves capable. In choosing to follow and emulate their Machiavellian double, they eagerly adjust themselves to the material world he prizes and seek their freedom in its rewards. In another context, Robert Heilman has said that an "unwillingness to accept the burden of being human means a minimizing of the morally and spiritually possible."[2] Webster's pragmatists seek such a diminished burden. In tragedy's real (because historical) world they attempt to exercise the moral as well as aesthetic prerogatives of farce. Steeling themselves against suffering and disillusionment, they must discover a capacity to suffer before reaching such knowledge as their last moments afford. They spend their plays learning they have a humanity to betray.

In this altered key, Webster continues Shakespeare's and Chapman's experiments in heroic tragedy, their interest in developing tragic significance out of conflicting generic perspectives and demands. Shakespeare's and Chapman's heroes steadily fall in our estimation, as the man behind the mask of greatness is revealed, only to rise again to a new, qualitatively revalued heroism. To prepare us for a tragedy of which the characters themselves believe corrupt humanity incapable, Webster must reveal his protagonists to be more, not less, than their own self-image. We must be led to see Flamineo and Bosola as panderers and murderers and yet also as frustrated moralists desperately suppressing the "knowledge" that would stifle action; Vittoria must seem selfish and willing to sacrifice husband, honor, and brother to her ambition and yet totally unlike the conventional whore of Monticelso's "character." Though their deeds subject them to the politicians' sanctions, they are not understood and cannot, finally, be commanded by the categories of self-confident Machiavels, time-servers, or moralists. They must learn, under pressure, to see the limits of their simplifying ethic; they must recognize the loss that detachment could not successfully trivialize and accept the burden of being fully human. They are at once a moral yardstick for their societies and, in subverting their own moral intelligence, both victims and examples of its corruption.

Flamineo, then Bosola, learn what both tricksters and Machiavels evade: each discovers that his liberating philosophy has in fact restricted self-expression, its certain "knowledge" left him empty and confused. The immaterial offered no hope in life, and at death the heavens reflect only the narrowness of his own prison. The screen he had interposed between us and the play's staged life dissolves, even as he drops the private barrier interposed between himself and the existential dilemmas of his own life. He loses distance on himself, and we face with him the hard mystery at life's core. With Flamineo especially, we are inside the straitened chambers of the cynic's fallen world; with him, we look briefly but longingly out at the world of human possibility, where we want to be.

Such a brief moment of truth brings no self-transformation, no triumphant harmony of inner contradictions. Moreover, in laying bare the dizzying, self-destructive world created by the Machiavel's practical realism, Webster stretches his generic experimentation and almost destroys the affective seriousness of his plays' ends. Although most completely in *The White Devil*, in both plays Webster's distinctive energy and power depend on fusing a tragic conception with farce's combination of amoral humor and witty inventiveness, and this fusion abides in the plays' conclusions. In *The White Devil*'s burlesque double "suicide" and in the final grotesque misprisions of *The Duchess of Malfi*, Webster farcically inverts the cool mastery that detachment and manipulative calculation seemed to ensure. In such bizarre night-pieces, all seem lost, equally distanced by the same comically lethal violence. Some distinctions remain, however. Stylized, even caricatured politicians do not become less powerful, or mere "painted devils," but they do reveal the cost of their obsessive ambition in human terms. Webster's would-be Machiavels escape their executioners' fully restricted humanity by accepting what they have suppressed and by facing, however briefly, the extent of their loss. From self-absorption and its progressive erosion of individuality Webster's protagonists, soon or late, declare themselves free.

The White Devil's dominant movement is toward a more profound rigidity; its protagonists' vibrant and irrepressible intelligence is extinguished. *The Duchess of Malfi*'s concluding events imply a more optimistic flexibility, despite the failure of the Duchess's life fully to transform Bosola or reach out to change the court. Instead of *The White Devil*'s discouragingly circular development, in which the final opposition of views echoes the deadlock of I.ii, the survivors in Malfi are granted a fresh start, one whose promise depends on the way corruption at the wellspring is destroyed. Bosola discovers a freedom Flamineo had lost. Despite his claim to be the stars' plaything, his confusion and uncertainty in the new revenger's role, Bosola gains some control through his willed refusal to accept the Machiavels' system of value and reward.

His action transforms "realist" politicians into over-confident fools and places them in the comic predicament which threatened Shakespeare's and Chapman's heroic protagonists. The play's optimism is guarded, its limits suggested by Bosola's disinclination to renounce worldly advancement, by his choice of the violent revenger's role, and by the problematic status of virtue and mercy in the new court. Still, Bosola asserts freedom and moral accountability as well as fatalism; he discovers through the Duchess new values and new meanings for "service." His claims, together with the Arragonian brothers' comic reduction, suggest that the egoists' pragmatic credo is not only dehumanizing but foolishly naïve, a species of comic self-delusion as well as a literally fatal mistake.

Heroic tragedy in Shakespeare and Chapman alters the old solitary-warrior ideal, and Webster extends this turn from simple martial and amatory prowess in his resolutely domestic and unheroic Duchess. If his antiheroic intriguers explore the inner cost of political pragmatism and reasonable goals, the Duchess's final integration of nobility and maternity, willfulness and humility, recalls his mentors' interest in self-transcendence as well as self-defeat. Despite her lowered rank and restricted court sphere, the Duchess, like Antony and Cleopatra, finds her goals unattainable but not unworthy. These protagonists all pass beyond recognition of failure. Under pressure they forge a new image; they momentarily fuse the seemingly incompatible elements whose disparate claims destroyed them. Tragic protagonists generally play the defiant dying hero for their executioners' benefit, but Antony, Cleopatra, and the Duchess of Malfi have a heavenly audience whose expectations they must also fulfill. As catalyst to an understanding beyond the worldly wisdom that makes each person his own god, life's final suffering frees them from the yoke of their own petty shifts, self-concern, and thirst for worldly honor or reputation. Released from their fallible humanity, the ideal of spirit they tarnished in life can be affirmed and finally possessed, in the only sense possible. In both plays that ideal ultimately rests on relationships with another, on a love whose full completeness can be envisioned beyond the physical world's corrosive confines. The dream of perfected mutuality in Antony's Elysium and in the Duchess's "eternal Church" validates the unheroic gropings, vacillating commitment, and temporal failure which the plays fully dramatize. These protagonists may not embody the ideal they pursue, but, like Bussy D'Ambois and even Coriolanus outside Rome, in their language and the shape they try to give their lives they hold that image before us.

The physical extent of such knowledge's transforming power is limited. As the social order collapses and perverts its most fundamental relationships of kinship, love, and mutual human responsibility, hope narrows to the regenerative possibilities of the individual soul. Webster's world, especially, offers little scope for political or spiritual aspiration; his plays lack old-fashioned "heroes" in Shakespeare's or Chapman's sense. Yet in his predecessors' generic cross-references Webster found the basic dialectic through which he could focus his more apolitical concerns and investigate the diminished creatures and straitened world that challenged his own ideal of spirit. Melodramatic, Italianate stories bring Webster's "historical" world closer to tragicomedy's primarily economic and social rather than political issues. Through them he could more fully explore the witty pragmatism which in heroic tragedy feeds on greatness. Webster's own generic mixture initially supports the trickster's primacy and leads us to accept his amused, detached perspective. As surrogate audience he brings himself close to us; as surrogate author he seems to share with us his privileged knowledge and "creative" manipulative power. He offers us in aesthetic terms the protective distance that rules his own interactions with others on the stage. Through such encouraged identification we are brought to suffer with him the new knowledge he so painfully and belatedly acquires. His discovery is limited, its worldly applicability ambiguous, yet it is all that matters. The figures left behind, both Machiavels and cautiously traditional moralists, are limited beings whose fates do not stir us. They are predictable, inflexible, incapable of illumination; indeed, they define that lesser, trivial world which absorbs *The Devil's Law-Case*.

Webster's would-be Machiavels set out to conquer the corrupt world on its own terms; his Duchess finally rejects the political and social world that denies her the unheroic, domestic felicity she seeks. In their various ways, all respond to the loss of a heroic world of daring exploits, superhuman virtues, and monolithic integrity. In the Jacobean plays I have discussed, the gradual erosion of heroic qualities and expansive vision is not an accident of selection. In the early seventeenth-century drama, tragic protagonists are forced to act in increasingly confusing and corrupt worlds—arenas that distort or inhibit heroic action and trivialize the transcendent aspiration they cannot understand. A diminished sphere of action reveals, or produces, a diminished race of heroes. Webster's protagonists suffer, with Shakespeare's and Chapman's, both personal entanglement and political restriction, but his concerns become increasingly private, contract toward familial relationships and domestic goals. His tragedies and later turn to tragicomedy reflect the reduced scope of later Jacobean drama as well as the rise of a Fletcherian aesthetic.[3]

Webster is an important, yet still transitional figure in drama's waning concern with the public consequences of those private relations that mold both the protagonist and the society he influences.[4] Unquestionably, the political sweep and importance of the plays' events have in Webster's tragedies declined, as have the stature and ambitions of his characters. Yet in comparison with Middleton's and Ford's later tragedies (with the possible exception of *Perkin Warbeck*), it is evident that Webster attaches greater significance to the fact that his stories take place at the commonwealth's moral and political source. Corruption there is dangerous because it is generated by society's most influential religious and political figures, and Webster's protagonists treat service to the politically and socially great as their key to advancement. Webster has not wholly overturned tragedy's traditional concerns. In Middleton and Ford this political-social extension, with its sense of urgency and impending catastrophe, is absent or attenuated to a muted and totally pervasive background.

More important, Webster's unheroic protagonists look backward, to a more inclusive and exalted vision; they know what they have lost. In the often contradictory accounts of experience offered in these plays, Webster suggests the individual's freedom to interpret, and so in a sense to create, his world. The chosen role may in the end confer neither expressive freedom nor practical control, yet recognition of failure does not in itself affirm human nobility. In his tragedies, at least, Webster's protagonists acknowledge responsibility for the quality of the life their deeds have shaped. Despite evident limits to the ego's absolute creative freedom, both personal and external, Webster preserves something of the scope, the mystery and wonder by which great drama touches our imagination. The plays do not encourage moral confusion, though their contradictions and tonal shifts cannot be easily assimilated. The standards by which we must evaluate do not depend upon final, summary comments; they are built into the plays themselves. Vitality, the exercise of one's intelligence and feelings, is at the center of all Webster's plays, and Webster binds this quality to heroic tragedy's affirmation of moral commitment, however fatal—to its transcendence of both heroic and antiheroic solipsism. Forcing our participation through the detached intriguer, the dramatic experience itself mediates between the moralists' prim disapproval and instinctive retreat from complexity and challenge, and the political egoists' pragmatically successful yet ultimately disintegrative activity. Webster shows us nothing startling about ourselves, discovers no new answer to the worldly knowledge that confounds our deepest needs.[5] He dramatizes simply the old paradox of strength and human potential bound to weakness, the importance of a few fundamental values—like love, care, and familial affection—on which "Compassionate Nature" can build.

Notes

1. Philip Edwards, *Shakespeare and the Confines of Art* (London: Methuen, 1968), p. 95. In this period a Shakespearean play "can be a resounding dramatic failure, filled to the seams with magnificent material which cannot be accommodated within the chosen shape. He requires a fiction which will digest all he knows, and there is tumult in his attempts, in these few plays, to create it" (p. 96).

2. Ibid., p. 14.

3. As Marco Mincoff observed some years ago, "There is no valid reason why Shakespeare should not serve as a portal to the understanding of his contemporaries. . . . After all it is probable that Shakespeare as the greatest dramatist of his age approached most closely to that unattainable ideal of drama that the playwrights of the Renaissance were striving after, and we are most likely to find developed in his works [their] common dramatic technique." See "Plot Construction in Shakespeare," *Annuaire de l'Université de Sofia: Faculté historico-philologique,* 37 (1941), pp. 4–5.

4. The Christian schema of temptations, in which Webster's characters become Satanic representatives, underlies Peter B. Murray's *A Study of John Webster* (The Hague: Mouton, 1969). In more restricted studies, D. C. Gunby sees a moralitylike opposition between good and evil, where the evil characters demonstrate that they are "hell-bound," in *Webster: "The White Devil,"* Studies in English Literature No. 45 (London: Edward Arnold, 1971), pp. 20 and 57–61. Joyce E. Peterson finds *The Duchess of Malfi* "old-fashioned" in its re-creation of "Commonweal tragedy"; Webster writes a sophisticated version of *Gorboduc* even as other playwrights "had turned to tragic genres concerned with the plight of the individual." See *Curs'd Example: "The Duchess of Malfi" and Commonweal Tragedy* (Columbia: University of Missouri Press, 1978), p. 12.

5. Although I applaud Ralph Berry's attempt to reevaluate Webster positively, as part of a broader European intellectual and artistic movement, I share neither his absorption with the visual arts (and translation of Wölfflin's formal patterns into dramatic imagery) nor his conclusions about Webster's themes or meaning. See *The Art of John Webster* (Oxford: At the Clarendon Press, 1972), esp. part 1.

INTRODUCTION

1. L. C. Knights helpfully investigated contemporary social and economic conditions in *Drama and Society in the Age of Jonson* (London: Chatto & Windus, 1937); Anthony Covatta provides a useful corrective in *Thomas Middleton's City Comedies* (Lewisburg, Pa.: Bucknell University Press, 1973), where he argues astutely against confusing comedy's everyday subject matter and topicality with a nineteenth-century idea of realism.

2. For the continued popularity of these moralized versions throughout the Jacobean period, see Alexander Leggatt's chapter "The Prodigal" in *Citizen Comedy in the Age of Shakespeare* (Toronto: University of Toronto Press, 1973), pp. 33–53.

3. Leo Salingar, *Shakespeare and the Traditions of Comedy* (London: Cambridge University Press, 1974), p. 325. Two strands of influence appear in the Renaissance's use of Roman New Comedy: "Jonson associated classical comedy with correction and satire, following a sixteenth-century tradition, while Shakespeare, also, however, following tradition, associated it with romance" (p. 77).

4. Rosalie Colie, *The Resources of Kind: Genre Theory in the Renaissance*, ed. Barbara K. Lewalski (Berkeley and Los Angeles: University of California Press, 1973), pp. 115–116. Colie concludes that the genre system offered "not a second world but an array of ways to look at the real world" and that in the Renaissance "the literary theory that underlies all others is *not* really expressed in its rich and varied criticism: namely, that a literary kind stands for a kind of subject, a kind of content, literary and intellectual; and also that some references to a subject or content may be taken as metaphors for a whole kind" (pp. 119 and 114). See also E. D. Hirsch, Jr., *Validity in Interpretation* (New Haven: Yale University Press, 1967), pp. 71–80.

5. Gabriele Bernhard Jackson explores this idea in Jonson's works in "Structural Interplay in Ben Jonson's Drama," *Two Renaissance Mythmakers: Christopher Marlowe and Ben Jonson*, ed. Alvin Kernan, English Institute Essays, n.s. 1 (Baltimore: Johns Hopkins University Press, 1977), p. 113. For a more general discussion, see Cyrus Hoy's *The Hyacinth Room: An Investigation into the Nature of Comedy, Tragedy, and Tragicomedy* (London: Chatto & Windus, 1964).

6. Some of the best discussions of the nature and history of the "Elizabethan play in two tones" are still A. P. Rossiter's. See *English Drama from Early Times to the Elizabethans* (1950; rpt. London: Hutchinson Universal Library, 1969), chap. 10 and epilogue; and the posthumously published *Angel with Horns*, ed. Graham Storey (1961; rpt. London: Longman, 1970), chap. 14.

7. See Michael Shapiro's *Children of the Revels: The Boy Companies of Shakespeare's Time and Their Plays* (New York: Columbia University Press,

1977), esp. chaps. 1 and 6, and Reavley Gair's more specific study, "The Presentation of Plays at Second Paul's: The Early Phase (1599–1602)," in *The Elizabethan Theatre VI*, ed. G. R. Hibbard (Hamden, Conn.: Archon, 1977), pp. 21–47. Arthur C. Kirsch, too, discusses the importance of the private theaters, especially in the rise of tragicomedy and satiric drama and in the creation "of a peculiarly self-conscious relationship between the audience and the play," in *Jacobean Dramatic Perspectives* (Charlottesville: University Press of Virginia, 1972), p. 5.

8. R. A. Foakes, "Tragedy at the Children's Theatres after 1600: A Challenge to the Adult Stage," in *The Elizabethan Theatre II*, ed. David Galloway (Hamden, Conn.: Archon, 1970), p. 39. For more specific instances of such cross-influence, see Foakes's later studies, "On Marston, *The Malcontent*, and *The Revenger's Tragedy*," in *The Elizabethan Theatre VI*, pp. 59–75, and his chapter on Shakespeare's problem plays and contemporary satirical comedy in *Shakespeare: The Dark Comedies to the Last Plays* (Charlottesville: University Press of Virginia, 1971).

9. Although his early dramatic work is usually associated with satiric comedy for the children's troupes, Middleton collaborated on *Caesar's Fall* for Henslowe in 1602 and, quite probably, wrote *The Revenger's Tragedy* and/or *The Second Maiden's Tragedy* (a play often mentioned in connection with Webster's *Duchess of Malfi*). The title page of *The Revenger's Tragedy* says it was acted by the King's Men. In his Revels edition of the play (London: Methuen, 1966), R. A. Foakes argues against Middletonian authorship (pp. xlviii–liv), yet evidence supporting Middleton's case has been offered by David J. Lake in *The Canon of Thomas Middleton's Plays* (Cambridge: Cambridge University Press, 1975) and by Peter B. Murray in *A Study of Cyril Tourneur* (Philadelphia: University of Pennsylvania Press, 1964), pp. 144–172. Cyrus Hoy assumes the case for Middletonian authorship proved; see "Critical and Aesthetic Problems of Collaboration in Renaissance Drama," *Research Opportunities in Renaissance Drama*, 19 (1976), p. 4. Lake, R. H. Barker ("The Authorship of the [sic] *Second Maiden's Tragedy* and *The Revenger's Tragedy*," *Shakespeare Association Bulletin*, 20 [1945], pp. 51–62 and 121–133) and Samuel Schoenbaum (*Middleton's Tragedies* [New York: Columbia University Press, 1955], pp. 183–202) defend Middletonian authorship of *The Second Maiden's Tragedy* as well. In her Revels edition of *The Second Maiden's Tragedy* (Baltimore: Johns Hopkins University Press, 1978), Anne Lancashire agrees on Middleton's probable authorship; Lancashire also ascertains that the play was initially performed by the King's Men, at Blackfriars, in the winter of 1611–1612 (p. 54). By this time Middleton had collaborated on *The Roaring Girl* for Prince Henry's Men, and would soon write *A Chaste Maid in Cheapside* for Henslowe and Lady Elizabeth's Men at the Swan.

10. See Clifford Leech, "The Dramatists' Independence," *Research Opportunities in Renaissance Drama*, 10 (1967), p. 17, and Shapiro's *Children of the Revels*, esp. chap. 6. This list might also include *The Second Maiden's Tragedy*.

11. It is not, of course, simply the unbelievable conjunctions of dramatists which surprise; we are amazed at the way in which distinctively different playwrights, as well as accepted couples like Beaumont and Fletcher, can so submerge their individual styles as to produce plays whose distribution of labor defies our analysis. Norman Rabkin has recorded some of our frustrations at this "great Elizabethan disappearing act" in "Problems in the Study of Collaboration," *Research Opportunities in Renaissance Drama*, 19 (1976), pp. 7–13.

12. Clifford Leech notes that, beyond personal and financial rivalry, aesthetic concerns piqued interest "because what had just previously been done opened up a new way of dramatic composition." See "Three Times *Ho* and a Brace of Widows: Some Plays for the Private Theatre," in *The Elizabethan Theatre III*, ed. David Galloway (Hamden, Conn.: Archon, 1973), p. 15.

13. Leech, "The Dramatists' Independence," p. 22.

14. Neil Carson discusses the significance of Webster's early collaborations, particularly *Westward Ho*, in "John Webster: The Apprentice Years," in *The Elizabethan Theatre VI*, pp. 76–87.

15. F. L. Lucas, *The Complete Works of John Webster*, 4 vols. (London: Chatto & Windus, 1927), 1:53–56. For closer analyses of the collaborations with Dekker, see ibid., vol. 4 (Appendix I), pp. 239–244, and Peter B. Murray, "The Collaboration of Dekker and Webster in *Northward Ho* and *Westward Ho*," *Publications of the Bibliographic Society of America*, 56 (1962), pp. 482–486; Murray allows Webster a stronger apprenticeship in comedy than Lucas, since Murray's conclusions increase the amount of Webster's contribution to about 40 percent for each play. A lucid survey of Webster's literary career, such as it is, appears in John Russell Brown's introduction to his Revels edition of *The White Devil* (1960; rpt., 2d ed., London: Methuen, 1968), pp. xvii–xxvi.

16. Neither date nor authorship of *Appius and Virginia* could be called a settled question. Most critics maintain that it must be either very early or very late. Lucas joins Stoll and Sykes in placing it at the end of Webster's career, in the mid 1620s, and Lucas maintains that, whatever the collaboration's nature, Webster dominates the final play (see *Complete Works*, 3: 121–130, 134–145); see also Fernand Lagarde's *John Webster*, 2 vols. (Toulouse: Association des Publications de la Faculté des Lettres et Sciences Humaines de Toulouse, 1968), 1:279–281. Rupert Brooke joins Chambers in assigning it to around 1608 and concludes that Webster had little, if any, part in the finished product; see *John Webster and the Elizabethan Drama* (New York: John Lane Co., 1916), Ap-

pendix A, pp. 165–210. Robert Dent, in *John Webster's Borrowing* (Berkeley and Los Angeles: University of California Press, 1960), maintains Webster's involvement but inclines toward the earlier date, on the basis of Webster's imitative practice (p. 62).

17. Brian Gibbons discovers close connections between Jonson's comical satires and *Antonio and Mellida*, as well as *What You Will, The Fawn,* and *The Malcontent;* see *Jacobean City Comedy: A Study of Satiric Plays by Jonson, Marston and Middleton* (London: Rupert Hart-Davis, 1968), p. 87. For the vexed relationship between *Antonio's Revenge* and *Hamlet,* see G. K. Hunter's edition of the Marston play for the Regents Renaissance series (Lincoln: University of Nebraska Press, 1965), pp. xviii–xxi. Both Hunter and Reavley Gair, the Revels editor of *Antonio's Revenge* (Manchester: Manchester University Press, 1978), think it most likely that Shakespeare and Marston wrote independently but used the same source, the so-called Ur-Hamlet.

18. For city comedy's satiric thrust, see Gibbons, *Jacobean City Comedy,* p. 24. City comedy's world is in Gibbons's view a world of Hobbesian economics, and the genre's finest products are the early (and, oddly, nonurban and Italianate) *Malcontent* and Jonson's later *Alchemist* (p. 17). The broader definition of this genre is from Leggatt's *Citizen Comedy in the Age of Shakespeare,* p. 10.

19. Personal relations between the men are unclear. Webster not only praises "Master Chapman" in the preface to *The White Devil;* in his funeral elegy he also refers to Chapman as Prince Henry's "sweet *Homer* and my frend" (1.267). *A Monumental Column* was entered in the Stationers' Register on 25 December 1612, though to what degree or how long they had been "friends" is unknown (see Lucas, *Complete Works,* 3:268).

20. See Foakes, "Tragedy at the Children's Theatres after 1600," pp. 42–43. Middleton's triumphs in city comedy do seem implicit in his earliest plays and may, as Gibbons maintains, develop naturally out of comical satire; for such theories, see Covatta, *Thomas Middleton's City Comedies,* and, for Jonson's chances of paternity, Gibbons, *Jacobean City Comedy,* pp. 25–26.

21. See the excellent introduction to Dent's *John Webster's Borrowing.* The nature of Webster's traceable borrowings suggests that passages were chosen for pithiness and striking expression, not because the source had anything to do with the Websterian play into which the plunder was to be inserted. Thus specific borrowings from playwrights whom we know Webster admired—like Jonson and Chapman—do not necessarily derive from those plays whose structure or concerns most closely approach Webster's. Though not so satisfyingly provable as specific borrowings, my contention is that in broader matters of inspiration and structure, Webster also built on others' groundwork.

22. In his commentary, Dent suggests specific borrowings from Jonson's *Sejanus* (in all of Webster's plays) and from *The Revenger's Tragedy* (in *The*

White Devil). I have referred to *The Revenger's Tragedy* as Middleton's rather than Tourneur's, partly on the basis of what seems to be an increasing acceptance of Middletonian authorship and partly to avoid cluttering my argument with a distracting number of different references. Nothing in my argument, however, depends on Middleton's authorship.

CHAPTER I

1. George R. Kernodle, "The Mannerist Stage of Comic Detachment," in *The Elizabethan Theatre III*, ed. David Galloway (Hamden, Conn.: Archon, 1973), p. 122.

2. Arnold Hauser, *Mannerism: The Crisis of the Renaissance and the Origin of Modern Art*, trans. Eric Mosbacher (New York: Alfred A. Knopf, 1965), part 1, p. 111.

3. Kernodle, "Mannerist Stage," p. 123. In *Mannerism,* Hauser argues that Mannerist art deliberately widens the distance between art and nature; fascinated by the "tension between its wilfulness and reality," its favorite subject is the dream, that "visionary fusion of semblance and reality" (pp. 29–30). See also Jackson I. Cope, *The Theater and the Dream: From Metaphor to Form in Renaissance Drama* (Baltimore: Johns Hopkins University Press, 1973).

4. Examining the author's control of viewpoint from Plautus to Restoration comedy, Eugene M. Waith discusses the way in which less central characters, such as Puck in *A Midsummer Night's Dream,* can dramatize (and thus control) the "distance between the one who laughs and the object of laughter." See "'Give Me Your Hands': Reflections on the Author's Agents in Comedy," in *The Author in His Work: Essays on a Problem in Criticism,* eds. Louis L. Martz and Aubrey Williams (New Haven: Yale University Press, 1978), p. 201.

5. Anthony Caputi's *John Marston, Satirist* (Ithaca: Cornell University Press, 1961) and Anthony Covatta's *Thomas Middleton's City Comedies* (Lewisburg, Pa.: Bucknell University Press, 1973) both trace in detail their authors' struggle to replace satire's didactic overseer and loose structure with a more fully integrated and dramatic action.

6. Peter Thorpe notes the implicit contradiction between the satirist's demand that men be complex and virtuous human beings (which presumes their free will) and satire's use of repetition, animal imagery, accusations of insanity and an "antiplot" whose movement does not lead to transformation (which suggests necessity and the permanence of innate human characteristics); see "Free Will, Necessity, and Satire," *Satire Newsletter,* 8 (1971), pp. 83–91. The tension between satire's ideal and comedy's norm has been explored most fully in Ben Jonson; see for instance Ian Donaldson's "Jonson and the Moralists" in *Two*

Renaissance Mythmakers: Christopher Marlowe and Ben Jonson, ed. Alvin Kernan, English Institute Essays, n.s. 1 (Baltimore: Johns Hopkins University Press, 1977), esp. p. 159.

7. Introduction to G. K. Hunter's Revels edition of *The Malcontent* (London: Methuen, 1975), p. lxii. Hunter's excellent discussion of satire and tragicomedy, and one mode of their fusion in *The Malcontent,* deserves full attention (pp. lxi–lxxiv).

8. My remarks on what I have called romance tragicomedy are based on pp. 7–15 of Arthur C. Kirsch's helpful *Jacobean Dramatic Perspectives* (Charlottesville: University Press of Virginia, 1972), though his initial discussion of tragicomic forms soon assumes that Renaissance English tragicomedy strives by its very nature to mirror and "celebrate man's deliverance from evil and sorrow and presents an action in which oppositions are being continuously *transformed*" (p. 15, my italics). Much closer to my own approach is Alexander Leggatt's in *"All's Well That Ends Well:* The Testing of Romance," *Modern Language Quarterly,* 32 (1971), for Leggatt feels that through "a positive and deliberate conflict" of two kinds of dramatic convention, the "values of romance are tested in a world of down-to-earth and often unpleasant realism" (p. 22).

9. While these plays share certain general features and reflect some degree of cross-influence as well as private inspiration, I am in no way trying to suggest that they constitute a genre, or even subgenre. I do not wish to force them to fit a pattern or judge some as successful exemplars and others as failures. Still pertinent is E. D. Hirsch's caveat on the dangers of "influence studies": "They tend to reduce the new genre to the preexisting conventions out of which it was formed. This is equivalent to identifying a metaphor with its elements instead of recognizing that every metaphor is a leap *ins Unbetretene.*" See *Validity in Interpretation* (New Haven: Yale University Press, 1967), p. 106.

10. Although I came to these ideas inductively, and here develop them largely from Kernodle's un-Marxist premise, Hauser's general discussions of this issue are still illuminating; see *Mannerism,* part 1, chaps. 7 ("Alienation as the Key to Mannerism") and 8 ("Narcissism as the Psychology of Alienation").

11. On this successful fusion of observer-judge and active protagonist, see Bernard Harris's New Mermaids edition of *The Malcontent* (London: Ernest Benn, 1967), pp. xxi–xxii, and Caputi's *John Marston, Satirist,* p. 188.

12. Hunter's Revels edition of *The Malcontent,* p. lxxiii. The clash between Malevole and Altofront, libertine and moralist—significant in Shakespeare's *Measure for Measure* and in Marston's own *Dutch Courtesan*—is dampened here by diminishing Altofront's appearances; as Hunter says, he seems to Malevole more "a set of assumptions about himself . . . than a set of characteristics" (p. lxviii). On the question of Altofront as the play's safety-valve, the means by which

tragicomic form can solve, rather than explore, the problem of his involvement with evil, see also T. F. Wharton, "*The Malcontent* and 'Dreams, Visions, Fantasies,'" *Essays in Criticism*, 24 (1974), pp. 261–274. In *John Marston of the Middle Temple* (Cambridge, Mass.: Harvard University Press, 1969), Philip Finkelpearl finds darker intimations of the impossibility of living as a "good prince" even when one has learned from one's mistakes: "You can be a philosophical monarch only if you act like a natural fool. You must temporize and pretend to play the game even if it means becoming something of a bawd" (p. 192).

13. The term "white Machiavel" is A. D. Nuttall's, from his discussion of Angelo and the Duke in "*Measure for Measure*: Quid pro Quo?" *Shakespeare Studies*, 4 (1968), p. 239.

14. See John J. O'Connor, "The Chief Source of Marston's *Dutch Courtesan*," *Studies in Philology*, 54 (1957), pp. 509–515. On Marston's careful provision of additional illustrations and variations on his chosen theme, see Paul M. Zall, "John Marston, Moralist," *ELH*, 20 (1953), pp. 186–193, and Gustav Cross, "Marston, Montaigne, and Morality: *The Dutch Courtesan* Reconsidered," *ELH*, 27 (1960), pp. 30–43.

15. J. W. Lever judiciously summarizes Shakespeare's amalgamation of Cinthio and Whetstone; see his Arden edition of *Measure for Measure* (London: Methuen, 1965), pp. xxxvi–xliv. All citations will be from this edition.

16. M. L. Wine's edition of *The Dutch Courtesan* for the Regents Renaissance Drama Series (Lincoln: University of Nebraska Press, 1965), I.ii.16. All citations will be from this edition.

17. The parallel defenses of brothels and bawds (I.i.118–120 and I.ii.41–43) suggest both young men's acceptance of the fallen world they share at the play's beginning. Peter Davison notes that Cocledemoy is thematically as well as structurally analogous to Freevill: "Cocledemoy is a *comic* version of Freevill—of the man who has come to terms with sexual desires." See the introduction to *The Dutch Courtesan*, Fountainwell Drama Texts (Berkeley and Los Angeles: University of California Press, 1968), p. 7.

18. Worth attention in this regard is Ian Donaldson's discussion of the disruptive comic energies Jonson unleashes in *Volpone*. See "*Volpone*: Quick and Dead," *Essays in Criticism*, 21 (1971), esp. p. 126; see also Covatta's *Thomas Middleton's City Comedies*, p. 47.

19. See Freud's chapters on "The Purposes of Jokes" and "The Mechanism of Pleasure and the Psychogenesis of Jokes" in *Jokes and Their Relation to the Unconscious* (1905) in *The Standard Edition of the Complete Psychological Works of Sigmund Freud* (hereafter referred to as *Freud*), trans. James Strachey, Anna Freud, Alix Strachey, and Alan Tyson, 24 vols. (1960; rpt. London: Hogarth Press, 1973), 8:90–139. Applying psychoanalytic insights, Erich Segal

has elucidated the appeal, and hence in part the technique, of Plautine comedy in *Roman Laughter: The Comedy of Plautus* (Cambridge, Mass.: Harvard University Press, 1968).

20. Farce's appeal is regressive. Eric Bentley likens farce to dreams and fantasies which allow scope to the childish ego's amoral desire for total gratification and in which, satisfyingly if temporarily, "one is permitted the outrage but is spared the consequences." See "The Psychology of Farce," Bentley's introduction to his edition of *"Let's Get a Divorce!" and Other Plays* (New York: Hill and Wang, 1958), p. xiii.

21. The inherent aggression in wit, that small-scale unmasking of public morality or individual hypocrisy, helps prepare us for the plots' aggressive action. Both Freud and Ernst Kris stress humor's importance in overcoming potentially painful emotions: a playful, festive attitude enables us to accept the invitation to common aggression and regression. For Kris's discussion, see "Ego Development and the Comic" in *Psychoanalytic Explorations in Art* (1952; rpt. New York: Schocken Books, 1964), pp. 204–216.

22. This view of Tharsalio is not widely shared. Though Thelma Herring observes that Tharsalio is both an eligible suitor and an "unmasker of comic pretentions" rather than a satirized atheist or Machiavel, she levels the play's total effect to that of satire, with no disturbing generic cross-signals; see "Chapman and an Aspect of Modern Criticism," *Renaissance Drama*, 8 (1965), p. 158. For very different interpretations of Tharsalio and Chapman's intentions, see Samuel Schoenbaum, "*The Widow's Tears* and the Other Chapman," *Huntington Library Quarterly*, 23 (1960), pp. 321–338; Henry M. Weidner, "Homer and the Fallen World: Focus of Satire in George Chapman's *The Widow's Tears*," *Journal of English and Germanic Philology*, 62 (1963), pp. 518–532; and Albert H. Tricomi, "The Social Disorder of Chapman's *The Widow's Tears*," *Journal of English and Germanic Philology*, 72 (1973), pp. 350–359.

23. Akihiro Yamada's edition of *The Widow's Tears* for The Revels Plays (London: Methuen, 1975), I.i.53–54 (and see also the exchange at I.i.68–73). All subsequent quotations from this play will be from Yamada's edition.

24. Chapman here inverts the opening soliloquy of his own *Bussy D'Ambois*, for Bussy renounces trust in Fortune and espouses Virtue. The private joke, which cues the opening's carefree tone, could have been shared by many in Chapman's audience. *The Widow's Tears* may have been Chapman's next play after *Bussy*, and although *Bussy* was first performed at Paul's, it seems to have migrated to the Blackfriars. There the same talented young actor, Nathan Field, probably gave both soliloquies; he was certainly remembered in later years for success in both roles. That Field's abilities were considerable is attested to by the many encomia which rank him with Burbage as one of the two greatest actors of the early seventeenth century; what such a talent, then seventeen or

eighteen, could do with Bussy or Tharsalio (or Freevill or Malevole-Alfront) can hardly be discussed, much less dismissed, in the terms usually applied to earlier plays performed by the children's troupes. For an account of Field's career and a list of the plays in which he probably had the leading role, see William Peery's introduction to his edition, *The Plays of Nathan Field* (Austin: University of Texas Press, 1950), esp. pp. 14 and 31–32.

25. For a fuller discussion of these "softening techniques" and a general review of the effects gained by Chapman's generic juxtapositions, see my article "The Boys from Ephesus: Farce, Freedom, and Limit in *The Widow's Tears,*" *Renaissance Drama,* 10 (1979), pp. 161–183.

26. In discussing Hal's wandering among his troops on the night before Agincourt, Anne Barton surveys the "surprising number of disguised kings to be found in those English history plays which have survived from the period 1587–1600"; though political necessity is occasionally the motive, a larger number, like Henry V, do it "as a caprice, for reasons that are fundamentally exploratory and quixotic." See "The King Disguised: Shakespeare's *Henry V* and the Comical History" in *The Triple Bond: Plays, Mainly Shakespearean, in Performance,* ed. Joseph G. Price (University Park: Pennsylvania State University Press, 1975), p. 93. Whatever the motive or outcome, these earlier plays "are fundamentally comical histories" whose optimism assumes the king's ability to solve his people's problems as well as to meet them comfortably as a man rather than a king. Barton's conclusion about Shakespeare's use of this motif in *Henry V* seems to me suggestive for his return to it in tragicomedy: his "conception of history, even when he was chronicling one of England's moments of glory, was fundamentally tragic" (p. 115).

27. Claudio, in much darker terms, agrees. Embarrassed at being publicly exhibited, he shares his society's ideals but concludes that men are incapable of self-control or moderation. Nature has its own way of enforcing continence, but its processes are mechanical and leave weak-willed man swinging helplessly between extremes: "So every scope by the immoderate use / Turns to restraint" (I.ii.119ff.). This acceptance of bodily determinism is also Freevill's (and Montaigne's): "Incontinence will force a continence; . . . Nothing is spoiled but by his proper might" (*DC,* II.i.120–122). Claudio's pessimism is more like Malheureux's, however, for both seem appalled to discover that physical desire compels shameful actions, that "there is no God in blood, no reason in desire" (*DC,* IV.ii.13). Because of its political and judicial framework, *Measure* suggests (though it ultimately denies) the logical conclusion: freedom ("scope") submits men to their bodies' tyranny; the body's health may depend on the political tyranny of legislated morality. In any case, concentration on physical dynamics leaves any question of the soul's health untouched.

28. Although I think he misreads the Duke's speeches in I.i as open explica-

tion of this idea, Terence Eagleton rightly sees the play's (and romantic comedy's) ideal as one in which private fulfillment can be found through public function and in which the individual's desires naturally and spontaneously issue in socially responsible action. See *Shakespeare and Society: Critical Studies in Shakespearean Drama* (New York: Schocken Books, 1967), p. 77 and the preceding discussion.

29. In Whetstone's *Promos and Cassandra* the low-life characters are kept completely separate from the brother-sister-deputy confrontations, but they do live out a story of their own. Shakespeare rejects the possibilities in Whetstone's connection between the prostitute Lamia, her witty servant Rosko, and Promos's right-hand man Phallax; Whetstone's subplot, in good Renaissance fashion, suggests the extent of corruption under Promos's rule, the close relation between sexual license and other forms of predatory chicanery, and (in the moralistic second part) the need for rulers to look closely to their henchmen. Whetstone's dedicatory letter interestingly defends certain structural choices on the basis of decorum. See Geoffrey Bullough, ed., *Narrative and Dramatic Sources of Shakespeare,* 8 vols. (London: Routledge and Kegan Paul, 1957–1975), 2:443. Vincentio is only a duke, but Shakespeare certainly elaborates the indignities he suffers in disguise and, in general, incorporates violations of decorum into his dramatic technique. It might also be noted that the care with which Shakespeare has excluded any suggestion of a green world is remarkable and, like Chapman's efforts in *The Widow's Tears,* atypical.

30. Lucio's coarse, particular idiom and the practical interest he shares with the Provost also allow Shakespeare to emphasize, by contrast, the absolutists' distance from the specifics of Claudio's case. Claudio remains abstract and depersonalized, brother or sinner; no one argues those special merits of his case which place him beyond the law's intended scope. The refuge found in abstractions is Shakespeare's addition. Both Cinthio's and Whetstone's heroines argue the *reasonable* grounds of extenuating circumstances; Shakespeare's characters here ignore the possibility of reasoned judicial distinctions and see no flexible mean between law and gratuitous personal pardon.

31. In *Shakespeare: The Dark Comedies to the Last Plays* (Charlottesville: University Press of Virginia, 1971), R. A. Foakes notes Vincentio's centrality throughout; because his presence in Vienna distances the emotionally charged events of act 2, we must "distinguish between the way the characters see themselves, and the pattern of expectation set up from the start of the action, with its promise of a comic resolution" (p. 21).

32. The 30 November 1957 *Time and Tide* reviewer for Margaret Webster's Old Vic production of *Measure for Measure* observed that "Miss Webster sees that it is not Angelo's conscience but the Duke's Wolfenden survey which is the crux of the play, and if you can make the Duke seem a true sociologist and not

a mere Arabian Nights *farceur* the usually intractable and tedious second half will come fully alive." Quoted by Jane Williamson in "The Duke and Isabella on the Modern Stage," *The Triple Bond*, p. 156.

33. The bed trick, staunchly defended on grounds of folkloric ubiquity as well as Renaissance acceptance of nonrealistic conventions, seems singularly appropriate for Vincentio, in many ways so remarkably like the young pranksters popular on the private stage. Despite the maturity in years attributed to Vincentio in the play, he shares their puckish delight in witty stratagems, their enjoyment of the process of deception as much as its goal. Part of our hesitation in seeing Vincentio as a providential stand-in lies in the conception of Providence he would illustrate. As William Empson says, "It seems hard not to regard him as a comic character," since "the higher you pitch the ethics of the Duke, the more surprising you must find his behaviour." See *The Structure of Complex Words* (New York: New Directions, n.d.), p. 281.

34. In discussing Middleton's city comedy, Covatta notes that irony expresses "the basic duality of comedy, its desire both to engage an audience in laughter and to afford it a respite from the rigors of social life"; irony refuses to judge reality and so allows us to enjoy the "success of a strictly practical mode of behavior," unconstrained by our normal moral imperatives. See *Thomas Middleton's City Comedies*, pp. 50 and 52.

35. In "John Marston, Moralist," Paul M. Zall suggests that Marston not only points out the discrepancy between neo-stoic ethics, which insists that reason rule passion, and natural law, which sees that both love and lust are "natural," but also offers norms for behavior proper to man's individual and social responsibilities: "The characters who illustrate this 'norm' are those who accept love as the natural passion it is, without compromising their virtue." He finds a dangerous irresponsibility in Freevill (p. 190).

36. Richard Horwich, "Wives, Courtesans, and the Economics of Love in Jacobean City Comedy," *Comparative Drama*, 7 (1973–1974), p. 296.

37. In a late essay, Freud calls humor the "triumph of narcissism, the victorious assertion of the ego's invulnerability," and a victory of the pleasure principle, which requires a "rejection of the claims of reality"; see "Humour (1927)" in *Freud*, 21:162–163. Our willingness to accept Tharsalio's solutions—either for himself or for Cynthia and Lysander—would in the theater, of course, vary according to the last scene's staging. Still, the violent hatred so recently displayed by both Lysander and his wife imposes some limit on the last scene's ability to suggest joyous conversion.

38. Herring sees a possible "parody of the conclusion of *Measure for Measure* in the final scene of *The Widow's Tears*." See "Chapman and an Aspect of Modern Criticism," p. 164.

39. Clifford Leech, "The 'Meaning' of *Measure for Measure*," *Shakespeare*

Survey, 3 (1950), p. 70. In "The Options of the Audience: Theory and Practice in Peter Brook's *Measure for Measure*," *Shakespeare Survey*, 25 (1972), Herbert S. Weil, Jr., considers the effect of reinstating in productions those dozen or so passages which "have seemed unplayable unless we are meant to laugh *at* the Duke and to find meaningful flaws in his personal private character as well as in his ability to rule." Weil concludes that to recognize "the Duke's function as near-omnipotent *deus ex machina* does not require us to accept his evaluations of other characters nor of himself. The discordance between a virtue claimed and the character whose actions we observe is one vital, recurring technique in *Measure for Measure*" (pp. 30 and 33). See also Weil's "Form and Contexts in *Measure for Measure*," *Critical Quarterly*, 12 (1970), pp. 55–72.

40. In "Quid pro Quo?" Nuttall sees vicariousness as the play's fundamental idea and notes that Angelo is seen as purely instrumental in I.i, "in himself a sort of surrogate human being" (p. 235).

41. In his Arden edition J. W. Lever observes that "in reality it is Lucio, not Escalus or Angelo, who serves here as the Duke's true deputy. . . . In the first two acts he is the indispensable go-between, passing from Claudio to Isabella, . . . drawing Isabella from her cloister, leading her to the presence of Angelo, and ensuring that she persists in her suit" (p. xcvi). Language, as well as function, associates these apparent opposites: the Duke's description of Angelo and the leonine characterization of the sleeping law to Friar Thomas (I.iii. 23–24, 50–53) are both echoed by Lucio to Isabella (I.iv.57–64).

42. In Marston's *What You Will* (1601), the Epicurean critic Quadratus offers a witty eulogy of "*Phantasticknesse.*" He associates *Phantasia incomplexa*—which Caputi describes as the "uncircumscribed or unfettered imagination" of the "wildly unconventional man" (*John Marston, Satirist*, p. 169)—with the creative and "bright immortal part of man" which separates us from beasts. See *The Plays of John Marston*, ed. H. Harvey Wood, 3 vols. (London: Oliver and Boyd, 1938), 2:250. The combination of frivolity and seriousness apparently recommended (the degree of irony is unclear) is embodied in Quadratus himself and perhaps also reflected in Lucio and Duke Vincentio. Certainly the term could carry meanings beyond mere foppishness. Webster reveals some interest in the "phantastique," for he includes the "character" of what he subtitles "An Improvident young Gallant" in his contribution to the sixth edition (1615) of Overbury's collection (see Lucas, *Complete Works*, 4:32–33); though impudent and scornful of conventional "honestie," Webster's representative figure lacks the witty intelligence of these earlier dramatic examples.

43. A. P. Rossiter, *Angel with Horns*, ed. Graham Storey (1961; rpt. London: Longman, 1970), p. 155. Rossiter quite rightly argues that Lucio simply hints a failure in self-transcendence that pervades the play's various love relationships, for both Claudio and Isabella, too, lack love's sympathetic imagination (p. 161).

44. Marco Mincoff, "*Measure for Measure:* A Question of Approach," *Shakespeare Studies,* 2 (1966), p. 146.

45. Mary Lascelles, *Shakespeare's "Measure for Measure"* (London: Athlone Press, 1953), p. 148. Lascelles catches Vincentio's detachment in another acute observation: comparing the strange near-isolation of this Duke with the comfortable centrality of the King in *All's Well That Ends Well,* she says, "There is a sense in which we may fairly say that the Duke does not *fill a place*" (p. 144).

46. The phrase is Nuttall's; he notes that the bed trick is a good example of expert comic plotting whose moral implications are appalling. See "Quid pro Quo?" p. 232.

47. As with Hamlet's "To be or not to be," Shakespeare here widens the description's scope; it becomes a universal vision encompassing more experience than the play's examples provide. From different premises, Rossiter reaches a similar conclusion. He notes in *Angel with Horns* that Barnardine puts the Duke in perspective by refusing to play the game: Barnardine is "the one positive: man without a mask, entirely assured, unstrippable, 'complete.' All the rest are doubters and seemers. Develop Barnadine [sic] and the Duke's 'Be absolute for death,' and you pass to Hobbes's picture of the world . . . where force and fraud are the only laws" (p. 167).

48. Tharsalio's witty "solution" is of course the most obvious statement of this demand; with the other intriguers it is implicit in their expectation of everyone's approval and positive admiration for their witty maneuvering. In *Mannerism,* Hauser deftly captures one root of our distance and distaste: "Humour reconciles itself to the alienation which tragedy is unable to accept, but is no less dependent on alienation and, like tragedy, expresses the sense of life of a generation dominated by it" (p. 141).

CHAPTER II

1. R. A. Foakes has fruitfully investigated Marston's extensive influence, both on plays written for the children's troupes and on satirical tragedy staged by the adults. In "Tragedy at the Children's Theatres after 1600: A Challenge to the Adult Stage," in *The Elizabethan Theatre II,* ed. David Galloway (Hamden, Conn.: Archon, 1970), p. 51, he notes that Shakespeare's company, pilferers of *The Malcontent,* offered both *Sejanus* and *The Revenger's Tragedy* between 1603 and 1606. See also Foakes's "On Marston, *The Malcontent,* and *The Revenger's Tragedy,*" in *The Elizabethan Theatre VI,* ed. G. R. Hibbard (Hamden, Conn.: Archon, 1977), pp. 59–75, and the chapter "Shakespeare and Satirical Tragedy" in *Shakespeare: The Dark Comedies to the Last Plays* (Charlottesville: University Press of Virginia, 1971).

2. Eric Bentley, following Stark Young, notes that tragedy has more in common with farce than with either *drame* or high romantic comedy, since its substructure of cosmic *lex talionis* merely gains intensity from farce's own unleashed human aggression. See *The Life of the Drama* (New York: Atheneum, 1964), p. 341. See also A. P. Rossiter's *Angel with Horns* (1961; rpt. London: Longman, 1970), pp. 269–273, and Bert O. States's *Irony and Drama: A Poetics* (Ithaca: Cornell University Press, 1971), p. 70.

3. In *The Multiple Plot in English Renaissance Drama* (Chicago: University of Chicago Press, 1971), Richard Levin examines *The Second Maiden's Tragedy*'s Lady as a kind of secular saint whose heroic death cleanses the corrupt court (p. 28). Anne Lancashire's investigation of the main-plot sources confirms his judgment, and she suggests extending the Lady's stature to that of a "Christ-figure." See "*The Second Maiden's Tragedy*: A Jacobean Saint's Life," *Renaissance English Studies*, 25 (1974), p. 277, and also the introduction to her Revels edition of the play (Baltimore: Johns Hopkins University Press, 1978).

4. Middleton collaborated with Webster, ca. 1621, on *Anything for a Quiet Life*, and soon contributed commendatory verses to the first quarto of *The Duchess of Malfi*. See F. L. Lucas, *The Complete Works of John Webster*, 4 vols. (London: Chatto & Windus, 1927), 2:34.

5. In *Shakespeare's Tragic Frontier* (Berkeley and Los Angeles: University of California Press, 1950), Willard Farnham cites Webster's *White Devil* and Chapman's *Bussy* and *Byron* plays as helping us "to understand the Jacobean quality in Shakespeare's last tragic world" (p. 12). In *The Tragic Satire of John Webster* (Berkeley and Los Angeles: University of California Press, 1955), Travis Bogard usefully discusses Webster's affinities with Chapman, though I think he wrongly identifies *The Revenge of Bussy D'Ambois* as the primary influence; see also M. C. Bradbrook's perceptive analysis of Webster's relation to Chapman's *Byron* plays, "Two Notes upon Webster," *Modern Language Review*, 42 (1947), pp. 281–294.

6. In contrast, G. K. Hunter thinks "Malevole's excellence is, as it were, outside himself. He is the mouthpiece of an unchanging though complex set of standards by which the fools *have* to be judged." See Hunter's introduction to his Revels edition of *The Malcontent* (London: Methuen, 1975), p. lix.

7. Hunter's comment on Antony is equally true of Coriolanus and Byron in peacetime politics and is close to our sense of Bussy, who tries to give substance to a heroic ideal (the Golden Age of "native noblesse") in an Iron present. Antony "is an exile from a world that we never see in the play, which existed splendidly in the past and will never be recovered again. . . . In the past it had seemed possible to be both glamorous and efficient, heroic and political. But Antony's 'heroic' gestures . . . are seen to be quite inappropriate to the present in which he lives." See "The Last Tragic Heroes" in *Later Shakespeare*, Strat-

ford-Upon-Avon Studies 8, J. R. Brown and B. Harris, eds. (London: Edward Arnold, 1966), pp. 21–22. See also Robert Ornstein's article in the same volume, "The Ethic of the Imagination: Love and Art in *Antony and Cleopatra*," pp. 35–37; and Millar MacLure, "Shakespeare and the Lonely Dragon," *University of Toronto Quarterly*, 24 (1954–1955), pp. 109–120.

8. "Historical realism," if you will, inspired the Machiavel's growth from the bogey-man Vice to the successful politician: the accent of Italianate evil is, by and large, replaced by the cool realism that made Prince Hal such a successful "man o' th' times." Alvin Kernan analyzes the increasingly "realistic" politicians of Shakespeare's history plays in "*The Henriad*: Shakespeare's Major History Plays," *Yale Review*, 59 (1969), pp. 3–32. See also Ornstein's discussion of the increasingly overt relation between Machiavel and the Renaissance's political "New Men, who subvert traditional aristocratic hierarchies," in *The Moral Vision of Jacobean Tragedy* (Madison: University of Wisconsin Press, 1965), chap. 1, esp. pp. 27 and 24–31; and Cyrus Hoy's "Jacobean Tragedy and the Mannerist Style," *Shakespeare Survey*, 26 (1973), pp. 49–67.

9. Maynard Mack, "The Jacobean Shakespeare: Some Observations on the Construction of the Tragedies," in *Jacobean Theatre*, Stratford-Upon-Avon Studies 1, ed. J. R. Brown and B. Harris (1960; rpt. New York: Capricorn Books, 1967), p. 15. The tragic protagonist may approach the status of comic butt, and this condition constitutes what Rossiter in *Angel with Horns* calls tragedy's "final alarmingness": not "loss of life," nor injustice, "but the threat of indignity, of the loss of heroic *existence*, by the mocking devaluation of those very qualities by which the hero commands our admiration" (p. 272). In defining the contrast as less between "good" and "evil" than between "values" and "non-values," Rossiter's approach resembles my own formulation of farce's challenge to tragic heroism. See also Lionel Trilling's observations in *Sincerity and Authenticity* (Cambridge: Harvard University Press, 1971), pp. 87–88.

10. At least one critic sees *The Revenger's Tragedy* as a sophisticated "black parody" of revenge plays and "a profound examination of the implications of the genre's immense popularity." See Leslie Sanders, "*The Revenger's Tragedy*: A Play on the Revenge Play," *Renaissance and Reformation*, 10 (1974), p. 25. Although some influence of *The Revenger's Tragedy* on Webster is obvious, especially in *The White Devil*, in this area Middleton provided no model.

11. In *Shakespeare: Seven Tragedies* (London: Macmillan, 1976), E. A. J. Honigmann notes that we "know how the Roman heroes appear to others from the outside, but, paradoxically, this knowledge conceals the inner man and helps to keep him at a distance" (p. viii). Foakes links this distancing both to the "problem" comedies and the late romances in *Shakespeare: The Dark Comedies to the Last Plays*, pp. 92–93.

12. In *The Tudor Play of Mind: Rhetorical Inquiry and the Development of Elizabethan Drama* (Berkeley and Los Angeles: University of California Press, 1978), Joel B. Altman traces the popularity of sophistic rhetorical structures for dramatists more interested in exploring ethical questions than moralizing them. Pursuing the same interests in later drama, in *The Rhetoric of Tragedy* (Amherst: University of Massachusetts Press, 1966), Charles Osborne McDonald is particularly acute on Chapman's "deliberate use of the antilogies 'built into' the sophistic tradition of rhetoric to create not only patterns of meaning but of form for his play" (p. 223).

13. Nicholas Brooke notes Chapman's effective sketch of a morality-play structure in this initial confrontation: stage directions describe figures of Poverty and Wealth, and Bussy clearly opposes humble virtue to corrupt ambition. See the introduction to Brooke's Revels edition of the original, 1607, version of *Bussy D'Ambois* (London: Methuen, 1964), p. xxviii; all subsequent quotations from the play will be from this edition. Brooke also notes that Chapman alters history to make his more general points: as an unemployed soldier and devotee of virtuous action, Chapman's Bussy bears little resemblance to the courtier and womanizer of recent French history. See Brooke's capsule account, pp. lix–lx.

14. In his introduction Brooke analyzes brilliantly the ways in which Bussy's prologue-soliloquy prepares us for the subsequent, contradictory perspectives on his actions: "Latent throughout is the implication of a healthy development of human powers, whose reach should be almost infinite; this is seen to be bafflingly impossible, but also to be the positive drive without which nothing has value. . . . [In Bussy] is explored precisely the conflict of the two meanings of 'virtue' which come out in his opening speech: his moral effort is to achieve the harmony of goodness and greatness, which from the beginning he indicates as impossible" (pp. xxxi and xxxiv). It is still an open question whether Chapman dramatizes a conflict between classical and Renaissance, humanist and Christian ideals.

15. The disparity between Bussy's claims and deeds is the play's most fully documented aspect. Most critics stress either language or action and see Bussy as exemplary, good or bad. In a less schematic study, "The Ironic Tragedies of Marston and Chapman: Notes on Jacobean Tragic Form," *Journal of English and Germanic Philology,* 69 (1970), pp. 613–630, Allen Bergson finds the ironic juxtaposition important, but feels such relentless undercutting produces a study in the failure of human aspirations. The most persuasive of those adopting a two-tier system, which sees Bussy acting simultaneously in the realms of the ideal and the real, is Eugene M. Waith. Waith recognizes that "purity of motive and corruption of act are brought out by the ambiguity of every major incident," but he feels rather that such paradoxes create "the moving dilemma

of a great-spirited man" trapped in "a world dominated by Machiavellian policy." See *The Herculean Hero in Marlowe, Chapman, Shakespeare and Dryden* (London: Chatto & Windus, 1962), p. 111.

16. Ennis Rees, *The Tragedies of George Chapman* (Cambridge, Mass.: Harvard University Press, 1954), p. 44.

17. In accepting Monsieur's crowns Bussy himself admitted the latent sexual implications of Monsieur's purchase. Seeing that Monsieur wants to corrupt his good intentions, to "sow" his crowns "upon my spirit" like "politic seed," Bussy still decides, "If I may . . . rise in Court with virtue, speed his plough" (I.i.119–126).

18. M. R. Ridley's Arden edition of *Antony and Cleopatra* (Cambridge, Mass.: Harvard University Press, 1954), I.i. 34–40, 4, 12–13. Subsequent citations will be to this edition.

19. Paul A. Jorgensen shows that in such a tradition the all-important question is, "Will Antony renounce his idleness, regain his lost soldiership, and become once more formidable in empire and war?" Shakespeare adds this tension to Plutarch's account, for Plutarch assumes Antony is beyond hope. See "Antony and the Protesting Soldiers: A Renaissance Tradition for the Structure of *Antony and Cleopatra*," in *Essays on Shakespeare*, ed. Gordon Smith (University Park: Pennsylvania State University Press, 1965), p. 165.

20. In *Poets on Fortune's Hill: Studies in Sidney, Shakespeare, Beaumont and Fletcher* (London: Faber and Faber, 1952), John F. Danby offers a long analysis of I.i similar to the one sketched here. William Rosen, too, in *Shakespeare and the Craft of Tragedy* (Cambridge, Mass.: Harvard University Press, 1960), sees the dominant mode of characterization in the play's first part as the "repeated framing of Antony's character and actions," and he suggests that it forces us to "assume the role of judge" and compare our view of Antony with that of his interpreters (pp. 129 and 135).

21. In *The Common Liar: An Essay on "Antony and Cleopatra"* (New Haven: Yale University Press, 1973), Janet Adelman explores devices by which Shakespeare dissociates us from the lovers and asks us to participate more often in the commentators' experience or adopt perspectives totally unrelated to the protagonists'. She goes on to note that "a dramatic structure in which the minor characters continually intervene between the protagonists and the audience is more characteristic of farce than it is of tragedy" (p. 50).

22. The illuminating background to this image, in Chapman as well as Shakespeare, is explored in the first two chapters of Waith's *Herculean Hero* and in chaps. 1–3 of Reuben A. Brower's *Hero and Saint: Shakespeare and the Graeco-Roman Heroic Tradition* (Oxford: At the Clarendon Press, 1971); see also the discussion at n. 7 just above.

23. Hunter, in "The Last Tragic Heroes," comments on the effect of con-

tinued play on *Antony* as both a name and an ideal of what the man once was and ought again to be: "The magic of an image of *Antony* has the power to hold the heroic past alive for the moment of the present; but the magic is a kind of confidence-trick. Nothing in the present really supports the idea" (p. 25).

24. That it is self-destruction, and only secondarily Caesar's luck, Shakespeare makes clear. The soldiers see that in fleeing Antony violates his own best qualities, and Antony speaks of his very hairs mutinying. Caesar later puts Antony's revolted soldiers in the van, "that Antony may seem to spend his fury / Upon himself" (IV.vi.10–11), and the figure of speech is literalized, of course, in Antony's suicide. Waith's discussion in *The Herculean Hero* of Antony's generosity is pertinent here: "Antony is spending his substance prodigally—in effect, giving himself away" (p. 115).

25. Analyzing Antony's concern with "disintegration and identity," Stephen A. Shapiro concludes that, paradoxically, the "richness of Antony's humanity increases with the instability of his attitudes"; see "The Varying Shore of the World: Ambivalence in *Antony and Cleopatra*," *Modern Language Quarterly*, 27 (1966), p. 24, and David Daiches, "Imagery and Meaning in *Antony and Cleopatra*," *English Studies*, 43 (1962), p. 355, from which Shapiro quotes the observation on Antony's humanity.

26. In "*Coriolanus*: Tragedy or Debate?" *Essays in Criticism*, 4 (1954), D. J. Enright notes "certain qualities of an intellectual debate" in the play and suggests that "the implications which the theme could carry for ordinary humanity are, as is the convention in debating, left tacitly aside" (pp. 4 and 10).

27. Philip Brockbank's Arden edition of *Coriolanus* (London: Methuen, 1976), I.i. 6–7, 29–30. Subsequent citations will be to this edition.

28. In *Shakespeare: A Survey* (New York: Hill and Wang, n.d.), p. 260, E. K. Chambers mentions in passing that in *Coriolanus* "the shattered ideal is that of honour. Beneath the mask of honour there lurks the subtle sin of egoism." Norman Rabkin lucidly analyzes the implications of what is, in I.ix, essentially a debate on the nature of honor, in *Shakespeare and the Common Understanding* (New York: Free Press, 1967), pp. 129–133. See also D. J. Gordon's excellent "Name and Fame: Shakespeare's Coriolanus," in *Papers, Mainly Shakespearean*, Aberdeen University Studies 147, ed. G. I. Duthie (London: Oliver and Boyd, 1964), pp. 40–57.

29. In *An Approach to Shakespeare* (2d ed., 1954; rpt. New York: Doubleday Anchor, 1956), Derek Traversi says that in this speech Coriolanus himself "caricatures his warlike valor" (p. 219); see also Rabkin's discussion in *Shakespeare and the Common Understanding*, esp. pp. 122–123. As Rossiter remarks in *Angel with Horns*, "Marcius's rages totter on the edge of a line which Jonson would have pushed them over—into ridicule" (p. 245).

30. Interpreting the play as satire, O. J. Campbell reduces Coriolanus to this

one comic role; see *Shakespeare's Satire* (New York: Oxford University Press, 1943), pp. 198–217. Noting that in the preface to *Man and Superman* G. B. Shaw calls *Coriolanus* "the greatest of Shakespeare's comedies," John Middleton Murry goes on to say that to "put the matter irreverently, Coriolanus is a big school-boy; Molière might have disposed of him better than Shakespeare." See *John Clare and Other Studies* (London and New York: Peter Nevill, 1950), pp. 222–223.

31. In "Voice and Deed in *Coriolanus*," Leonard Dean observes that "the opposition between *voice* and *deed* deepens into the metaphor of play-acting," which also applies to Coriolanus's final submission: as a "dull actor," the "man who had thought to preserve the integrity of his essential nature by refusing to play-act now unconsciously speaks of that 'integrity' itself as another role." See *University of Kansas City Review*, 21 (1955), pp. 177 and 183–184.

32. In *Shakespeare's Military World* (Berkeley and Los Angeles: University of California Press, 1956), Paul A. Jorgensen notes that Plutarch stresses the political circumstances behind Coriolanus's history; depriving Coriolanus of the eloquence and willingness for peacetime political office accorded him by Plutarch, Shakespeare wholly alters the story's significance (pp. 299 and 313). See also M. W. MacCallum, *Shakespeare's Roman Plays and Their Background* (1910; rpt. London: Macmillan, 1925), p. 510.

33. I have not here followed Brockbank, who, with Style and Tucker Brooke, reassigns this line to Coriolanus's excited soldiers. The emendation is an interesting one, and does give the crowd Shakespearean words to "*shout*," but I do not find it fully persuasive; see Brockbank's discussion of i.vi.75ff. on p. 138 of his Arden edition.

34. Traversi, *An Approach to Shakespeare*, p. 226. Wilson Knight long ago noted the absence, in Coriolanus's mechanical fighting, of the "glamour of romance, like Antony's"; see *The Imperial Theme* (1931; rpt. London: Methuen, 1951), p. 168. See also Brockbank's introduction, where he nicely catches the complex effect of imagery deifying mechanization: "The protesting hyperboles belong both to the tragic and to the comic imagination" (p. 51).

35. In this Coriolanus simply makes total the depersonalization of others that marked his refusal of communal meanings in the marketplace and his reversal of Rome's banishment in "a magnificent gesture, asserting himself as a subject and objectifying the whole city: 'I banish you.'" So Terence Eagleton, in *Shakespeare and Society* (New York: Schocken, 1967), p. 113. See also James L. Calderwood, "*Coriolanus*: Wordless Meanings and Meaningless Words," in *Essays in Shakespearean Criticism*, J. L. Calderwood and H. E. Toliver, eds. (Englewood Cliffs, N.J.: Prentice-Hall, 1970), esp. pp. 554–555.

36. The "chorus" of Monsieur and Guise (act 5) and Henry's eulogy (act 3) seem to be Chapman's version of a Shakespearean device—a "dream of D'Am-

bois" or, as Cleopatra would have it, of one "past the size of dreaming"; see Millar Maclure's discussion in *George Chapman: A Critical Study* (Toronto: University of Toronto Press, 1966), p. 123. L. C. Knights discusses Cleopatra's figure as one "disengaged from, or glimpsed through," the play's Antony; see "On the Tragedy of Antony and Cleopatra," *Scrutiny*, 16 (1949), p. 322.

37. Waith, *The Herculean Hero*, p. 114.

38. Adelman, in *The Common Liar*, is more positive about Antony's final stature than I, but her account of Antony well describes the ideal glimpsed through him and adumbrated in Cleopatra's dream: "If at the start of the play Antony overflows the measure, by its end he has become the measure: at his death, the odds is gone" (p. 139). William Blissett adds, tellingly, that in her effect on Dolabella we see that the "stature of Antony, the fascination of Cleopatra, are still being freshly revealed in act five"; see "Dramatic Irony in *Antony and Cleopatra*," *Shakespeare Quarterly*, 18 (1967), p. 164.

39. This tendency to abstraction pervades the play. Descriptions and debates about Envy, Honour, Sin, Justice, Great Men, and Nature abound, and everyone seems determined to place his private actions in the largest possible moral framework. The technique is less academic and pedantic than it sounds, and in this play, at least, Chapman gains some of the energizing tension between the passionate individual and a self-conscious awareness of significance that distinguishes Shakespeare's Hal, Falstaff, and Hamlet.

40. Monsieur's and the Guise's theories also, of course, absolve Bussy of responsibility for his own end and blunt his ethical criticism of their society. Bussy's satiric stance rests on a belief in man's accountability for his physical and moral life, his right and obligation to be a law unto himself in a corrupt society. Monsieur's explanation would reduce Bussy and everyone else to the status of fate's ministers. Tamyra's and the Friar's belief in physiological determinism varies the justification but would also rob Bussy of tragic stature: if "our affections' storm, / Rais'd in our blood, no Reason can reform," then Bussy, like Coriolanus or Antony, becomes simply his body's puppet (II.ii.186–187).

41. Danby, in *Poets on Fortune's Hill*, observes that Caesar is in the line of Shakespearean politicians, but now taken for granted as "part of the structure of things. . . . The politician is a perfectly normal person. . . . To be normal like him . . . two conditions are necessary. First, one must sacrifice the other half of life [for politics is only half]; then, one must be prepared to make complete submission" (pp. 143–144). Thomas McFarland finds Caesar's qualities to be similar but more disturbing: "confidence in the reality of the world, willingness to live in the future, inability to love"; see "Antony and Octavius," *Yale Review*, 48 (1958), pp. 212 and 219.

42. MacLure captures this sense of awesome but delusive self-dramatization in *George Chapman:* the hero is possessed "not by a theory but by a *daimon,*

the author, so to speak, of a private play in which the protagonist, looking constantly in a mirror to see the world, sees all but himself out of focus" (p. 111); in *Hero and Saint* Brower calls Coriolanus a man "whose true love is his own heroic image" (p. 380). On the self-absorption and alienation of Shakespeare's late, "fully Jacobean tragedies," see also Hoy's "Jacobean Tragedy and the Mannerist Style," pp. 58–61.

43. In *The Story of the Night: Studies in Shakespeare's Major Tragedies* (Lincoln: University of Nebraska Press, 1961), John Holloway emphasizes the lovers' "sense of having the rôle of greatness to live up to" and their attraction to each other's nobility, their dwelling on it even more than their love "at the moment of disaster and crisis" (pp. 102–103). See also Dorothea Krook, *Elements of Tragedy* (New Haven: Yale University Press, 1969), pp. 210n. and 226.

44. Although recent critics have tended to take Cleopatra more or less at her word, Honigmann feels that, on the contrary, she strains too hard and gets carried away with her own hyperbole: in *Shakespeare: Seven Tragedies* he suggests that her "ineradicable love of pose and spectacle" casts doubt upon her "ennoblement" (pp. 163–164). For a different but related view, see L. J. Mills, "Cleopatra's Tragedy," *Shakespeare Quarterly*, 11 (1960), pp. 147–162. Hoy ("Jacobean Tragedy and the Mannerist Style") balances both sides nicely: "Both lovers are prepared to die, as they have lived, by love, and their tragic stature consists in their readiness to accept their fate, but they do not accept their fate without a certain amount of imaginative re-adjustment of the realities that have overtaken them" (p. 64).

45. In his introduction to the play Brooke, too, sees in Bussy's final speeches a progressive self-awareness: "The Stoical fortitude suggests Seneca; the complaint to heaven, Hercules: hence the translated lines. Bussy, whose initial despair led to belief in Monsieur's chance-ruled life, has come to see himself as a successful hero in Guise's terms—a noble death is the end for which Nature designed him." But the "splendid" gesture is false to the play's complexity, and in "the egotism of his noble death he ignores the suffering of the lives for which he has become responsible" (p. li).

46. Shakespeare's departures from North make problematic the private victory of the authoritarian mother over the fractious child. For North's Volumnia, honest judgment and duty are not separate and equal grounds of appeal ("And therefore, it is not only honest, but due unto me, that without compulsion I should obtaine my so just and reasonable request of thee"). Her mention of nobility also shades immediately into noble men's duty to parents; she fails to mention at all either mercy or the kind of honor that emulates the gods' graces. In North's translation Volumnia's personal victory is explicitly acknowledged by her son: "Oh mother, said he, . . . I see my self vanquished by you alone."

All quotations from North's translation of Plutarch are on p. 363 of the Arden edition's appendix.

47. Arnold Stein, "The Image of Antony: Lyric and Tragic Imagination," *Kenyon Review,* 21 (1959), p. 605.

48. All quotations are from "The Last Tragic Heroes," p. 18. Though Hunter's analysis is brilliant, I obviously do not share his conclusion that Shakespeare's last tragedies offer us, finally, only the "alternative heroisms of stone or water" (p. 25).

49. The dying hero is the repository of whatever moral order these plays discover, despite his natural ethics' coincidence with fundamental, traditional Christian virtues. On this point, see Harold Wilson, *On the Design of Shakespearean Tragedy* (Toronto: University of Toronto Press, 1957), p. 213. In this sense the plays are both secular and strangely modern. Strikingly apt is Friedrich Duerrenmatt's discussion of the possibility of tragedy in our secular and anti-heroic world, where "there are no more guilty and also, no responsible men." If "tragedy presupposes guilt, despair, moderation, lucidity, vision, a sense of responsibility," for us "guilt can exist only as a personal achievement, as a religious deed." Duerrenmatt maintains that "the tragic is still possible even if pure tragedy is not," and we can achieve it "out of comedy." Man can still be shown as a "courageous being" and, within such a being, "the lost world order is restored." See "Problems of the Theatre," *Tulane Drama Review,* 3 (1958), pp. 20–21.

CHAPTER III

1. In "The Date of Chapman's *Bussy D'Ambois,*" *Modern Language Review,* 3 (1908), pp. 126–140, T. M. Parrott argues for a revival of *Bussy,* as well as *The Widow's Tears,* by the Queen's Revels' children at Whitefriars around 1610. Accepting Parrott's thesis, Albert H. Tricomi presents the case for tandem performances of *Bussy* with its sequel; see "The Revised *Bussy D'Ambois* and *The Revenge of Bussy D'Ambois:* Joint Performance in Thematic Counterpoint," *English Language Notes,* 9 (1971–1972), pp. 253–262. While there is no external evidence for such a revival, strong additional circumstantial evidence is offered in Albert R. Braunmuller's "Chapman's *Bussy D'Ambois* and Field's *Amends for Ladies,*" *Notes and Queries,* n.s. 26 (1979), pp. 401–403.

2. J. R. Mulryne's focus on Webster's use of comedy leads him to brilliant discussions of dramatic technique. In his Regents Renaissance edition of *The White Devil* (Lincoln: University of Nebraska Press, 1969), Mulryne observes that "although *The White Devil* is cast, however unsystematically, in the mold

of the Revenge play, its pedigree of feeling, if not form, can be better traced through comedy than through tragedy." Mulryne cogently locates the audience's problem in the "difficulty" in reconciling "the resulting comic detachment with what we can only take to be the play's ultimate seriousness" (p. xxii). See also "*The White Devil* and *The Duchess of Malfi*" in *Jacobean Theatre*, Stratford-Upon-Avon Studies 1, eds. J. R. Brown and B. Harris (1960, rev. 1965; rpt. New York: Capricorn, 1967), pp. 201–225. Examining Webster's early work with Dekker, Neil Carson finds some interesting precedents for Webster's later dramatic technique; see "John Webster: The Apprentice Years," *The Elizabethan Theatre VI*, ed. G. R. Hibbard (Hamden, Conn.: Archon, 1977), pp. 76–87, and also Inga-Stina Ewbank, "Webster's Realism, or, 'A Cunning Piece Wrought Perspective'" in the Mermaid Critical Commentaries volume *John Webster*, ed. Brian Morris (London: Ernest Benn, 1970), p. 165.

3. Harold Jenkins, "The Tragedy of Revenge in Shakespeare and Webster," *Shakespeare Survey*, 14 (1961), p. 49. The extension to Shakespeare's last tragedies may seem tenuous—though one of Caesar's stated motives for pursuing Antony is to do Octavia justice, and Aufidius in some sense revenges the betrayed Volscians as well as his own hurt pride—but the idea of reversal does help illuminate the altered conception of the tragic protagonist and his place in the world. In "'Quaintly Done': A Reading of *The White Devil*," *Essays and Studies*, n.s. 19 (1966), Roma Gill correctly sees Websterian tragedy as "an unusual and unequal mixture" of Kydian revenge tragedy and the psychological probing of motives which we accept in Middleton; the third component she finds in Webster—"a disturbing moral ambiguity"—is not "his alone" (p. 42).

4. In his Mermaid Critical Commentaries article, "Webster and the Uses of Tragicomedy," Mulryne argues that Webster diverts his plays from tragedy to tragicomedy and that the employment of tragicomic tensions explains the "division of response" and "genuine ambivalence of feeling" we experience in both plays (p. 138). Despite the similarity of Mulryne's title to my own interests, I think his reading errs in locating the plays' dynamic in a conflict between instinct and moral sense, rather than between the moral certainties our minds favor and contradictory ambivalences with which the world (and the "realistic" farceur) counter that simplification. The latter tension is not necessarily limited to personal confrontations, though the plays are full of those; it also exists within the main characters themselves and endows them with tragic potential.

5. Printed in 1612, quite probably (according to J. R. Brown) from a manuscript supplied by Webster himself, *The White Devil* appeared without act or scene divisions. The play's first sweeping movement, ending with the climactic mother-son interview, is conventionally designated as act 1. The text to which I will refer is J. R. Brown's edition for The Revels Plays (2nd ed., 1966; rpt.

London: Methuen, 1968). While I have adopted Brown's orthography in des-
ignating Webster's dramatis personae, I have not standardized the variety of
spellings which appear in the cited critical articles.

6. In a characteristically perceptive essay, "The Tragedy of Blood," *Scrutiny*,
8 (1939), James Smith notes that they "are mocking rather than rebuking
Ludovico; or if they rebuke him at all, it is for not being sufficiently hypocritical
as they are. . . . The dialogue is an artifice—hence its artificial structure; and by
it the speakers intend that artifice shall be recommended" (p. 269).

7. Robert Dent sees Flamineo's early speeches on women as one indication of
his complexity: "In these initial speeches his cynical joviality allows him to
minimize the evil of his activity, to affect a nonchalance in evil he thinks a sign
of sophistication, and to pretend (in vain) an easy familiarity with Brachiano as
of two men of the world conversing with one another." See *John Webster's
Borrowing* (Berkeley and Los Angeles: University of California Press, 1960), p.
29.

8. Two attitudes toward love confront each other, but neither can be said to
"prove" the other wrong. As B. J. Layman says, "When we perceive how
Webster contrives for the two charged voices of mask wearer and mask stripper
to exist side by side without canceling each other out, we move very close to the
essential poetic structure of the drama." See "The Equilibrium of Opposites in
The White Devil: A Reinterpretation," *PMLA*, 74 (1959), p. 342. In establishing the "elements of domestic drama" in both Webster's Italianate tragedies in
her essay "Webster's Realism," Inga-Stina Ewbank astutely notes that Webster
undermines the heroic tone by modulating from "the triple-pillar idiom of
Antony and Cleopatra" to the "definitely bourgeois" discussion of shifting shirts
after tennis in II.i (p. 172).

9. Both Gill and Elizabeth M. Brennan note that Camillo is a stock comic
figure, and both conclude that his comic impotence encourages sympathy for
Vittoria's adultery. See "'Quaintly Done,'" p. 46, and Brennan, "'An Understanding Auditory': An Audience for John Webster," in the Mermaid Critical
Commentaries volume *John Webster*, p. 14. Such sympathy for the young wife
of an impotent cuckold surely exists, but only so long as the context is one of
city comedy; it is a response appropriate to a comic handling of adultery, not
murder.

10. Rupert Brooke, *John Webster and the Elizabethan Drama* (New York:
John Lane Co., 1916), p. 145; see also Clifford Leech's early but excellent
discussion of Flamineo as both creative actor and voyeur, in *John Webster: A
Critical Study* (London: Hogarth Press, 1951), pp. 49–51. John F. McElroy
shares my sense that Flamineo enjoys his role "not only because it offers him a
means of validating his own very low estimate of human nature, but because it

emotionally distances him from an otherwise demeaning situation"; see *"The White Devil, Women Beware Women,* and the Limitations of Rationalist Criticism," *Studies in English Literature, 1500–1900,* 19 (1979), p. 308.

11. Observing that "Harold Jenkins is virtually alone in rejecting Flamineo's interpretation" of Vittoria's dream, Robert Dent maintains that both views are defensible because Webster encourages the "audience to suspend judgment," though they "would wait in vain" for proof; see "The White Devil, or Vittoria Corombona?" *Renaissance Drama,* 9 (1966), p. 193, but also idem, *John Webster's Borrowing,* pp. 87–88. In the notes to his text of the play Brown agrees that there are two ways of interpreting Vittoria's dream (see n. to 1.ii.243). Pertinent here is A. J. Smith's observation that the "notorious ambiguity of the motives and characters of *The White Devil* comes back to the language and the way it pushes one away; we can't place these people because they don't tell us about themselves"; see "The Power of *The White Devil"* in the Mermaid Critical Commentaries volume *John Webster,* p. 78.

12. In the introduction to his edition Brown notes that "whatever action takes place, there is always some one observing and commenting upon it" (p. xlv). This particular scene is extravagant in its plethora of commentators, but elsewhere, too, the clash of perspectives generates uncertainty: "The comments do not simplify the play for us, they involve us in it, and make us question the implications of its action and dialogue" (pp. li–lii).

13. If one thinks Flamineo understands his world and voices Webster's point of view, it follows that in this scene he silences his mother with "truth," reveals the necessity for his own behavior, and delineates Webster's vision. The most extensive and persuasive argument for Flamineo as Webster's tragic chorus is Travis Bogard's in *The Tragic Satire of John Webster* (Berkeley and Los Angeles: University of California Press, 1955).

14. Smith, in "The Power of *The White Devil,"* aptly characterizes the seemingly objective language especially prominent in such confrontations: the language points outward rather than inward, often by "some relatively impersonal and public manner of reference such as proverbial lore. These speeches work above all to offer a context of reference and action, present a certain account of the world; through them the characters of the play are always offering to define the kind of world they inhabit, or the kind of world they think they know and can manipulate" (p. 78). For a related view of Flamineo as a "rationalizing thinker" who "cannot quite get rid of the notion that the traditional virtues have value," see Peter B. Murray's *A Study of John Webster* (The Hague: Mouton, 1969), p. 46.

15. As Gunnar Boklund says, "There is something bordering on smugness in the remarks of Isabella, Cornelia and Marcello; if the irresponsibility of such virtue is not implied in Webster's presentation, the impracticability of it most

certainly is"; see *The Sources of "The White Devil"* (Uppsala: Lundequistska Bokhandeln, 1957), p. 177. See also J. R. Mulryne's introduction to his Regents Renaissance edition of *The White Devil*, p. xxi.

16. Mulryne, "Webster and the Uses of Tragicomedy," p. 145; but see also Boklund, *The Sources of "The White Devil,"* pp. 158–159, and Leech, *John Webster: A Critical Study*, p. 47.

17. The quoted phrase is from J. R. Mulryne's Regents Renaissance edition of *The White Devil*, p. xxii. Sensibly taming Ralph Berry's discussion of "baroque" elements in Webster, as laid out in *The Art of John Webster* (Oxford: At the Clarendon Press, 1972), Carson discusses "the alternation between moments which involve us totally in the emotions and fortunes of the characters, and passages that invite us to remain detached, critical, and reflective"; see "John Webster: The Apprentice Years," p. 86.

18. Many commentators feel that the murder-by-dumbshow successfully distances us from the victims' innocence and suffering and allows us to continue sympathizing with the lovers, even as we see the deed for which revenge will later be exacted. See Ian Scott-Kilvert, *John Webster*, Writers and Their Work No. 175 (London: British Council, 1964), pp. 19–20; Brown's Revels edition, p. xliv; and Mulryne, "*The White Devil* and *The Duchess of Malfi*," pp. 203–204.

19. I am almost alone in sharing Robert Dent's sense of the ironic distance between Webster and his dramatic creation. As "a lover of craft with too turbulent a spirit to be successfully crafty," Flamineo lacks self-control and self-knowledge. Dent concludes that it "would be truer to say that Flamineo is of all men the most deceived, the least objective, in really essential matters, and that much of his cynicism is but an inverted species of cant. . . . He knows neither himself, his fellows, nor the world"; see *John Webster's Borrowing*, p. 30. See also Robert Ornstein, *The Moral Vision of Jacobean Tragedy* (Madison: University of Wisconsin Press, 1965) p. 138.

20. In her excellent discussion in "Webster's Realism" of Webster's energetic use of language, his masterful pitting of one idiom against another, Inga-Stina Ewbank notes that "the trial scene, which has tremendous linguistic vitality, is in a sense also a scene about the uses and possibilities of language" (p. 176). In *The Moral Vision of Jacobean Tragedy*, Ornstein, too, asserts that the critical debate about Vittoria's moral stature during the trial is misdirected, for although she seems "to nullify the charges hurled against her, it is not because she is more than innocent, but because innocence and guilt are not the primary issues in her arraignment" (p. 132).

21. W. A. Edwards's complaint about Webster's "conceited" style denies the dramatic interest of characters who are self-conscious virtuosi and the fact that rhetorical self-consciousness is precisely the point. His description of the style's

effect is, however, completely accurate: "The style of the conceited character-writer . . . is the style of an objective, rather cynical observer, commenting and reflecting upon men and actions, and constantly invites admiration for the elegance of its manner. It tends towards epigram and maxim, and uses simile rather than metaphor. . . . For dramatic utterance such a style of writing is too formal, too far from speech-idiom." Since the Cardinal's character of a whore is composed of disconnected observations, "we are left thinking of the last epigram and trying vainly to recollect the others. At the end of his speech we lack any clear conception of the whore, and are conscious only of an admiration for the Cardinal's talent as a wit." See "Revaluations (I): John Webster," *Scrutiny*, 2 (1933), p. 17.

22. The phrase is Irving Ribner's, from *Jacobean Tragedy: The Quest for Moral Order* (London: Methuen, 1962), p. 102. See also H. Bruce Franklin's excellent discussion of the trial's complex rhetorical poses, in "The Trial Scene of Webster's *The White Devil* Examined in Terms of Renaissance Rhetoric," *Studies in English Literature, 1500–1900*, 1 (1961), p. 51.

23. In "The Power of *The White Devil*" Smith develops the analogy and locates part of the play's disturbing tone in the fact that "there is something inherently farcical both in the view that characters take to each other and in the playwright's attitude to all of them. We see them struggling to control their world by deriding it, while he persistently betrays their assurance with his ironies" (p. 89).

24. The Machiavellian world of great princes to which Lodovico, Vittoria, and Flamineo aspire is indeed governed by what Ornstein in *The Moral Vision of Jacobean Tragedy* calls "the blind determinism of the emancipated will" (p. 138). Smith, too, in "The Power of *The White Devil*," sees the attempt to impose one's will on others as the play's theme: the world of power "is a special case only in its writing large of human will, in the freedom it gives men to do as we would" (p. 81).

25. Mulryne, "*The White Devil* and *The Duchess of Malfi*," p. 207.

26. If the trial has exposed one public use of language, the "curious dialogue between Flamineo and Lodovico after Vittoria's trial is a very blatant demonstration of language as attitudinising—one which in itself undercuts the verbal activity of the malcontent critic." Ewbank ("Webster's Realism") sees this scene's emphasis on "language as a self-conscious device" as characteristic of *The White Devil*; it is part of the power struggle in a world of *Realpolitik* and "it is, above all a way of hiding the truth" (p. 175).

27. In *John Webster's Borrowing*, Dent notes Marcia Lee Anderson's comparison of this scene with the "strict friendship" between Malevole and Bilioso in Marston's *Malcontent*, i.i. (p. 118). More pertinent, I think, is the calculated rogues' banter between Malevole and Mendoza in the same play (ii.v), though

the witty duel between rogues, each adopting hypocritical poses to gull the other, is also a standard comic situation in Middleton's city comedies. Given the underlying aggression in *The White Devil*'s scene, and Lodovico's destiny as Flamineo's murderer, Webster may also have had in mind the "flyting" between Bussy and Monsieur in Chapman's *Bussy D'Ambois*. For some suggestive remarks on similarities between Flamineo, Bosola, Freevill, and Malevole, see G. K. Hunter's "English Folly and Italian Vice: The Moral Landscape of John Marston," in *Jacobean Theatre*, pp. 104–105 and 110.

28. Boklund, *The Sources of "The White Devil,"* p. 167.

29. Monticelso's sudden access of virtue as Pope Paul IV is the only apparently unmotivated, Fletcherian transformation in a play where inconsistencies generally contribute to complexity of character. The conversion both introduces traditional moral values to challenge the revengers and illustrates virtue's ineffectiveness in the face of Francisco's passion and cunning. Certainly Webster builds much of his tension as well as his characterization on debates and confrontations between differing perspectives; in this instance, structural requirements seem to have taken precedence over consistency of characterization.

30. Francisco's aphorisms here, or in his "good prince" speech to Monticelso (IV.i), are of the same character as Flamineo's—the linguistic expression of the role they are acting within the play. Indeed, Layman points out in "The Equilibrium of Opposites" that "much of the most orotund moralizing, as well as gnomic wisdom, comes off the tongues of the artful deceivers hard at their game" (p. 336). As R. A. Foakes observes of the dramatic function of *sententiae* in *The Revenger's Tragedy*, "their triteness, their inadequacy as moral comment, their insufficiency in any perspective outside the immediate one, are what makes them the vehicle of much of the play's deepest irony." See Foakes's introduction to his Revels edition of *The Revenger's Tragedy* (London: Methuen, 1966), p. xxxiv.

31. In "Shakespeare and the Drama of His Time," in *Shakespeare: Aspects of Influence,* Harvard English Studies 7, ed. G. B. Evans (Cambridge, Mass.: Harvard University Press, 1976), pp. 21–42, Cyrus Hoy complains that in modeling his play on *Antony and Cleopatra*, Webster missed the point. He fails "to follow the death of the tragic hero with a closing movement which would depict the agony and death of the tragic heroine. . . . Vittoria is absent from much of the finale that ought rightly to be hers, and when at last she is brought on the scene, she is made to share it with Flamineo, whose role here as elsewhere overshadows hers" (p. 37).

32. In contrast, Leonora Leet Brodwin sees Bracciano as "totally devoid of narcissism," a man who would "never reduce [Vittoria's] individuality to that of a possessed thing"; see *Elizabethan Love Tragedy: 1587–1625* (New York: New York University Press, 1971), p. 274. Brodwin may have found her in-

spiration in F. L. Lucas, who feels that "few virtues are as moving as the courage and devotion of these lovers, who have been so ruthless and guilty in all else." See *The Complete Works of John Webster,* 4 vols. (London: Chatto & Windus, 1927), 1:96.

33. A staging consonant with this interpretation could emphasize the acceptance of kinship and momentary creation of familial identity. Flamineo's answer to Vittoria's confusion, "Then cast anchor," might indicate his offer of more than proverbial consolation. Brother and sister could come together as a physical unit, supporting each other as they face death; Flamineo docs not assert his solipsistic absoluteness until after he thinks his sister dead.

34. Strict moralistic interpreters of *The White Devil* see both Flamineo and Vittoria as damned and their deaths wholly without moral value. At the end they exhibit *only* the hardening effects of the life of sin, and the tragic meaning of their last speeches lies in their revelation of the "hopeless feeling of exclusion that is suffered by those who selfishly and willfully divorce themselves from their proper place in the human community"; see Peter B. Murray, *A Study of John Webster* (The Hague: Mouton, 1969), p. 99. See also E. B. Benjamin's "Patterns of Morality in *The White Devil,*" *English Studies,* 46 (1965), pp. 1–15; D. C. Gunby, *Webster: "The White Devil,"* Studies in English Literature No. 45 (London: Edward Arnold, 1971); and Ian Jack, "The Case of John Webster," *Scrutiny,* 16 (1949), pp. 38–43.

35. Structure thus enhances the effect of Webster's "satiric counterpointing" and allows Webster's plays to achieve what Bogard (in *Tragic Satire*) calls "the generalized and universal level" of pure tragedy (p. 5). See also Douglas Cole, "The Comic Accomplice in Elizabethan Revenge Tragedy," *Renaissance Drama,* 9 (1966), p. 138.

36. In *King Lear in Our Time* (Berkeley and Los Angeles: University of California Press, 1965), Maynard Mack says of tragedy that it "never tells us what to think; it shows us what we are and may be." Mack's conclusion about *King Lear* is close to my own sense of the tragic value in Flamineo's and Vittoria's deaths and explains why I reject the idea of mortality itself as being the most important "fact" of experience for Webster: "If there is any 'remorseless process' in *King Lear,* it is one that begs us to seek the meaning of our human fate not in what becomes of us, but in what we become. Death . . . is miscellaneous and commonplace; it is life whose quality may be made noble and distinctive" (p. 117). Although I disagree with his analyses of Webster's and Chapman's plays, my sense of what is and is not melodrama stems, at least in part, from the early and lasting impression made by Robert B. Heilman's *Tragedy and Melodrama* (Seattle: University of Washington Press, 1968), esp. chap. 3.

CHAPTER IV

1. Allen Bergson, "The Ironic Tragedies of Marston and Chapman: Notes on Jacobean Tragic Form," *Journal of English and Germanic Philology,* 69 (1970), continuation of n. 4, p. 615.

2. In his Revels Plays edition of *The Duchess of Malfi* (London: Methuen, 1964), John Russell Brown notes that one of the contradictions suggesting Bosola's complexity is his apparent indifference to the advancement he seeks: "Despite the energy of his railing and his service for Ferdinand, there is almost nothing he wants: his 'garb' of melancholy sits naturally upon him after his preferment, as before" (p. li). All references to *The Duchess of Malfi* will be to this edition.

3. Robert Ornstein, *The Moral Vision of Jacobean Tragedy* (Madison: University of Wisconsin Press, 1965), p. 144.

4. In *The Cankered Muse: Satire of the English Renaissance* (New Haven: Yale University Press, 1959), Alvin Kernan traces this side of Bosola's lineage and calls Bosola the "*ideal* Elizabethan satirist," a "textbook model" (p. 233). Fernand Lagarde is more accurate, I think, in seeing the function of the satiric aspects as one of liberating Webster from conventional, sentimental responses to his material and thus allowing him greater originality; see *John Webster,* 2 vols. (Toulouse: Association des Publications de la Faculté des Lettres et Sciences Humaines de Toulouse, 1968), 2:910–911.

5. In "A Contemporary View of *The Duchess of Malfi,*" *Comparative Drama,* 3 (1969), pp. 297–307, Louis D. Giannetti discusses the tableaux groupings of 1.i, with Bosola moving physically and morally between them. Giannetti's analysis of physical stage action usefully highlights the way Bosola serves as a go-between for the play's worlds as well as for the play and its theater audience (p. 301).

6. At one time it was felt certain that this speech represented a late revival's addition (ca. 1617), topically referring to the Concini affair which had recently stirred the French court; see especially E. E. Stoll, *John Webster* (Boston: Alfred Mudge, 1905). This no longer seems a necessary conclusion, and in his edition Brown argues persuasively for the speech's dramatic rather than topical pertinence (pp. xxv–xxvi). Whatever the speech's source, its placement makes it a significant part of Webster's play as we have it.

7. Roger Warren points out that the discussion of horses and riding, too, helps create a "poised and elegant, often witty" court atmosphere. At greater length and with more than two hypocritical courtiers, Webster strives here to communicate the sense of a busy, normal rather than grotesque, background; as Warren says, "we only come to Ferdinand's savagery by degrees, and . . . even

then, we are constantly reminded of other considerations." See "*The Duchess of Malfi* on the Stage" in the Mermaid Critical Commentaries volume *John Webster*, ed. Brian Morris (London: Ernest Benn, 1970), pp. 47–48.

8. As J. R. Mulryne astutely notes, the bond between these siblings is "a matter of 'blood,' in all the Elizabethan senses of that term. . . . The Duchess, by acts of choice and by eddies of temperament, is firmly knit to the world that destroys her." See "Webster and the Uses of Tragicomedy," in the Mermaid Critical Commentaries *John Webster*, p. 153. See also Alexander W. Allison, "Ethical Themes in *The Duchess of Malfi,*" *Studies in English Literature, 1500–1900*, 4 (1964), pp. 263–273.

9. As with the circuitous and often contradictory evaluations of Bosola, Webster offers us apparently irreconcilable views of both the Duchess's actions and her character. Clifford Leech usefully discusses Webster's divergent perspectives and suggests that this technique "brings her close to us" and involves our sympathies; see *Webster: "The Duchess of Malfi,"* Barron's Studies in English Literature No. 8 (Great Neck, N.Y.: Barron's Educational Series, 1963), p. 49.

10. Jane Marie Luecke is right to see the heroine as "rather a woman than a duchess; she seeks rather to lose herself in the social act of sex-marriage-childbearing, and she places herself in an 'abnormal but usual' social situation by committing the social error of marrying below her class—all of which is the specific matter of comedy rather than of tragedy"; see "*The Duchess of Malfi:* Comic and Satiric Confusion in a Tragedy," *Studies in English Literature, 1500–1900*, 4 (1964), p. 277. Although Luecke overstates the case for romantic "comedy," certainly part of the fourth act's power derives from our feeling, at some deep level, that "for her transgression of a social convention, this woman is forced to pay not comic consequences but the tragic extreme" (pp. 277–278).

11. On the imagery's suggestions of death as well as love, see especially Hereward T. Price, "The Function of Imagery in Webster," in *Elizabethan Drama: Modern Essays in Criticism*, ed. R. J. Kaufmann (New York: Oxford University Press, 1961), p. 241; but also Inga-Stina Ekeblad [Ewbank], "The 'Impure Art' of John Webster," in "*The Duchess of Malfi,*" ed. Norman Rabkin, Twentieth Century Interpretations (Englewood Cliffs, N.J.: Prentice-Hall, 1968), p. 63; and Gunnar Boklund, "*The Duchess of Malfi*": *Sources, Themes, Characters* (Cambridge, Mass.: Harvard University Press, 1962), p. 92.

12. Accounts of "contemporary opinion" differ from critic to critic. Frank W. Wadsworth, searching Renaissance literature for "a more modern and democratic voice," manages to find several and presents them in "Webster's *Duchess of Malfi* in the Light of Some Contemporary Ideas on Marriage and Remarriage," *Philological Quarterly*, 35 (1956), esp. p. 402; William Empson's bluff approach wittily dismisses detractors of the Duchess in "Mine Eyes Dazzle," *Essays in Criticism*, 14 (1964), pp. 80–86. James L. Calderwood, on the other

hand, believes that any audience would strongly condemn the Duchess's violation of degree, for in marrying Antonio she threatens the cosmological as well as the social order; see "*The Duchess of Malfi*: Styles of Ceremony," *Essays in Criticism*, 12 (1962), pp. 133–147. In *Curs'd Example: "The Duchess of Malfi" and Commonweal Tragedy* (Columbia: University of Missouri Press, 1978), Joyce E. Peterson agrees. In his Revels edition, Brown comes closest to the effect of Webster's ambiguous treatment: "There is no clear judgement in the play, only that Bosola and Ferdinand at last declare her to be innocent" (p. liv).

13. Clifford Leech, "An Addendum on Webster's Duchess," *Philological Quarterly*, 37 (1958), p. 255.

14. With the wooing scene, Webster has introduced a new element, one that cannot be fully accounted for by the play's preceding discussions but which challenges the court's idea of love, marriage, and human relatedness. No colossus "past the size of dreaming," the Duchess displays a different, wholly domestic and apolitical heroism. In her fine Mermaid Critical Commentaries essay, "Webster's Realism, or, 'A Cunning Piece Wrought Perspective,'" Inga-Stina Ewbank notes that "the relationship of Antonio and the Duchess . . . comes to form a strain of simplicity, of almost bourgeois sentiment, which establishes a viewpoint and a value" (p. 173).

15. Brown, Revels introduction, p. xlvi. Ferdinand shares his sister's sense of humor: he mocks her *magnanima menzogna* in the "politic equivocations" of his letter requesting Antonio's return, and again later when he offers her the dead-man's hand (iv.i).

16. Critical views of Antonio run the full spectrum. In "Some Contemporary Ideas" Wadsworth tries at length to prove that, barring his social standing, Antonio was fashioned as both the ideal Renaissance husband and an exemplar of "patience and fortitude" (p. 405); Ornstein, however, finds Antonio completely overshadowed by the woman who wooed him, an almost faceless man whose "contemptible death is appropriate," as he says in *The Moral Vision of Jacobean Tragedy* (p. 144). Analyzing the play's relation to its sources in *Sources, Thomas, Characters*, Boklund perhaps wisely splits the difference: he sees Antonio as a carefully presented average man, sympathetic though a "hesitant falterer" far less heroic or ambitious than the sources' major-domo (p. 93).

17. The violent sexuality and disproportion of Ferdinand's outrage, combined with the voyeuristic description of her probable sexual partners and confused desire to prolong his horror, all suggest that incestuous love motivates his hysteria. Such possibilities are discussed at some length by Clifford Leech in *Webster: "The Duchess of Malfi"* and in *John Webster: A Critical Study* (London: Hogarth Press, 1951). McD. Emslie also explores the suggestion of incest in "Motives of Malfi," *Essays in Criticism*, 9 (1959), pp. 391–405; see especially p. 395 for Emslie's discussion of the line hinting at Ferdinand's perverse

desire for the continuation of his sister's affair. Then, too, as Brown notes in his edition, "a hidden motivation for Ferdinand is in keeping with the general mode of characterization" (p. lii).

18. Ferdinand's examples suggest, indeed, the kind of play to which the Duchess is temperamentally suited. In one sense at least she is, as Ornstein says in *The Moral Vision of Jacobean Tragedy*, "a heroine of Shakespearean romantic comedy, graceful, witty, wanton and innocent at the same time, who woos and wins her husband in spite of himself"; this characterization, he maintains, also suggests Webster's boldness as a tragedian (p. 147).

19. Many critics find the madmen an apt symbol of Webster's fragmented world and a proleptic introduction to the chaos of act 5. For an interpretation of the madmen's masque as Ferdinand's delayed and demonic celebration of his sister's marriage, see Inga-Stina Ekeblad's "The 'Impure Art' of John Webster."

20. There is some doubt about the guilt for which the Duchess feels she needs "heaven's scorge-stick" (III.v.81). She may refer to that life of constant deception to which efforts at preserving position and honor led her; she certainly knows that Bosola and her brothers merely "counterfeit heaven's thunder" (III.v.100). M. C. Bradbrook suggests that it "is through the awakening of responsibility that the Duchess develops into a tragic figure." This acceptance of her fate as a necessary "scorge-stick" marks an important change in her response, a coming to terms with her deeds: "She never acknowledges that her brothers have the right to judge her; but she does acknowledge that she is in need of a corrected judgment." See *Themes and Conventions of Elizabethan Tragedy* (1935; rpt. Cambridge: Cambridge University Press, 1960), pp. 203–204.

21. Bosola's shape-changing may lack the trickster's gusto and playfully self-conscious theatricality, but it is just as necessary to his sense of identity. Bosola's various roles—from Paduan scholar and later intelligencer to the fourth act's formal disguise as old man/tombmaker/bellman—are all self-protective attempts to live with his divided nature. In *The Art of John Webster* (Oxford: At the Clarendon Press, 1972), Ralph Berry calls "the most important characteristic of Bosola . . . his behaviour [as] a series of role-playing changes," for it is the result of having chosen "a course of action that is ultimately opposed to his inner values" (p. 139). See also C. G. Thayer, "The Ambiguity of Bosola," *Studies in Philology*, 54 (1957), pp. 162–171, and Irving Ribner, *Jacobean Tragedy: The Quest for Moral Order* (London: Methuen, 1962), esp. pp. 110–115.

22. Discussing Webster's use of language, in "Webster's Realism," Ewbank notes that the Duchess's plain answers do not merely discredit Bosola's words. Both simplicity and complexity are necessary to the process of defining a truth or experience that exists, finally, beyond words: "She is both 'a box of worm-

seed' and 'thy duchess,' both a grey-haired woman who cannot sleep and 'Duchess of Malfi still.' Each of them may see only, or mainly, one side of the dialectic, but we see the whole dramatic image" and the views become superimposed upon one another (p. 178).

23. Ornstein rightly questions the prevalent idea of the Duchess as a symbol of solitary integrity whose famous cry defeats the chaos that surrounds and threatens her. In *The Moral Vision of Jacobean Tragedy* he maintains that the "Duchess' strength is not a lonely existential awareness of self but a remembrance of love, expressed in her parting words to Cariola and in her answers to Bosola. . . . Webster's other heroes and heroines die obsessed with their sins and follies, projecting their individual experiences as the pattern of man's fate. The Duchess is the only one to move out of self" (p. 148).

24. Boklund, *Sources, Themes, Characters,* p. 169. In Boklund's view the final theme is one of "unrelieved futility," and we must "realize that the pattern is not a moral one" (pp. 129–130).

25. In "*The Duchess of Malfi*: Act V and Genre," *Genre,* 3 (1970), pp. 351–363, Normand Berlin usefully discusses Webster's comic distancing. See also Brown's introduction to his Revels Plays edition, and Lois Potter, "Realism Versus Nightmare: Problems of Staging *The Duchess of Malfi*," in *The Triple Bond: Plays, Mainly Shakespearean, in Performance,* ed. Joseph G. Price (University Park: Pennsylvania State University Press, 1975), pp. 170–189.

26. Although the echo scene focuses on Antonio's melancholy, Cecil W. Davies may be correct in seeing that the "true marriage of Antonio and the Duchess is surely symbolized in the way in which his own words become her warning to him." See "The Structure of *The Duchess of Malfi*: An Approach," *English,* 12 (1958), p. 90.

27. In *The Moral Vision of Jacobean Tragedy* Ornstein forges rather too tight a negative similarity between Antonio and Bosola; they do, however, both seek "security" above all and, ironically, "neither Antonio's honesty nor Bosola's policy secure them against their fates." As he points out, "it is hardly an accident that they cause each other's death, for in life they were brothers under the skin, men who committed spiritual suicide before a sword-thrust ended their miserable lives" (p. 142).

28. In *Webster: "The Duchess of Malfi,"* Leech's analysis of the Bosola who pursues revenge in act 5 is acute: though sympathizing with Antonio and dedicated to a woman he hoped would save his soul, Bosola is seen "slaying an innocent servant without compunction, mistakenly killing Antonio, complaining always of being neglected. As an instrument of justice he is pitifully imperfect, while he had shown address as tormentor and executioner" (p. 27).

29. As Boklund puts it in *Sources, Themes, Characters,* the "ground between the extreme moral alternatives, which was left unexplored in *The White Devil,*

is now invaded by the Duchess, and the validity of the experiment is belatedly recognized both by Bosola and the audience" (p. 169). While Boklund holds that the Duchess's solution remains private and of "strictly limited pertinence," in "Intelligence in *The Duchess of Malfi*," in the Mermaid Critical Commentaries *John Webster*, pp. 95–112, Nigel Alexander argues persuasively for broader relevance.

CHAPTER V

1. In his perceptive essay "*The Devil's Law-Case*: An End or a Beginning?" in *John Webster*, ed. Brian Morris (London: Ernest Benn, 1970), pp. 113–130, Gunnar Boklund notes this play's similarity to *Measure for Measure;* he also insists that to make "Websterian sense" of *The Devil's Law-Case* one must consider it in relation to the earlier tragedies, "not only in style and workmanship but above all in theme." Characters and problems are more purely domestic and the play is concerned with "the trivial side of life . . . but this does not make it a trivial play" (pp. 128–129). On this latter point see also Fernand Lagarde's discussion in *John Webster*, 2 vols. (Toulouse: Association des Publications de la Faculté des Lettres et Sciences Humaines de Toulouse, 1968), 1:457–485.

2. Cyrus Hoy observes that Fletcherian tragicomedy did not sit well with those of Shakespeare's contemporaries "accustomed to take a more problematic view of things than [such] tragicomedy ever permits." Neither Webster nor Middleton were "at ease with the form as it develops in its new and voguish aspect," and *The Devil's Law-Case* and *More Dissemblers Besides Women* fail "not because they are bad imitations of Fletcher but because they treat of subjects of Shakespearean complexity with a Fletcherian inconsequence." See "Shakespeare and the Drama of His Time," in *Shakespeare: Aspects of Influence*, Harvard English Studies 7, ed. G. B. Evans (Cambridge, Mass.: Harvard University Press, 1976), p. 35.

3. In "*The Devil's Law-Case*: An Interpretation," *Modern Language Review*, 63 (1968), pp. 545–558, D. C. Gunby interprets the play's "miraculous" cures and final unraveling as heaven's direct intervention; see also Peter B. Murray, *A Study of John Webster* (The Hague: Mouton, 1969), pp. 185–215. Agreeing that *The Devil's Law-Case* is a relatively simple moral *exemplum*, Ralph Berry finds its concern "is, quite simply, its literal content," the law; we see here most clearly the moralist who in all his plays is "fascinated with the problem of calibrating punishment to offence." See *The Art of John Webster* (Oxford: At the Clarendon Press, 1972), pp. 153 and 167.

4. Marlowe's influence is everywhere apparent, in verbal echoes as well as in

44

character and plot allusions. See F. L. Lucas, *The Complete Works of John Webster*, 4 vols. (London: Chatto & Windus, 1927), 2:217–218; Frances A. Shirley's Regents Renaissance edition of *The Devil's Law-Case* (Lincoln: University of Nebraska Press, 1972), pp. xviii–xix; and G. E. Bentley, *The Jacobean and Caroline Stage*, 7 vols. (Oxford: At the Clarendon Press, 1941–1968), 5:1251. All references to *The Devil's Law-Case* will be to Shirley's edition, which employs modern spelling.

5. Robert Dent discusses Webster's indebtedness to *The Devil is an Ass* (acted 1616) in *John Webster's Borrowing* (Berkeley and Los Angeles: University of California Press, 1960), pp. 58–59 and Commentary.

6. In *A Study of John Webster* Murray goes on to praise Webster's plotting in this play as an "over-looked" beauty (p. 187). He discusses balance in plotting and Webster's skill in dovetailing his many schemes: "In one plot Romelio seeks to make his illegitimate child the heir of riches, in the other, Leonora seeks to make her legitimate son lose his rightful inheritance" (p. 193).

7. In "Interpretation," Gunby maintains that Romelio is clearly under the Devil's influence and is identified by Webster with antireligion; Gunby calls the play "a study of pride humbled," whose action reveals a "providentially organized campaign to reclaim Romelio" (pp. 550 and 553).

8. As Lagarde astutely observes in *John Webster*, "Jolenta, dont la première apparition comme soeur rebelle et amante éplorée séduit, adopte avec aisance une conduite et un langage qui devraient lui répugner et où l'on peut voir quelque équivoque; elle est soeur de Romelio et fille de Leonora; à la moindre contrariété les forces contenues se manifestent. La famille entière partage cette volonté inflexible d'atteindre ce qu'elle appelle le bonheur au mépris des obstacles et des conventions sociales; alors reparaît la vigueur de la meilleure tradition webstérienne" (1:473). Jolenta's disillusionment and ready acquiescence in her brother's plans perhaps suggest the misanthropic trickster's original motivation: finding the race of men false, she vows to retaliate by being false to it. Like Romelio, she uses her new "credo" to amuse herself; in her "fantastical sorrow" she wittily contemplates her "part," the petticoat's "quilted preface" and the "qualms and swoundings" necessary to carry it off (iii.iii.185–200). Both Jolenta and her mother come to share Romelio's cynicism and, hence, his ethics.

9. While making a slightly different point, in "An End or a Beginning?" Boklund notes that Jolenta too serves as ethical commentator on Romelio's actions: "What he calls 'A piece of Art' is to her 'Rather a damnable cunning, / To have me goe about to giv't away, / Without consent of my soule'" (pp. 123–124).

10. The method is typically Websterian. In *The White Devil*, iv.i, Francisco persuades Monticelso that, far from intending revenge, he is a model prince

who fears God and cares for the welfare of his subjects; the "good prince" speech is a ruse immediately rejected in Francisco's private plans, but through it Webster suggests the standards by which we judge Francisco's real designs.

11. Cf. *Volpone,* ed. A. B. Kernan (New Haven: Yale University Press, 1962): "Yet, I glory / More in the cunning purchase of my wealth / Than in the glad possession . . ." (1.i.30–32).

CONCLUSION

1. In "Ben Jonson and the Centered Self," *Studies in English Literature, 1500–1900,* 10 (1970), pp. 325–348, Thomas M. Greene discusses the search for a protean, perpetually transforming self as an escape from self, since to be everything to everyone is to be nothing. Also pertinent to my discussion of Webster is Greene's conclusion in "The Flexibility of the Self in Renaissance Literature," in *The Disciplines of Criticism: Essays in Literary Theory, Interpretation, and History,* ed. Peter Demetz, Thomas Greene, and Lowry Nelson, Jr. (New Haven: Yale University Press, 1968): "Renaissance speculation on the theme of flexibility reaches a natural end point with the plays of Shakespeare, dramatizing as they do the painful difficulty of moral ascent and the happy success of lateral resourcefulness. . . . His theater is a theater of horizontal maneuverings and adaptations, and so ushers in the modern era we still inhabit" (p. 262). See also A. Bartlett Giamatti's "Proteus Unbound: Some Versions of the Sea God in the Renaissance," in the same volume, esp. pp. 459–466, and, for a very different but interestingly related view, Richard A. Lanham, *The Motives of Eloquence: Literary Rhetoric in the Renaissance* (New Haven: Yale University Press, 1976), esp. chap. 1, and chap. 4's for remarks on the tragicomedy of Shakespeare's *Venus and Adonis.*

2. Robert B. Heilman, *Magic in the Web: Action and Language in "Othello"* (Louisville: University Press of Kentucky, 1956), p. 112. In *Tragedy and Melodrama: Versions of Experience* (Seattle: University of Washington Press, 1968) Heilman rightly maintains that the tragic hero must be intelligent, capable of tragic knowledge: though he "may try to escape self-knowledge, he cannot be incapable of it; in the effort at flight lies tragedy, in incapability, at most, an ironic drama of ignorance" (p. 16).

3. In "Renaissance and Restoration Dramatic Plotting," *Renaissance Drama,* 9 (1966), pp. 247–264, Cyrus Hoy traces seventeenth-century drama's slide toward a tragedy of "frankly romantic" subject matter and a tragicomedy that festoons a "slender . . . often distinctly elegant structure of comic intrigue and romantic purpose with great garlands of tragic, or quasi-tragic, or pseudo-tragic passion" (pp. 249 and 250). While developing the romantic love-motif in ways

fundamentally different from its later simplified use as the spark of love/honor dilemmas, Webster obviously contributes to the development of romantic love as tragedy's primary subject; he helps prepare a soil later tilled by Fletcher, Middleton, Massinger, Shirley, and Ford. See also Hoy's "Artifice and Reality and the Decline of Jacobean Drama," *Research Opportunities in Renaissance Drama,* 13–14 (1970–1971), pp. 169–180.

4. Discussing Renaissance tragedy's increasing subjectivity of approach, its progressively restricted vision, Marco Mincoff notes that scarcely a generation after Shakespeare the religious pull no longer balances the idea of human beings bound by social ties. The sense not only of superhuman powers in the background but also of the mystery of life fades, and in tragedy all over Europe the love/honor conflict opposes passion with a fundamentally social code: "As the theatre became more and more a form of upper-class entertainment, the concept of morality as a social rather than a religious obligation imposed itself." See "Shakespeare, Fletcher, and Baroque Tragedy," *Shakespeare Survey,* 20 (1967), p. 3.

5. As Raymond Williams astutely remarks, "Order, in tragedy, is the *result* of the action, even where it entirely corresponds, in an abstract way, with a pre-existing conventional belief. It is not so much that the order is illustrated as that it is recreated. In any living belief, this is always the relation between experience and conviction. Specifically, in tragedy, the creation of order is directly related to the fact of disorder, through which the action moves. Whatever the character of the order that is finally affirmed, it has been literally created in this particular action." See *Modern Tragedy* (Stanford: Stanford University Press, 1966), p. 52.

Index